ROUTLEDGE LIBRARY EDITIONS: SMALL BUSINESS

Volume 9

NEW FIRMS AND REGIONAL DEVELOPMENT IN EUROPE

NEW FIRMS AND REGIONAL DEVELOPMENT IN EUROPE

Edited by
DR. DAVID KEEBLE & EGBERT WEVER

Routledge
Taylor & Francis Group

LONDON AND NEW YORK

First published in 1986 by Croom Helm Ltd

This edition first published in 2016
by Routledge
2 Park Square, Milton Park, Abingdon, Oxon OX14 4RN

and by Routledge
711 Third Avenue, New York, NY 10017

Routledge is an imprint of the Taylor & Francis Group, an informa business

British Library Cataloguing in Publication Data
A catalogue record for this book is available from the British Library

ISBN: 978-1-138-67308-3 (Set)
ISBN: 978-1-315-54266-9 (Set) (ebk)
ISBN: 978-1-138-67718-0 (Volume 9) (hbk)
ISBN: 978-1-138-67730-2 (Volume 9) (pbk)
ISBN: 978-1-315-55962-9 (Volume 9) (ebk)

Publisher's Note
The publisher has gone to great lengths to ensure the quality of this reprint but points out that some imperfections in the original copies may be apparent.

Disclaimer
The publisher has made every effort to trace copyright holders and would welcome correspondence from those they have been unable to trace.

New Firms and Regional Development in Europe

Edited by Dr. David Keeble & Egbert Wever

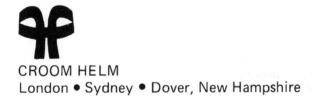

CROOM HELM
London • Sydney • Dover, New Hampshire

© 1986 David Keeble and Egbert Wever
Croom Helm Ltd, Provident House, Burrell Row,
Beckenham, Kent BR3 1AT
Croom Helm Australia Pty Ltd, Suite 4, 6th Floor,
64-76 Kippax Street, Surry Hills, NSW 2010, Australia

British Library Cataloguing in Publication Data

New firms and regional development in Europe.
   1. Regional planning – European Economic Community
   countries 2. New business enterprises – European
   Economic Community countries 3. European Economic
   Community countries – Economic conditions –
   Regional disparities
   I. Keeble, David   II. Wever, Egbert
   338.7'094   HC241.2

   ISBN 0-7099-1577-2

Croom Helm, 51 Washington Street, Dover,
New Hampshire 03820, USA

Library of Congress Cataloging in Publication Data
Main entry under title:

New firms and regional development.

   Includes index.
   1. Small business—Europe—addresses, essays, lectures.
2. New business enterprises—Europe—addresses, essays,
lectures. 3. Europe—industries—location—addresses,
essays, lectures. I. Keeble, David. II. Wever, E.
HD2346.E9N48   1986   38.7'1'094   85-28372
ISBN 0-7099-1577-2

Printed and bound in Great Britain by
Biddles Ltd, Guildford and King's Lynn

CONTENTS

Preface

CONTENTS

PREFACE

Since the early 1970s, nearly all European Community countries have experienced a surprising resurgence in the numbers of small and new businesses in both manufacturing and service industry. The reasons for, significance, and impact of this phenomenon are a matter of considerable current debate and controversy, not least amongst geographers and economists. The research into new and small firms which has been carried out in different European countries reveals, for example, that firm formation rates often vary substantially between different regions, and between urban and rural areas. Regions recording high rates are by no means always the traditionally most economically dominant and prosperous metropolitan centres.

The research conducted has not yet provided a general explanation for observed urban and regional differences in new firm formation rates. This partly reflects the fact that the investigations differ widely in spatial scale, in industrial sectors considered, in the definition of a new firm, and other respects. These differences, together with the growing interest in new and small firms, were the basis of a major initiative by the Industrial Study Group of the Institute of British Geographers and the Economic Geography Group of the Royal Dutch Geographical Society in March 1985. The aim of this initiative was the bringing together for a two-day conference in Utrecht of leading researchers in this field from virtually all the European Community countries. As the first EC-wide conference on this theme, the meeting attracted considerable interest, as evidenced by reports in the United Kingdom Times and participation by senior British and Dutch government researchers. The number of participants had indeed to be restricted, to allow in-depth discussion to take place among the researchers who attended.

We realise that the phenomenon and academic research on new firms are both very recent in most European countries. The papers presented at the conference therefore raised far more questions than they answered, not least concerning the wide variations in observed patterns and possible causes in different countries. Nonetheless, the conference was extremely valuable in providing an up-to-date overview of the new firm formation process at the urban and regional scale in the different countries of the European Community. Even more important, arising from this overview it is possible to identify certain interesting new research directions. The overview provided by the conference and these new research directions together represent the chief motive in publishing most of the Utrecht papers in this volume, in order to make it possible for a wider audience to see what is going on in this field.

The Utrecht conference was generously sponsored by the UK Economic and Social Research Council, the IBG, the Dutch Ministry of Economic Affairs, the Dutch National Physical Planning Agency, the Union of Dutch Chambers of Commerce and the Departments of Geography of the Universities of Utrecht and Cambridge. Without the helpful financial support of these organisations, the conference could not have taken place. Sincere thanks must also go to colleague professor Marc de Smidt, the local organiser, for his excellent conference arrangements. We should like to place on record our appreciation of the help afforded by the Department of Geography and Planning of the University of Nijmegen in preparing the camera-ready text.

Our final wish is that this book will stimulate ongoing discussions and deeper understanding of the new firm formation process at the urban and regional scale in the member countries of the European Community.

Cambridge   Nijmegen
David Keeble   Egbert Wever

Chapter one

INTRODUCTION

David Keeble
Egbert Wever

Introductory Remarks

Differences in the extent of unemployment between
regions are regarded as a problem in most Western
European countries. The regional policies which
have resulted aim to bring the number of workers in
a region more into line with the number of jobs
available there. In most countries, this has
involved a strategy of taking 'work to the
workers'. By applying particular policy measures,
governments have attempted to create additional
employment in those regions where the shortage of
jobs is greatest. The object has generally been to
make such regions more attractive as a location for
'new' firms and employment. Until recently this
meant persuading existing companies to relocate
their activities in a problem assisted area, or
more commonly to establish a branch plant there.
Initially preoccupied with manufacturing
activities, regional policy has since the 1960s
been extended to embrace certain service
industries, so far with only limited success.

In all European countries, the policy of
finding an external solution for regional
employment problems has however in recent years
become less and less successful. Deepening
recession and a generally poor economic climate
have greatly reduced opportunities for attracting
branch plants. The number of relocations of
existing plants to problem areas has also
diminished. One reason for this is that the most
important push-factor for long-distance industrial
migration, a shortage of labour in the major origin
areas, has disappeared. Another closely connected
reason is the growth of high unemployment in the
traditional origin areas, such as the big cities of

1

northern Europe, themselves. Local authorities there are often now actively promoting the retention of local industry and employment, in contrast to the situation only a decade or so ago. The result of these changes is that no region, least of all the problem areas, can rely any longer solely on an external solution for solving their employment problems.

In consequence, regional policies are increasingly emphasising the need to harness the indigenous potential of the problem areas. One approach to this is by stimulating innovation (in a very broad sense) within the region's existing plants. This reorientation is to a certain extent reflected in the growing attention economic geographers are now giving to the relations between innovation, technology and regional development. The other approach to increasing the indigenous economic potential of a region is to stimulate local entrepreneurship. The growing interest in the phenomenon of new firm formation within the framework of regional policy provides much of the context for this book. However, the interest shown by economic geographers and regional economists in new firm formation is not only prompted by the role new firms play in regional policy. Perhaps even more important is the broadly-accepted argument that large corporations will not be able, at least in the foreseeable future, to provide enough jobs for the working populations of our European countries. Since David Birch published his research on 'the job generation process' in 1979, many other commentators have also suggested that newly-created small firms can make an important contribution to the creation of new jobs. Even when such expectations are pitched too high, which they often are, this possibility explains the interest in new firm formation shown by politicians, development agencies, journalists and scientists.

New Firm Formation: A Framework

This book focusses on new firms and research by economic geographers and regional economists on their spatial distribution in the countries of the European Community. Essentially, however, we can distinguish two different sorts of new firms. Both play an important role in regional policies. The first category consists of the relocated firm and the newly-established branch plant of a firm

already operating elsewhere. For the destination region these are new firms, although the companies to which they belong did already exist elsewhere before. This category is the more traditional focus of regional policy. Much geographical and economic research has already been devoted to these firms and their importance for economic development and employment in destination regions. Some of the more characteristic research questions investigated by economic geographers include the following:
- does this category of new firms contribute to the diversification of the regional economy?
- what impacts do these firms exert on the destination region by the salaries paid to local workers, by the material and non-material linkages, etc.?
- are there negative effects on the destination region because of external control?
- what are the motives for relocation (push and pull factors) and what factors influence the locational choice of branch plants?
- what was the nature of the search procedure for the new location?
- did the relocated firm meet problems in its new location and was its choice on balance satisfactory?

The considerable volume of firm migration which occurred in Europe in the 1960s and early 1970s stimulated a great deal of research into the above questions, as for example that reported in Klaassen and Molle (1983). In view of our already-extensive knowledge of migrant new firms, this category will not be considered further here.

The central theme of this book concerns the second category of new firms, namely those which did not exist before and which are set up by their founders as independent businesses. Connected with this kind of new firms is the concept of the 'entrepreneur'. In considering the importance of new independent firms of this type for urban and regional economic development, several aspects can be distinguished. Moreover, each of these aspects has a spatial dimension. Fig. 1 gives an overview of the discussion in the remainder of this section.

Perhaps the most obvious starting-point for considering new enterprise creation and the stimulation of entrepreneurship is the question, why does someone set up his own business, despite all the risks of such a venture? Some interesting ideas here can be derived from Shapero (1983). He distinguishes four main motives which can stimulate

Introduction

Fig. 1. The new firm formation process.

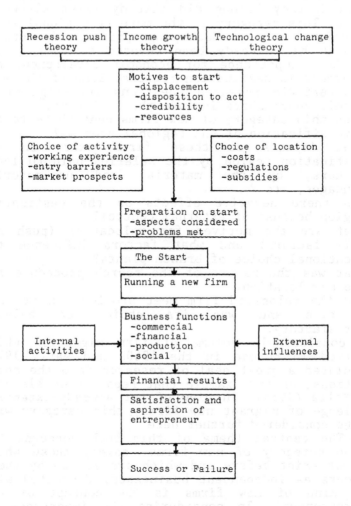

an individual to start a firm. The first of these is called the <u>displacement</u> factor. This usually explains the precise timing of business formation. Sometimes the firm founder has very little choice in this respect. Many refugees, for example, start their own firm because they have no other obvious way to survive. In the same way, longterm unemployment, or the threat of it, can stimulate people to start up in business for themselves. To Shapero such negative firm formation motives are very important: 'threat works more than incentive'.

Introduction

Of course there are also more positive motives for starting a new firm. It may be that these positive motives are more important than negative stimuli in our West European welfare states. Examples of positive factors are the desire to be recognised as a craftsman, the wish to use one's capacities to the full, the ambition to be one's own boss, and the urge to become rich.

The second main motive Shapero calls the disposition to act. Many people feel the need, for one reason or another, to change something in their lives. However, not every refugee, long term unemployed person or frustrated employee, feeling that need decides to start a firm. Those who do take that step want freedom and independence more than anything else. Therefore a good reason for wanting to start will only lead to a new firm in reality if the entrepreneur has the appropriate personality.

The third main motive is called credibility. The decision to set up a new firm will be influenced not only by the personality of the potential entrepreneur, but also by the social position and esteem enjoyed by businessmen in a particular society. In some 'social climates' entrepreneurship will flourish more than in others. In a society where employment in the civil service confers high social status and economic security, the pull of entrepreneurship will be diminished. Shapero himself gives the following very illustrative example: 'In Italy, I found that a man of education who started a small business lost social status. In the USA, that man is a folk-hero'. Political opinions and attitudes can also play a role. Someone who proclaims the class struggle and moves in like-minded circles is unlikely to participate in setting-up a new capitalist enterprise. The reverse is also true. Many new firm founders come from families, a member of which is already a businessman and which provide encouragement and social support. This is especially important in the context of a Western European society in which someone who fails in business loses status.

The last main motive identified by Shapero is the availability of resources. This can be regarded as the more material stimulus provided by a given local, regional or national environment. Such stimuli can perhaps help a potential new firm to cross the notorious threshold of successful new enterprise formation by reducing risks and costs either nationally or in particular regions (for example, by special financial and tax incentives, management and marketing counselling, or subsidised housing costs). From the policy perspective, this last motive is of particular interest because of the possibility of public intervention. However, in explaining regional variations in numbers of new firms, the availability of resources appears to be a much less significant influence than the 'social climate' or credibility factor. In traditional new firm studies focussing on the urban incubator hypothesis, for example, perhaps too much attention has been paid to material and too little attention to social stimuli.

The decision to set up one's own firm leads inevitably to a further series of questions. The first of these is 'what type of firm will I start?' In many cases the answer to this question is already given, in that the entrepreneur has only a limited choice. The most important factor here is the previous experience of the new firm founder. The overwhelming majority of founders inevitably set up businesses in activities in which they have working experience. This also means that in general new firms conform to the existing regional economic structure. In the short-run at least, their contribution to diversification may therefore be modest. On the other hand, this does not mean that similar numbers of new firms are founded in all industrial sectors. The most important reason for this seems to be the presence or absence of barriers to entry. For a potential entrepreneur who has been a blue-collar worker in a blast furnace setting up a new firm will be more difficult than for a similar worker experienced in the clothing industry. To some extent this may also explain why the influence of demand factors appears to be relatively limited. A number of stagnating or declining sectors are for example characterised by low entry barriers and therefore by many new firm start-ups. The fact that a potential entrepreneur believes that he will succeed where others have failed will also diminish the influence of market demand on new firm formation rates. As sectors dominated by small firms are at the same time usually characterised by low entry barriers, this may be one reason why many new firm founders have gained their previous work experience in small and medium-sized firms. It may of course also be true that work experience in small firms is more varied and provides better allround training for becoming an independent businessman. In a region which possesses many small firms the credibility factor may also be important, in that there are more examples of successful 'role models' and mentors whom potential founders can copy than in an area where the majority are employed in one or two large companies.

The next question which the potential entrepreneur has to answer is 'where do I set up my firm?' To an even greater extent than with firm type, the founder usually has little choice in this respect. Most entrepreneurs set up their new firms in the area in which they already live. The new independent firm is therefore a genuinely endogenous answer to regional unemployment problems. Of course this does not mean that new firms in a particular region are only established by residents who were born and bred in the area. Many recent new firms in rural areas of northern Europe appear in fact to have been set up by migrants coming from large cities, and who have moved to these rural areas because of their more attractive living conditions.

Having answered the questions 'shall I start?', 'which activity shall I undertake?', and 'where do I start?', the new firm founder must finally prepare detailed plans for his new business. This is the point at which optimistic hopes and broad expectations must be translated into operational realities. Which aspects have to be taken into account? What knowledge do I have myself? Where can I obtain information from others? Can I really earn a living by establishing a new business? How do I obtain capital to start? Even at this late stage, some potential founders will give up. This may be because their plans were not realistic enough, or because they come to feel that after all, they lack the necessary ability or experience to be successful. On the other hand, those who retain confidence in their plans and succeed in overcoming all the pre-start problems which inevitably occur (finance, premises, etc.) really will establish a new business. For these entrepreneurs, the phase of running the new firm begins.

In this phase, and assuming reasonable success in producing and marketing goods or services, the entrepreneur evolves gradually into the manager, even when he works alone or only with the help of family labour. More and more time is spent on the four main business functions, the commercial, financial, production and social function. To guarantee the continuity if not growth of the firm the owner is confronted with such questions as 'how and where can I find new clients?', 'how can I finance new production facilities?', 'do I have to move to a better location?', 'how can I maintain a technical lead over my competitors?', 'can I afford to expand, and if so do I need to employ extra workers?' New firm formation is only a beginning: for the entrepreneur, his employees, and the region in which he operates, successful solutions to questions of this kind are in the long-term even more important.

The model of new firm formation outlined in Fig. 1 thus provides a useful inductively-developed framework for many of the issues considered in later chapters. However, recent research also provides more general, sometimes deductive, perspectives on new firm formation in Europe. The following sections thus attempt to provide a succinct but wide-ranging review of recent research, as a further context for the detailed case studies of new firm creation and its relationship to regional policy in the different European countries presented in the rest of the book.

The Resurgence Of New Small Firms In Europe

A major reason for current interest in the formation of new, independent small businesses is the clear evidence of a substantial resurgence in the numbers of such firms in most European countries since the 1960s, after decades of decline. While the timing of the reversal has varied between countries, being earliest in the United Kingdom and Italy, and most recent in West Germany and Belgium, its reality has been clearly documented by workers such as Baroin and Fracheboud (1983), Greffe (1984), Aydalot (1983), Storey (1982, 1984) and Gudgin (1984). The UK case is vividly illustrated by Fig. 2 and Table 1. The latter shows that the 1980s have witnessed a considerable and growing volume and surplus (births minus deaths) of new companies in the UK, in a variety of sectors. According to this data, the total stock of companies in the UK increased by 8 per cent between 1980 and 1983, with a 10 per cent increase in the manufacturing sector alone. The great majority of these are undoubtedly very small,

Introduction

Fig. 2. Small Manufacturing Establishments (Ten employees or less) in the United Kingdom, 1930-1980.

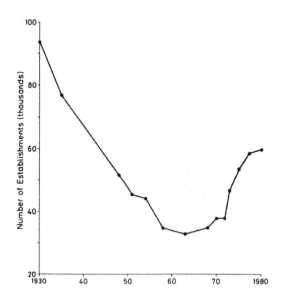

independent businesses (Gudgin 1984). Exactly the same trend is evident in France, where new firm creations in manufacturing industry have increased considerably since the mid-1970s, with a 22 per cent increase in the three years 1980-82 alone! Despite notoriously high death rates, the stock of new small companies is thus now growing in most European countries, with the possible exception of West Germany (chapter twelve).

In the UK if not elsewhere, this new firm resurgence has been accompanied by some political rhetoric and arguable claims concerning the importance of new small firms in long-run industrial regeneration. Leaving rhetoric aside, the new firm resurgence phenomenon is nonetheless clearly of considerable intrinsic interest, in terms not least of its possible causes, variation between cities and regions, and local impact. These three issues are therefore addressed, as an introduction to subsequent chapters, in this introductory chapter.

Explanations for the resurgence of new small businesses since the 1960s range from Storey's list (1984) of eight possible causal factors to Gudgin's

(1984) single mono-causal 'recession push' theory. The former list includes the role of increased oil prices since 1973 in inhibiting large-scale production in capital-intensive plants, and in increasing transport costs and hence encouraging more geographically-dispersed small-scale production. Storey also suggests that growing international competition - from Japan and the Third World - has hit particular European industries in which large firms are dominant, and that in the 1970s increasing managerial diseconomies of scale may have favoured small-scale production. However, these piece-meal explanations do not seem sufficiently fundamental or radical convincingly to account for the kind of reversal indicated by Fig. 2. Discussion here will therefore focus on three far more basic, structural, theories of new firm resurgence which are also touched on by Storey (1982, 203-4: 1984). These are 'recession push' theory, 'income growth' theory, and 'technological change' theory. Some attention will also be paid to recent arguments over large firm fragmentation policies, and to the role of government policies.

Recession push theory has been advocated in the UK by Gudgin (1984) and Binks and Coyne (1983), and at the wider European level by Baroin and Fracheboud (1983, 56). This theory argues that new firm resurgence primarily reflects the impact of deepening recession in Europe since the 1960s, which has operated in two ways. First, redundancy, threatened unemployment, and recession-induced blocking of promotion prospects push more potential entrepreneurs to establish their own businesses than is the case in periods of economic growth and job security. The last of these mechanisms is presumably the most important, since UK studies show that under 10 per cent of new firms are actually started by people who were previously unemployed (Gudgin 1984, Keeble and Gould 1985). Recession push theory therefore focusses attention on Shapero's displacement factor, as motivating entrepreneurship. Secondly, enforced rationalisation and withdrawal of large firms from less profitable activities which are peripheral to their main operations may leave vacant market niches which can be taken over by more flexible and specialist new firms with lower overhead costs. Recession push theory is supported by Fothergill and Gudgin's (1982) identification of a close temporal relationship between fluctuating firm

Introduction

Table 1. The Growth of New Firms in the United
Kingdom in the 1980s.

	Manufacturing[1]		Finance, Property Profess. Services[2]		Other Services[3]	
	New Firms	Surplus[4]	New Firms	Surplus	New Firms	Surplus
1980	14,487	1,374	10,436	3,155	22,442	5,366
1981	14,744	3,308	9,189	2,886	22,416	7,863
1982	16,542	2,808	9,659	2,054	25,319	6,815
1983	18,962	5,961	11,107	4,171	26,598	9,589

1: plus gas, electricity and water
2: insurance, banking, finance and property services, and
professional and scientific services (accountancy,
educational, medical, legal, etc.)
3: transport and telecommunications (excl. road transport),
business services, miscellaneous services (leisure,
entertainment, consumer services, etc.)
4: new business registrations for VAT purposes; for full
definition, see Ganguly, 1982.

Source:. Ganguly 1984, 1985

formation rates and unemployment levels in the East
Midlands between 1945 and 1975, and by Atkins,
Binks and Vale's claim (1983) that over half of all
entrepreneurs establishing new manufacturing firms
in Nottingham since 1978 were 'pushed' to do so by
recession-induced pressures. The latter is a much
higher proportion than that recorded by earlier
studies. The very substantial recent growth in
self-employment in countries such as the UK
(Clement 1984), where the number of self-employed
workers increased by 22 per cent between 1979 and
1983 after declining between 1971 and 1979, also
fits this kind of explanation.

On the other hand, other evidence appears to
run counter to recession theory. Particularly
telling here is Binks' more recent finding (Binks
and Jennings 1983) that when adjusted for time-
series autocorrelation, econometric analysis of
rates of new company registration and unemployment
levels in Britain between 1971 and 1981 indicates
that recent steep increases in unemployment have
apparently significantly depressed, not enhanced,
rates of new firm formation. Equally, recent East
Anglian new firm founder research (Keeble and Gould
1985) reveals that in this high firm formation rate

11

region, very little impact of recession can be identified in the actual decisions taken by new firm founders to establish their businesses. This is especially true in the case of Cambridgeshire, which has one of the highest rates of new manufacturing firm formation in the UK. So while recession-push theory is probably one important explanation for new firm resurgence, especially in industrial northern Europe, more long-run structural considerations almost certainly also need to be incorporated in full understanding of this phenomenon. Such structural considerations are the focus of 'income growth' and 'technological change' theories.

The first of these, which is noted by Storey (1982, 204), is perhaps most widely associated with work on the Italian small firm phenomenon by Brusco (1982, Brusco and Sabel 1981). Brusco's work shows clearly that a major reason for "the proliferation of small enterprises" and associated "decentralisation of the productive structure in... Italy.... can be found in the emergence since the mid-1960s of a significant demand for more varied and customised goods, produced in short series, alongside that for standardised goods" (Brusco 1982, 171). This structural change in market demand of course chiefly reflects a substantial increase in real household incomes over the last thirty years in all European countries, notwithstanding recession[2]. Substantial income growth, coupled with widening cultural tastes[3], has fuelled an "expansion in the market for sophisticated products" and "an increasingly pronounced....consumer demand for quality and variety" (Brusco 1982, 180). However, as Brusco convincingly documents, short-series, customised goods can be produced just as efficiently - if not more efficiently - by small firms as by large. Growth in demand for more sophisticated products has thus created numerous market niches capable of exploitation by new small businesses. Brusco's theory was developed in relation to manufacturing firms, and finds its fullest expression in the Italian small firm 'industrial district' model outlined in chapter nine. But it is of course equally applicable to the service sector, whose products often command particularly high income elasticities of demand, and where barriers to new firm entry - in activities as diverse as, for example, tennis coaching, restaurants, language schools, management consultancy, and insurance broking - are often low.

Introduction

Income growth theory thus constitutes a particularly convincing and plausible structural explanation for new, small firm resurgence in affluent northern Europe since the 1960s.

The second structural explanation is 'technological change' theory. As noted, various recent workers, notably Mensch (1979), Hall (1981) and Freeman (1983, 1984), have argued that the deepening European-wide recession of the 1970s and 1980s appears to conform to a Kondratiev-type long wave pattern of boom then slump, which Schumpeter (1939) explained, in relation of course to previous long waves, as a result of bursts of radical technological innovation followed by longer periods of innovation exploitation and eventual decline through market-swamping as a result of competitive imitation. Bursts of innovation, or 'technological revolutions' (Freeman 1984) are then the only way forward for continued capitalist economic growth. Such revolutions are characterised, as for example by electrical power in the 20th century, by widespread impacts, which not only create wholly new industries but affect and transform many existing, more traditional, ones. Freeman argues that the 1980s are witnessing just such a technological revolution, in the form of radical technological change in micro-electronics, which is altering production technology, labour skill requirements, and the economics, organisation and flexibility of production in a very wide range of manufacturing and service industries. Rapid recent technological innovation in micro-electronics, in Freeman's judgement, does therefore provide the basis for "the new technological paradigm for the 5th Kondratiev".

The question which of course arises at this point is whether one possible organisational change associated with the impact of the micro-electronics revolution in Europe is the growth of numerous new, small firms as part of a more decentralised, technologically-flexible, system of production of goods and services. The possible impact of micro-electronics and new information technology on the development of a more dispersed, small-scale production system has recently been attested by both electronic industry and labour market researchers (Town and Country Planning 1985). Equally, however, it can be argued that the speed and nature of the micro-electronics revolution are directly creating a host of new product, process and market opportunities which are particularly

suited to exploitation by small firms set up by
skilled or research-based entrepreneurs. The
mushroom growth of US semiconductor firms, and of
UK hardware and software computer firms provides
empirical evidence supporting this hypothesis. But
it is also possible that micro-processor technology
is facilitating new firm establishment and growth
in apparently low-technology industries. An
excellent example here is the Cambridge mechanical
engineering firm of Domino Printing Sciences, set
up in 1978 by its founder Greame Minto to
manufacture micro-processor controlled ink jet
printers for the food industry, and now employing
160 workers with a 1985 worldwide turnover of over
£ 10 million. While intrinsically more difficult to
quantify, the impact of recent technological change
on new firm formation in traditional industries may
thus well be as important, overall, as with the
more obvious and easily-documented 'high-
technology' industries.

Together, recession push, income growth and
technological change theories do seem to provide a
convincing explanation for new firm resurgence in
Europe. This view is not however accepted by all
commentators. From a radical or marxist
perspective, for example, continuing capital
accumulation and centralisation in large capitalist
organisations, and the resultant demise of small
independent firms, are generally seen as
inevitable, and part of the inexorable logic and
contradictions of competitive capitalist evolution.
Not surprisingly, therefore, some radical workers
have recently argued (Shutt and Whittington 1984)
that small firm resurgence is largely 'illusory',
in the sense that many apparently new, independent
businesses are a direct result of deliberate
fragmentation policies by large firms, under
conditions of great demand and innovation
uncertainty and increasing difficulty of control
over the labour process. Shutt and Whittington thus
claim (1984, 22) that "the general increase in
small units can be at least partly explained by the
deliberate strategies of large firms shifting
production....into small firms and smaller plants"
which are fundamentally dependent on or directly
controlled by the large firm sector.

To the extent that Shutt and Whittington's
argument includes recession-induced withdrawal of
larger firms from peripheral activities, thus
leaving vacant market niches for new firms, it of
course supports the general recession theory put

forward earlier. Equally, there is no doubt, as
Mason and Harrison (1985) have recently documented,
that certain larger firm policies such as
franchising or facilitation of management buyouts
(Wright, Coyne and Lockley 1984) do help to enlarge
the stock of small businesses. This said, however,
the large firm fragmentation argument seems very
difficult to accept as more than a minor aspect of
recent small business resurgence. The sheer volume
of new company formations in countries such as the
UK is now so great (650 thousand, 1980-83, for
example; Ganguly 1984) as to render very
implausible its ascription to deliberate policies
by relatively small numbers of large firms.
Moreover, recent research on the nature and process
of new firm formation does not reveal any general
scenario of large-firm dependence or initiation.
Thus only 17 per cent of the large random sample of
new East Anglian manufacturing firms interviewed by
Keeble and Gould in 1983 reported any substantial
(50 per cent or more) dependency for sales on a
single large customer. Nearly three-quarters of the
firms reported dependency levels of less than 33
per cent, with nearly half less than 20 per cent.
Even when extended to dependency on several key
customers, a clear majority of new firms (nearly
three-fifths) did not regard themselves as large-
firm dependent. Finally, the great majority (nearly
two-thirds) of new firm founders had been employed
in a small (less than 100 workers), not large, firm
immediately prior to setting up their own business.
A mere 10 per cent had worked in genuinely large
companies (500 or more employees). So again the
influence of large firms seems far more limited
than the large firm fragmentation policy argument
suggests.

An alternative view, perhaps more common on
the right of the political spectrum in the UK case
at least, is that new firm resurgence owes much to
recent government policy initiatives, aimed at
freeing market imbalances which unfairly disfavour
small companies relative to large, and directly
encouraging entrepreneurship and the availability
of venture capital. The recent surge of government
interest in Europe in small firm policies is fully
acknowledged in this book, as for example in the
chapters by Mason-Harrison and Donckels-Bert. In
the UK case, the post-1979 Conservative government
claimed by 1984 to have initiated over 100 separate
measures aimed at helping small, and by implication
often new, businesses, including financial aid to

business formation by workers unemployed for more than three months, and tax incentives for the provision of start-up capital by private investors. The former was assisting over 50,000 self-employed individuals and new firm founders by mid-1985, while the latter provided £73 million of investment capital in 1983-84, the bulk (57 per cent) of which went to start-up firms (The Treasury 1984, The Times 1984). Such measures are now common throughout Europe, as for example in France (Duche and Savey 1984) and West Germany (Hull 1983, 169-171). However, while they have no doubt enhanced and publicised new firm formation, it is not realistic to regard them as a fundamental cause of post-1970 small firm resurgence, given the latter's scale and timing, which generally predates any significant government policy initiatives. As argued earlier, the causes are more deeply rooted in the changing nature and economic performance of Europe's highly industrialised and affluent economies.

New Firm Formation: Spatial Dimension

New small firms have, not surprisingly, attracted considerable recent interest from national and European Community regional policymakers concerned with rising regional unemployment and the drying-up of previous migration flows of large-firm branch plants to less prosperous regions. Thus the revised European Regional Development Fund regulations adopted by the EC Council of Ministers with effect from January 1985 expressly emphasise the aim of "greater exploitation of the potential for internally generated development of regions". Greater Fund aid will therefore go to "measures for assisting undertakings, especially small and medium-sized undertakings" already operating in less prosperous regions, for such purposes as technology transfer, management advice, and provision of start-up capital. However, there is growing evidence that many regions, especially declining old industrial regions, are precisely the areas in which new business formation and entrepreneurship are least common. What therefore is already known about the actual urban and regional distribution of new firms in European countries, and what theoretical explanations for these patterns are available?

As the chapters in this book indicate, the

geography of recent new firm formation in European Community countries is perhaps best documented for the United Kingdom, France, the Netherlands, and Ireland, particularly with regard to new manufacturing businesses. From studies in these and other countries, three main generalisations can perhaps be made. First, Europe's largest diversified cities and their surrounding metropolitan regions tend to exhibit high rates - and large volumes - of new firm formation, in both manufacturing and service industries.

Secondly, high rates, though lower volumes, are characteristic of a number of previously unindustrialised, rural regions. The most striking examples here are the rural regions of southern France (the Midi), various regions of Britain (the South West, East Anglia, West Midlands and central Wales, the Scottish Highlands), north-central Ireland, Denmark's Jutland, and Adriatic central Italy (Umbria, Marche, Abruzzi). These cases are documented in subsequent chapters. While high rates in some areas owe something to low base levels of existing industry, this rural region pattern does nonetheless seem to be novel to the 1970s and 1980s, and in several cases is associated with a striking reversal in previous rural depopulation and migration flows. This is true in the British and French cases, for example. The region's socio-cultural heritage and type of agriculture appear to be associated factors in other countries.

The third generalisation is that the lowest rates - and small volumes - of new manufacturing firm formation are now to be found in Europe's old specialised urban-industrial regions, as part of a syndrome of structual industrial decline (coal, steel, heavy engineering, shipbuilding, textiles), high and rising levels of unemployment, and net outmigration of population (Robert 1984). While this pattern must reflect in some way inherited over-specialisation on declining manufacturing and mining industries, it is noteworthy that many much less-specialised cities in northern Europe - Dublin, Copenhagen, Manchester, Edinburgh - are also characterised by low firm formation rates. This suggests that the relative dearth of entrepreneurial activity in Europe's old industrial regions may be as much associated with the urban, as with the industrial character of these areas.

The above three generalisations are very broad, and subject to exceptions. In particular, a rural, unindustrialised environment is no guarantee whatsoever of above-average entrepreneurial or firm formation activity, particularly in the case of such peripheral, isolated regions as the Mezzogiorno, rural Greece, or south-west Ireland. These regions all have low enterprise creation rates. But there is nonetheless a degree of similarity of experience in different countries which leads naturally to consideration of possible broad, theoretical causes of the variations observed. For convenience, the available theories may be discussed under three headings, of structural, socio-cultural, and economic theories.[4]

Structural theory embraces the impact both of sectoral and plant size structures on the geography of new firm formation. Clearly, as noted in the introduction to this chapter, differences in production technology, barriers to entry, and market growth result in different propensities for new firm formation in different industries, which impact on cities and regions through differences in local sectoral specialisation. New enterprise creation rates in communities dominated by iron and steel or petrochemical complexes are bound to be lower than in areas specialising in clothing manufacturing, diversified electronics production, or tourism. However, even more important, according to Gudgin (1978), Storey (1982) and Lloyd and Mason (1984), is the effect of regional plant or firm size structures. Empirical research shows clearly that most founders come from small or at most medium-sized plants and firms, in which they have received far more appropriate experience and training for entrepreneurship than is the case with large, more hierarchical and occupationally-segmented, establishments. Fothergill and Gudgin (1982, 132) thus argue that the chief single factor in UK variations in new manufacturing firm formation rates is "the extent to which local manufacturing employment is concentrated in large plants". Their structural theory yields good predictive estimates on firm creation in such different regions as Leicestershire and Teesside.

Socio-cultural theory represents a second major area of current investigation into the causes of regional variations in enterprise formation, and is in fact discussed in several chapters in this book. This approach views the rate of firm formation as strongly influenced by the existing socio-economic mix and characteristics of the resident population of a locality or region, through its impact on the supply of local potential entrepreneurs. In the context of concern with the local 'social climate' for entrepreneurship noted in the introduction, two rather different socio-cultural explanations for variations in enterprise creation in different European countries have recently been put forward.

First, research in the UK, France and the Netherlands lends considerable support to the view that an important determinant of such variations is the occupational structure of the local population, especially with regard to any relative concentration of non-manual, managerial or professional workers, possessing higher educational qualifications. The latter are viewed as more likely to establish viable enterprises with survival and growth potential. Thus Whittington (1984) has found a significant statistical relationship between regional firm birth rates and the proportion of non-manual workers in the UK as a whole; while Keeble and Gould (1984, 1985, Gould and Keeble 1984) demonstrate a similar association within East Anglia, and show that the region's, and especially Cambridgeshire's high firm birth rate reflects an unusually large proportion of highly qualified and educated entrepreneurs. The latter's concentration in the area in turn reflects the great importance of environmentally-induced population migration into East Anglia, which has been spearheaded by more skilled, highly-qualified and higher-income individuals. Thus 56 per cent of all East Anglian new firm founders (70 per cent in Cambridgeshire) in the 1970s were previous immigrants to the area, while 65 per cent of these immigrants (79 per cent in Cambridgeshire) had been greatly influenced in their move by the region's perceived high residential amenity and environmental quality as a place to live. Such environmentally-influenced migration appears to have become of growing significance in many European countries since the 1960s, with respect to a range of scenically-attractive rural, small-town, or climatically-favoured areas, such as the Midi and Grenoble regions of France, Bavaria and southern Germany bordering the Alps (Merritt 1985), and southwest England, East Anglia, rural Wales, and the Scottish Highlands in Britain (Jones, Caird and Ford 1984). Fuelled by rising real incomes, greatly improved communications (motorways, air transport, telecommunications), and a growing dissatisfaction with the quality of life in large, congested urban regions, environmentally-related migration may thus represent a new and significant basis for small firm development, self-employment[5], and economic growth in previously unindustrialised communities and regions.

The second socio-cultural explanation is rather different, in arguing that high rates of new firm formation in other, more agriculturally-based, rural regions stem from a local tradition of self-employment, enterprise and indigenous economic initiative associated with particular forms of agricultural tenure, such as the 'metayage' (share-cropping) system. In the Danish case, for example, Illeris draws attention to the prevalence in Jutland of what Danish ethnologists have termed the 'self-employment life mode', rooted in an historic social context of independent and self-reliant small farmers. Brusco develops a very similar argument for new firm formation in the former metayage agricultural regions of Emilia-Romagna, Tuscany, Umbria and the Marche, arguing that the absence of small-firm 'industrial districts' in the Mezzogiorno is basically to be explained by the region's different type of agricultural land tenure and historic rural social formation. Lastly, and at the opposite end of the scale, a dearth of entrepreneurship and new firm formation in industrial South Wales[6] is ascribed by Morgan and Sayer (1984, 6) to a legacy of externally-controlled 19th-century industrial specialization on coal and steel which has left the social structure of the region "overwhelmingly proletarian" and lacking in any "indigenous 'business class'" of managers, owners and local entrepreneurs. Quite independently, then, these three groups of workers all focus attention on historically-conditioned differences in social class composition as a key influence on new enterprise formation in particular regions, especially agricultural regions, of Europe.

The third type of spatial new firm formation theory may be termed economic. This refers to theoretical explanations which focus on the economics of new firms, in terms of the local or regional availability of factors of production such as premises or capital, and demand for new firm products from particular geographical markets. Shapero's 'availability of resources' factor is an example of this kind of approach, as are government policies (Chisholm 1984). As noted earlier, this kind of theory possesses a natural appeal to regional policy makers, in that it suggests instruments and levers whereby government can influence local or regional enterprise creation. Thus one of Oakey's (1984) main conclusions in his study of high-technology new firms in South East England, Scotland, and California, is that a minority of firms in the last of these areas has benefited significantly from the availability of venture capital, which has until recently been lacking in Britain. He therefore argues that government provision of venture capital in depressed regions could be an effective regional new firm policy, by "ensuring that the minority of high technology small firms that are born in largely hostile innovation environments are compensated by a locally superior environment for investment finance" (Oakey 1984, 158).

Oakey's work thus provides some support for the view that local factor supply conditions may influence new firm formation and survival rates. This seems to be most strikingly true of the development of local 'technology oriented complexes', compromising a growing cluster of new small businesses engaged in high-technology activities (micro-electronics, computer hardware and software, lasers, robotics, bio-technology, and so on). Epitomised by Silicon Valley in California, TOC's are perhaps recognisable in different forms in Europe, notably in the Cambridge and Berkshire regions of the UK, the Enschede area of the Netherlands, Toulouse and Grenoble in France[7], and southern Bavaria centred on Munich. Significantly, all these are regions of relatively high residential amenity and environmental attractiveness to highly-qualified research scientists and engineers. But in addition, in several cases a fundamental role has been played by local universities and research institutions, out of which have come entrepreneurs, skilled manpower, new technologies and scientific innovations (Segal Quince and Partners 1985). In this particular and dramatic form of localised new firm resurgence, the local factor supply of ideas, innovations, skills and entrepreneurs provided by a major university or concentration of R and D activity may thus be of key significance.

Lastly, economic theorists also argue that variations in regional market demand can play a significant role in influencing the geography of new enterprise creation (Lloyd and Mason 1984, 210, Rothwell 1982, 366). This theoretical argument is based upon the fact that many new small businesses tend initially at least to serve a restricted geographical market (Gudgin 1978, 106, Lloyd and Mason 1984, 216). Differences in the level, nature and growth of local and regional demand for goods and services are therefore viewed as of considerable importance in determining business start-up and survival rates in different areas. Regional market growth itself may of course reflect a variety of processes, including large firm restructuring, public sector spending, and population trends reflecting environmentally influenced migration. Heavy concentration of UK government defence procurement and equipment expenditure in South East and South West England[8], for example, has recently been stressed as a key factor in the growth of new and multiplant electronics firms in the so-called M4 corridor between London and Bristol (Breheny and McQuaid 1985). More generally, market demand arguments do seem to fit observed patterns of new manufacturing firm formation in the UK, most notably in relation to the broad contrast between relatively buoyant southern (South East, South West, East Anglia), and depressed northern (North West, Yorkshire and Humberside, North, Scotland) regional economies. The regional market factor is however likely to be of greatest importance for new service industry firms, given the general necessity of face-to-face contact and direct provision to clients of most services. This view is certainly consistent with the observed distribution of new firms by sector in the UK case. Thus the South East, the country's largest, most affluent and economically buoyant regional market, accounted for a significantly higher share of the UK's new service businesses in 1980-1983, even than of new manufacturing firms[9], notwithstanding its already exceptionally high creation rate in the latter case.

The above discussion of the three categories of theoretical explanation for observed geographical variations in enterprise creation in Europe suggests that all three are likely to be involved, but to a varying degree of importance and sometimes only in relation to particular cases. Very low firm formation rates in old urban-industrial areas may thus primarily reflect sectoral and plant-size structural factors, perhaps aggravated by social class and depressed regional market conditions. High rates in Europe's largest, diversified metropolitan centres may be due to a combination of especially favourable occupational and establishment size structures and buoyant regional demand, with factor supply advantages of secondary significance. The striking recent phenomenon of rural region new firm creation is perhaps chiefly to be understood in terms of socio-cultural considerations. In some regions this involves environmentally-stimulated migration of higher-income professional and managerial workers, whereas in others it reflects a local entrepreneurial tradition rooted in particular agricultural societies. High technology rural region new firms may also be influenced by special factor supply conditions related to university and R and D activity. These judgements are of course tentative, and much more detailed research is needed to test their validity or otherwise in different European cities and regions.

Significance Of New Firms For Urban And Regional Development

The preceding sections of course have so far begged a very important question. Given their generally small size and share of output and employment, are new firms of any real significance for European urban and regional economic development? A negative judgement on this question is suggested by various evidence and arguments. Despite new firm resurgence in Europe since the 1960s, the average size of such firms and contribution to employment and output is generally very small. As Gould and Keeble (1984) show in the East Anglian case, for example, new independent manufacturing firms set up between 1971 and 1981 and surviving to the latter date employed on average only 12 workers each, and accounted for only 4.7 per cent of total 1981 regional manufacturing employment. In the Irish case (O'Farrell and Crouchley 1984), average new manufacturing firm size 1973-81 was exactly similar (12 workers), though larger numbers of such firms yielded a greater, though still very limited, share (7.5 per cent, 1981) of national manufacturing jobs.

These are fairly unimpressive statistics, reflecting the fact that most new firms do not grow to any size, supply local rather than national or international markets, and are established by 'jobber' or 'craftsmen' entrepreneurs with strictly limited horizons and expertise, rather than by 'marketeer' or 'opportunist' founders possessing managerial qualifications and a motivation for growth (Gudgin 1978, 97-100, Storey 1982, 14). Investment, product development and marketing behaviour are frequently inefficient and inadequate (Hankinson 1984). All these factors also contribute to the high death rate common amongst new firms. Thus Gudgin's work (1978, 178) on Leicestershire shows that 25 per cent of all new manufacturing plants set up 1947-57 had closed by 1957, with 66 per cent closing by 1970.

These negative judgements possess considerable force, and at the very least provide an essential counterweight to recent political rhetoric on the presumed merits of new small businesses. However, there also exist positive arguments and aspects of new firm formation which suggest that this phenomenon does justify balanced academic and government interest from the regional development perspective in the Europe of the 1980s. First, academic research, including that presented in this book, suggests that whatever its short-term contribution, in the long-term new firm creation can have an appreciable effect on regional job creation, production and economic prosperity. Thus as Gudgin (1984) demonstrates for Leicestershire, over a thirty-year period (1947-79), new companies can contribute up to one-quarter of total manufacturing employment, and spearhead a major shift in industrial structure, in this case away from specialization in textiles and clothing towards a more diversified, engineering-focussed economy. This is particularly true of areas which develop as 'technology oriented complexes', or where a significant number of 'high-flier' new companies do achieve rapid growth. Thus in the Cambridge region, only four new high-technology firms had, through rapid growth, created as many jobs by 1985 (800) as Gould and Keeble (1984) found for 1981 in all such firms in the whole of East Anglia. Equally, no less than a quarter (4,000) of all Cambridge's current high-technology jobs are in new independent companies set up in only the last ten years, since 1974 (Segal Quince and Partners 1985). The growth of new small firms in the Italian 'industrial districts' studied by Brusco also supports this view of the possible long-term regional significance of new business formation.

A second consideration is that new firm growth does seem to be an integral part of a broader

Introduction

structural shift in European economies which has resulted in a diminished contribution to employment and output by large companies. Indeed, it is very remarkable that in each of at least three countries, the UK (Frank, Miall and Rees 1984), West Germany (Hull 1983, 163) and France (Duche and Savey 1984, 6-7), the later 1970s and early 1980s have witnessed a striking and consistent continuum in rate of employment change with size of manufacturing firm. In each case, the larger the firm size category, the greater the rate of employment <u>loss</u>, while the smaller the firm size category, the greater the rate of employment <u>gain</u>. The latter is almost certainly a reflection of increased new firm formation and young firm growth. The role of such firms as an integral component of broader and radical structural change in European manufacturing may thus be of greater interest than narrow assessment of their activities alone suggests.

A third important issue is the possible significant role of new firms in technological change and innovation, the latter having important implications for long-term regional economic growth. Certainly Brusco (1982) argues that small new Italian firms have exhibited considerable technical ingenuity and innovation potential, which helps to explain the growth of the 'industrial district' phenomenon. Equally, Rothwell (1982, 366) claims that "technology-based new small firms do play an important part in the emergence of new technologies and in economic growth". This view is supported empirically by Segal Quince and Partners' detailed study (1985) of 'the Cambridge Phenomenon', and by Oakey's research (1984, 69) on small high-technology firms in the instrument and electronics industries. The latter found a very high - 76 per cent - new product innovation rate during the previous five-year period amongst the 174 firms surveyed, with a striking 24 per cent rate for the most radical type of innovation possible ("totally new product in new field of technology").

The two final positive arguments concern the role of new firms in the growth of the service sector, and in rural region development. Most of the negative judgements noted earlier are in fact explicitly or implicitly based on consideration of new manufacturing firms. In the case of many growing private sector service industries, however, it may plausibly be argued that new firms are probably of quite considerable job creation and output significance even in the short-run. Though detailed empirical research is lacking, this is certainly suggested by the low average firm size and entry barriers in many consumer and producer service activities. These help explain the high rates of recent new service firm formation. The coincidence of recent growth in the surplus (births minus deaths) of new service firms in countries such as the UK (Table 1) with aggregate employment expansion in private sector services, both nationally and regionally, is also consistent with this view.

Lastly, while it may be true that new firm formation policies in old industrial regions confront major problems of hostile environments, this is almost certainly less valid with regard to regional policies aimed at Europe's low-income rural regions. Some of the latter, notably in central and Adriatic Italy, southern France, and parts of rural Ireland, already exhibit above-average firm formation rates. And the barriers to new firm development noted earlier, such as large plant dominance, capital-intensive industrial structures, socio-cultural considerations and market demand, are probably less extreme, or more amenable to policy intervention, in rural areas than in declining urban-industrial regions. For all these reasons, urban and regional variations in new firm formation, survival and growth in Europe do warrant serious academic and government interest.

Contents And Future Research Directions

The remaining chapters of this book address the issue of urban and regional variations in new firm formation in each of the countries of the European Community except Luxemburg. All draw on and report recent empirical research, including the results of primary surveys of new firm development and entrepreneurship carried out by the authors themselves. While primarily concerned with establishing the nature and dimensions of regional variation in new firm formation, as an essential basis for any understanding of the regional significance of this phenomenon, most chapters also consider possible causes and discuss implications for government policy. Theoretical issues and models of new and small firm development also receive attention in particular contributions, such as those by De Jong/Lambooy on urban incubation theory, Illeris on ethnological 'life-mode' concepts, Brusco on different models of new, small firm evolution in Italy, and Keeble/Kelly on technological change theory. As noted earlier, the overwhelming majority of new firms are also small firms. This explains why, in several cases, authors focus their attention on small firm development as a broader area of enquiry than just new firm formation. This of course also reflects the absence of data on specifically new firms in several cases, as for example with Korte's Community-wide regional analysis and Dokopoulou's research on Greece.

What general conclusions, especially for future research in this field, can be drawn from the ensuing chapters? Certainly this book bears witness to the fascinating variety and complexity of both trends and research on new small firms in the different Community countries. So generalisations are not easy, and are bound to be subjective. Nonetheless, five points can be made, particularly with regard to possible directions for future research.

First, the chapters in this book provide ample evidence that the creation and development of small new independent businesses is now very much back on the research agenda for social science enquiry in general, and investigation by urban and regional researchers in particular, because of the growing firm formation rates and small firm employment levels which are being recorded by most EC countries, at a time when many large corporations have been rationalising their activities and reducing their work forces. From the perspective of regional policy and theory, workers such as Aydalot (1983) thus now even argue that in the 1980s, "large companies that contract their employment needs can no longer control regional development. This responsibility has passed into the hands of the regions themselves", via the creation of new, small enterprises. And in consequence, "we have to make a transition from a theory of localizing large business to a theory of local dynamics, a theory involving the role of the local environment in creating new activities". Aydalot thus sees the whole issue and debate over 'branch-plant' regional economies as a 1960s phenomenon. The new regional issue for the 1980s is in his view the study of why certain, usually previously un-industrialised, regions (such as the French Midi) are generating

spontaneously large numbers of new, small-scale
independent firms. In this context, Aydalot's
suggestion that high rates of new firm formation
are of greater significance as <u>indicators</u> of
regional dynamism, rather than causes, is also
worthy of note.

The second conclusion suggested by this book
is that traditional industrial location theories,
based on assumptions of rational and deliberate
firm location optimisation, and the careful
weighing-up of costs and benefits in different
locations, are inapplicable to the new firm
phenomenon. While attempts to fit aspects of such
traditional theories can be made, as with
explanations based on Shapero's 'availability of
resources' approach and interest in urban
incubation theory, it seems clear that the causes
of the fascinating regional variations in new firm
formation and small firm development identified in
subsequent chapters lie primarily in the nature of
the local population, economy and society. Regional
histories of industrial and agricultural
development, and the changing social composition of
different areas, are much more relevant than the
availability of capital or premises to
understanding why some regions generate many, and
others few, new businesses. Traditional location
theory is also inadequate in that it of course
tells us nothing about the broad macro-economic
forces - recession, rising incomes, technological
change - stimulating a general European resurgence
in numbers of new small firms. Any theoretical
understanding of the regional dimension of new firm
development must also take account of the causes of
this resurgence.

A third point concerns the similarities and
differences of empirical patterns identified in the
different national studies. As noted earlier, broad
generalisations are evident, and can be
substantiated with regard to three different
categories of European regions, namely old
urban-industrial regions, the largest metropolitan
centres, and many rural, previously unindustrialised areas. However, to take the last
category as an example, it was also noted that
there are various exceptions to the pattern of
above-average new firm formation rates in rural
areas. Some of them are regions - the Mezzogiorno,
South-West Ireland, the Greek islands - which are
extremely isolated and peripheral to the main foci
of European economic activity. But others - the

rural problem areas of the Netherlands, for example - are far more accessible. In the light of earlier comments, it seems highly probable that these differences reflect underlying differences in the socio-economic character of these different rural areas, in terms of occupational and social class structures, the impact - positive and negative - of population migration, the nature of agriculture, and so on. In turn, this suggests that there is a clear need for co-ordinated international comparative research on different rural regions, to identify differences in socio-economic structure and their relationship to new business formation and regional dynamism or stagnation.

In addressing the issue of regional policy towards new firms, the chapters in this book provide considerable evidence of the major constraints which must inhibit government efforts in the European Community countries to promote higher rates of new firm births in particular problem regions. O'Farrell's chapter on the Irish case is particularly telling here. However, as Wever has pointed out with respect to the Netherlands, urban and regional policy makers concerned with local job creation are more likely to be able to intervene to promote the viability and growth of <u>existing</u> small companies than to stimulate increased <u>new</u> firm formation rates - although even the former poses major policy problems of instruments, targeting and effectiveness. West German research by Hjern and Hull (1984) has however recently argued from a series of detailed local area case studies that the planned development of sensitive and active small firm local 'assistance agencies', especially in small-town environments where such agencies can achieve high visibility to client populations, has had a marked effect in promoting above-average small firm growth and diminishing business failure rates. The actual and potential role of local/small business assistance structures in different urban and regional environments thus warrants research priority from the policy perspective.

Lastly, though not an issue considered in any detail in the following chapters, there seems to be growing evidence that new firm resurgence is part of a more general trend, at national, regional and local scales, towards more decentralised, small-scale forms of economic organisation and employment structures in advanced capitalist societies. This kind of point, made recently by two of the

Introduction

contributors to this book (Mason and Harrison 1985) in a Progress in Human Geography review of small firm research, thus suggests the need for research on the urban and regional incidence and significance of growing levels of self-employment, of co-operative businesses, of franchising operations, and of other types of decentralised economic activity, in both an organisational and geographical sense. The significance of such activities for so-called counter-urbanisation processes and rural region/small town population and employment growth is as yet largely unexplored by urban and regional researchers.

Notes

1. We are indebted to Professor Philippe Aydalot and Mr. Claude Pottier for this unpublished CEPME (Credit d'Equipement aux Petites et Moyennes Entreprises) data.
2. For example, by + 87 per cent per head in the ten-member European Community between 1960 and 1980, measured at constant prices and in purchasing power parities: see Keeble, 1985B.
3. Arguably as a result of such factors as mass television ownership, and increasing foreign travel, both in turn permitted only by rising real incomes.
4. The first two of these were grouped together as 'behavioural' approaches in Keeble 1985B. In that chapter, 'economic' theory was discussed solely in terms of market demand variations, whereas here factor supply differences are also included under this heading.
5. It is noteworthy that the three UK regions with the highest shares of self-employment in the civilian labour force by 1983 were the South West, East Anglia and Wales (Clement 1984). These are precisely the regions which have experienced the greatest rates of population in-migration over the last decade, much of it arguably for environmental reasons.
6. South Wales new production firm formation rate 1980-83 was only 6.08, lower than all other UK regions except Scotland and Northern England.
7. The famous Sophia-Antipolis high-technology park near Valbonne in the Alpes-Maritimes appears as yet not to be a spontaneously-evolving, new firm-based, TOC, but a large-firm branch unit implantation. Present activity may however

provide the basis for a future, more integrated and indigenous complex.
8. In 1977-78, government defence procurement expenditure in South East England was £1,176 million or 42 per cent of the national total, with the South West accounting for a further £410 million (15 per cent). This compares with total government expenditure on regional policy in the whole of Britain in that year of only £483 million, spread between a number of regions (Scotland, Wales, the North, Merseyside).
9. The South East's share of total UK new companies in 'other services', 1980-83, was 48 per cent, and in 'financial and professional' services 50 per cent. This compares with its 38 per cent share of new manufacturing companies (and 30 per cent share of the UK population). Source: Ganguly 1985.

References

Atkins, T., M. Binks and P. Vale (1983) 'New Firms and Employment Creation', SSRC Newsletter, 49, pp. 22-23

Aydalot, P. (1983) New Spatial Dynamisms in Western Europe: the French Case, Université de Paris 1 Panthéon-Sorbonne, Centre Economie-Espace-Environnement

Baroin, D. and P. Fracheboud (1983) 'Les PME en Europe: et Leur Contribution à l'Emploi', Notes et Etudes Documentaires, La Documentation Francaise, Nos 4715-6

Binks, M. and J. Coyne (1983) 'The Birth of Enterprise', Institute of Economic Affairs, Hobart Papers, No 98

Binks, M. and A. Jennings (1983) New Firms as a Source of Industrial Regeneration, Nottingham University Small Firms Unit

Breheny, M.J. and R.W. McQuaid (1985) 'The M4 Corridor: Patterns and Causes of Growth in High Technology Industries', University of Reading Geographical Papers, No 87

Brusco, S. (1982) 'The Emilian Model: Productive Decentralisation and Social Integration', Cambridge Journal of Economics, 6, pp. 167-184

Brusco, S. and C. Sabel (1981) 'Artisan Production and Economic Growth' in F. Wilkinson (ed.), The Dynamics of Labour Market Segmentation, Academic Press, London, pp. 99-113

Cheshire, P., D. Hay and G. Carbonaro (1984) The Decline of Urban Regions in the EEC: Some

Recent Evidence and the Scope for Community
Policy, Joint Centre for Land Development
Studies, Reading University

Chisholm, M. (1984) 'The Development Commission's
Factory Programme', Regional Studies, 18, pp.
514-517

Clement, B. (1984) 'Service Sectors Benefit as More
Workers Go It Alone to Beat Recession', The
Times, October 15, 4

Duche, G. and S. Savey, (1984) Nouvelle
Organisation de la Production et PME; Vers un
Nouveau Système Industriel, Université Paul
Valéry, Montpellier

Fothergill, S. and G. Gudgin (1982) Unequal Growth:
Urban and Regional Employment Change in the
UK, Heinemann, London

Frank, C.E.J., R.H.C. Miall and R.D. Rees (1984)
'Issues in Small Firms Research of Relevance
to Policy Making', Regional Studies, 18, pp.
257-266

Freeman, C. (1983) Long Waves in the World Economy,
Butterworths, London

Freeman, C. (1984) The Role of Technical Change in
National Economic Development, Science Policy
Research Unit, University of Sussex

Ganguly, P. (1982) 'Births and Deaths of Firms in
the UK in 1980', British Business, January 29

Ganguly, P. (1984) 'Business Starts and Stops:
Regional Analyses by Turnover Size and Sector
1980-83', British Business, November 2

Ganguly, P. (1985) 'Business Starts and Stops: UK
County Analysis 1980-83', British Business,
January 18

Gould, A. and D. Keeble (1984) 'New Firms and Rural
Industrialization in East Anglia', Regional
Studies, 18, pp. 189-201

Greffe, X. (1984) Les P.M.E. Créent-Elles Des
Emplois? Economica, Paris

Gudgin, G. (1978) Industrial Location Processes and
Regional Employment Growth, Saxon House,
Farnborough

Gudgin, G. (1984) Employment Creation by Small and
Medium Sized Firms in the U.K., Department of
Applied Economics, University of Cambridge

Hall, P. (1981) 'The Geography of the Fifth
Kondratieff Cycle', New Society, March 26, pp.
535-537

Hankinson, A. (1984) 'Small Firms' Investment: A
Search for the Motivations', International
Small Business Journal, 2, pp. 11-24

Hjern, B. and C. Hull (1984) Beyond Bureaucracy and

Market: Helping Small Firms Grow, International Institute of Management, Science Center, Berlin

Hull, C. (1983) 'Federal Republic of Germany', in D.J. Storey (ed.), The Small Firm: an International Survey, Croom Helm, London, 153-178

Jones, H., J. Caird and N. Ford (1984) 'A Home in the Highlands', Town and Country Planning, 53, pp. 326-327

Keeble, D. (1985A) 'Industrial Change in the United Kingdom', in W.F. Lever (ed.), Industrial Change in the United Kingdom, Longman, Harlow, chapter 1

Keeble, D. (1985B) 'The Changing Spatial Structure of Economic Activity and Metropolitan Decline in the United Kingdom', in H-J Ewers (ed.), The Future of the Metropolis, De Gruyter, Berlin

Keeble, D. and A. Gould (1984) New Manufacturing Firms and Entrepreneurship in East Anglia: Final Report to the Economic and Social Research Council, Department of Geography, University of Cambridge

Keeble, D. and A. Gould (1985) 'Entrepreneurship and Manufacturing Firm Formation in Rural Regions: the East Anglian Case', in M.J. Healey and B.W. Ilbery (eds.), Industrialization of the Countryside, Geobooks, Norwich

Klaassen, L.H. and W.M.T. Molle (1983) Industrial Mobility and Migration in the European Community, Gower, Aldershot

Lloyd, P.E. and C.M. Mason (1984) 'Spatial Variations in New Firm Formation in the United Kingdom: Comparative Evidence from Merseyside, Greater Manchester and South Hampshire', Regional Studies, 18, pp. 207-220

Mason, C.M. and R.T. Harrison (1985) 'The Geography of Small Firms in the UK: Towards a Research Agenda', Progress in Human Geography, 9, pp. 1-37

Mensch, G. (1979) Stalemate in Technology: Innovations Overcome the Depression, Ballinger, New York

Merritt, G. (1985) 'Siemens Leads Bavarian Boom', The Sunday Times, July 14, 61

Morgan, K. and A. Sayer (1984) 'A 'Modern' Industry in a 'Mature' Region: the Re-making of Management-Labour Relations', University of Sussex, Urban and Regional Studies Working

Paper, 39

Oakey, R. (1984) High-Technology Small Firms:
Innovation and Regional Development in Britain
and the United States, Frances Pinter, London

O'Farrell, P.N. and R. Crouchley (1984) 'An
Industrial and Spatial Analysis of New Firm
Formation in Ireland', Regional Studies, 18,
pp. 221-236

Perez, C. (1983) 'Structural Change and the
Assimilation of New Technologies in the
Economic and Social System', Futures, 15, pp.
357-375

Robert, J. (1984) Technical Report on What is at
Stake in the Traditional Industrial Regions of
Europe, Région Nord-Pas de Calais

Rothwell, R. (1982) 'The Role of Technology in
Industrial Change: Implications for Regional
Policy', Regional Studies, 16, pp. 361-369

Schumpeter, J.A. (1939) Business Cycles: a
Theoretical, Historical and Statistical
Analysis of the Capitalist Process,
McGraw-Hill, New York

Segal Quince and Partners (1985) The Cambridge
Phenomenon: The Growth of High-Technology
Industry in a University Town, Cambridge

Shapero, A. (1983) New Business Formation, Enschede

Shutt, J. and R. Whittington (1984) 'Large Firm
Strategies and the Rise of Small Units: the
Illusion of Small Firm Job Generation',
University of Manchester, School of Geography
Working Paper 15

Storey, D.J. (1982) Entrepreneurship and the New
Firm, Croom Helm, Beckenham

Storey, D.J. (1984) Business Competitiveness: the
Role of Small Firms, University of
Newcastle-upon-Tyne, Centre for Urban and
Regional Development Studies

The Times (1984) Small Businesses: A Special
Report, June 21

The Treasury (1984) 'Helping Markets Work Better':
and 'The Business Expansion Scheme', Economic
Progress Report, 173, pp. 1-6

Town and Country Planning (1985) 'Planning for the
Future', Town and Country Planning, 54, esp.
111-122

Whittington, R.C. (1984) 'Regional Bias in New Firm
Formation in the UK', Regional Studies, 18,
pp. 253-256

Wright, M., J. Coyne and H. Lockley (1984)
'Regional Aspects of Management Buyouts: Some
Evidence', Regional Studies, 18, pp. 428-431

Chapter two

SMALL AND MEDIUM-SIZED ESTABLISHMENTS IN WESTERN
EUROPE

Werner B. Korte

Introduction

Regional patterns and trends of small and medium-sized enterprises are becoming increasingly important in the framework of the regional policies pursued by the various member countries of the European Community. The lack of success of traditional instruments, aimed at the transfer of industrial activity to assisted regions, has led to the recognition of the relevance of indigenous potential from both the regional policy and regional science perspectives. This shift in emphasis has generated a series of investigations into forms and conditions of promotion of indigenous regional development. Although much neglected in empirical studies[1], in this connection small and medium-sized enterprises (subsequently referred to as SMEs) play a key role. Whereas transfer-related policies aim at the attraction of large companies, the creation or extension of SMEs in backward or depressed regions is arguably the only feasible basis for indigenous regional economic development.

It is against this background that this chapter is to be viewed. The main focus lies on the empirical investigation of regional patterns and trends of SMEs in Europe. The first section briefly reviews certain theoretical considerations which are relevant in this context. Subsequent sections then describe the statistical basis of the analysis, and present original empirical results concerning the nature of recent regional trends and patterns of SMEs, especially in the manufacturing sector, across the European Community as a whole. Finally the main conclusions are summarized.

EEC

Background

There are widely divergent estimates of the ability of SMEs to adjust to economic change, of their role with regard to innovation, and of their job creation potential. It is therefore not possible, nor would it be meaningful, to base the present study on a simple, one-dimensional set of hypotheses.

It can be argued that economic recessions mainly affect regions with enterprises that are largely export-oriented. Since most export-oriented enterprises are larger companies which have so far generally been able to benefit from the advantages of central locations, in the form of the main, densely populated and industrialized regions of particular countries, an economic recession will first affect these regions. However, as a result of their structure and the selective regional effects of anticyclical economic policy measures, these regions will also be the first to recover in an upswing phase.

SMEs, on the other hand, are generally considered to be a stabilizing factor in employment, and according to the 'medium-sized enterprise hypothesis' they may contribute to maintaining or increasing employment, rather than to its reduction. That means that they will be less affected in times of recession and may maintain output and employment better than large firms, so that regions where the enterprise structure is largely that of SMEs will also record a better economic performance.

Similar views are expressed by Kamp (1981) on the relation between regional and sectoral unemployment and regional enterprise size structure in his very detailed study of regions and sectors in the Federal Republic of Germany.

A recent study on regional unemployment in the FRG reaches similar conclusions on the significance of establishment size structure (DFG 1979). It states that:
- regions with continued high unemployment and a large share of persons employed in SMEs exhibit the lowest growth rates of unemployment in times of recession;
- the 'medium-sized enterprise hypothesis' does apply to some regions, but not all; and
- there is at least some connection between the share of employment in large-scale enterprises and regional unemployment.

36

If SMEs are located mainly in structurally weak areas while large enterprises tend to be in densely populated areas (growth poles), it may be assumed that the geographical distribution of enterprises does initially tend to favour innovation advantages (agglomeration advantages). The 'dynamic spread of ideas and values' (Myrdal 1959), i.e. the diffusion of innovation, is firstly between large enterprises in growth centres (densely populated areas) or between these centres. Only in later stages do the innovations reach peripheral rural areas. This means that SMEs located there do not share in this until very much later.

During the 1960s and early 1970s, many enterprises were active in establishing branch plants in structurally weak areas. Besides lower labour costs the state aided the enterprises with massive incentive and promotion programmes, in the Federal Republic of Germany, for instance, with the Act on the Promotion of Border Areas.

SMEs in industries located primarily in rural areas may preserve jobs more because they belong to large firms which have been stepping up their presence in these areas, than because of a better indigenous small firm performance. This may even be true where declining sectors, including declining service sectors, are involved. The problem of the 'extended workbench' (as branch plants are sometimes called) therefore deserves special consideration, because a balanced or positive situation in a regional economy and on a rural labour market can be reversed through branch establishments. Friedmann speaks of a certain 'colonial' exploitation between the growth poles and the hinterland. "The dominance of the pole prevents independent development in the hinterland. The pole 'colonialises' the hinterland by the establishment of branchplants, because it passes on the costs of cyclical and structural adjustment to the hinterland and because if there is a crisis the branchplant is closed first, i.e. the incidence of crisis costs tend to be higher in the hinterland" (Fürst et al. 1976).

It is against the background of these few general remarks that the regional distribution and trends of SMEs are examined subsequently.

Statistical Basis

The data used for the empirical analysis come from

two sources, namely EEC statistics (Eurostat 1981) and official national statistics (Appendix 1). It is necessary to use two sources, because the EEC data are not detailed enough; no data is available, for example, for employment in establishments with less than 10 employees. The use of Community statistics in addition to national statistics is necessary because the national data are often not comparable in terms of definitions.

A sub-division of the data by industries is only possible for a few countries so that a comparative analysis is limited to a simple breakdown in 'manufacturing' and 'services'. Here too, however, problems arise in that often data are not available for the service sector in adequate regional differentiation and according to size category of establishments; in some cases only global data are given. Moreover, the reference years of the available national data vary greatly from one country to another.

Fig. 1 displays the available national data. There are considerable variations between the EEC data and the official statistics of member states. For example, the number employed in manufacturing (not including electricity, gas and water) in the Federal Republic of Germany in 1978 was according to the EEC statistics (EEC 1972 and 1978) 8,895,111. According to the Statistical Yearbook for the Federal Republic of Germany the same figure for 1978 was only 8,668,000. A comparison with the EUROSTAT statistics merely adds to the confusion, since the figure here is substantially greater, at 10,452,000. Still another set of EEC statistics (Regional Statistics of the DG XVI) gives 10,741,000. The situation is similar for France[2], where the figures vary between 5,830,079 and 7,625,000.

Taking the data-related problems into consideration, we proceeded as follows:
- A set of data was produced for a global analysis of the structure and development of employment from 1972 to 1978 for establishment size categories 10-49 and 50, differentiated according to NACE groups 2000, 3000, 4000 and 5000 and on the basis of the regions on level I;
- An analysis was made of the structure and development of employment from 1972 to 1978 in establishment size category 10-49 in level I regions differentiated according to NACE groups;
- A set of data was compiled for an analysis of the structure and development of employment for the

Fig. 1. Establishment Size Categories in the Official Statistics of EEC-Member States (Regional Level I).

Country	Year	Size Groups								
F.R.G. [1]	1970		1-9		10-49	50-99	100-199	200-499	500-999	≥1000
	1975		1-9		10-49	50-99	100-199	200-499	500-999	≥1000
Denmark	1970		6-9	10-19	20-49	50-99	100-199	200-499	≥500	
	1980		6-9	10-19	20-49	50-99	100-199	200-499	≥500	
France	1978	1-4	5-9	10-19	20-49	50-99	100-199	200-499	≥500	
	1981		1-9		10-49		50-199	200-499	≥500	
Luxemburg	1975				20-49	50-99	100-199	200-499	500-999	≥1000
	1978				20-49	50-99	100-199	200-499	500-999	≥1000
Greece	1963	1-4	5-9		10-49	≥50				
	1973	1-4	5-9		10-49	≥50				
	1978	1-4	5-9		10-49	≥50				
Netherlands	1970				10-49	50-99	100-199	200-499	≥500	
	1974		1-9	≥10						
	1981		1-9	≥10						
	1981			10-19	20-49	50-99	100-199	200-499	≥500	
Italy	1971		1-9	10-19	20-49	50-99	100-199	200-499	500-999	≥1000
	1981		1-9	10-19	20-49	50-99	100-199	200-499	500-999	≥1000
Ireland	1981				3-49	50-99	100-199	200-499	≥500	
Belgium [2]	1973	1-4	5-9	10-19	20-49	50-99	100-199	200-499	500-999	≥1000
	1982	1-4	5-9	10-19	20-49	50-99	100-199	200-499	500-999	≥1000
United Kingdom [3]	1976	1-10		11-24	25-49	50-99	100-199	200-499	500-999	≥1000
	1978	1-10		11-24	25-49	50-99	100-199	200-499	500-999	≥1000

1) Regional Level II
2) Total (no regional differentiation)
3) Total (no regional differentiation)

seventies and early eighties, with an attempt at further differentiation according to establishment size categories on the basis of the regions on level II, differentiated according to industries;
- A detailed analysis was made of the structure and development of employment in the seventies and early eighties in level II regions.

Overview Of Trends And Distribution Of Employment By Size Of Establishment

An overall picture at Community level of the distribution of employment and the relative importance of small and medium-sized enterprises and establishments is displayed in Fig. 2.

At the level of member states it appears that, in general, manufacturing employment is dominated by larger establishments (1000 employees and over), with the notable exception of Denmark where enterprises with 10-49 employees are dominant. The largest concentration of employment in enterprises with 1000 employees and over can be found in the

Fig. 2. Distribution of Employment in Enterprises and Establishments by their Size at European Level 1978*.

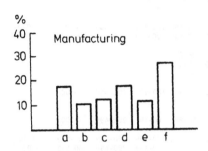 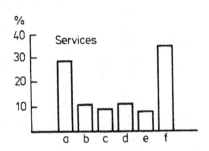

a) 10 - 49 employees   d)   200 - 499 employees
b) 50 - 99 employees   e)   500 - 1000 employees
c) 100 - 199 employees   f) 1000 and over employees

* The EEC-average for the service sector does not include Greece, the U.K., Ireland and Luxemburg. The EEC-average for manufacturing excludes Ireland, Luxemburg and Greece.
Source: EUROSTAT, Labour Cost Survey 1978

Federal Republic of Germany (37% of total employment in establishments with 1000 employees and over) and in the U.K. (32%).

The recent distribution of employment by size of enterprise in the tertiary sector shows that in comparison to the distribution in manufacturing, employment in services is much more polarized. In all Member States for which data are available, establishments with 10-49 and 1000 employees and over assume the highest shares of employment. Whereas employment in establishments within the four groups with 50-999 employees hardly exceeds 10% of the total in each case, employment in the 10-49 and the 1000 and over groups accounts in both cases for over 20% in all Member States, even exceeding 30% in most of them.

With regard to trends of employment, in general, a correlation seems to exist between changes in the composition of employment by size of

establishment of enterprises, and aggregate changes
in employment. Tendencies towards concentration
occurred mostly in those countries and industries
which experienced relatively small losses of
employment. Deconcentration in turn was found in
those countries in which industries suffered rather
large losses in manufacturing employment.

Generalization of these findings with regard
to size and industry-related changes of
manufacturing employment may shed more light on
this correlation. We are basically dealing here
with two groups of countries: the United Kingdom,
Belgium, Denmark, the Netherlands and the Federal
Republic of Germany, where trends towards
deconcentration became apparent or where the
largest businesses suffered relative losses of
employment, and France and Italy where clear trends
towards high increases in employment in large
establishments were observed, while relative losses
were found in the smallest units. In this second
group, reductions of employment in manufacturing
industries were fairly low. In France, the level of
national manufacturing employment decreased by only
0.6% p.a. during 1970-1979, while in Italy it even
showed a slight increase of +0.1% p.a. By
countrast, in the first group of countries, which
showed trends towards deconcentration and a growing
relative importance of small establishments,
manufacturing employment decreased during the
seventies by rates varying between -1.4% p.a. and
-2.0% p.a.

This finding of an interdependence between
volume and size specific changes of employment -
reductions of employment associated with relative
growth of small businesses, and increases with
relative growth of large businesses - clearly needs
further investigation. The available literature
does however seem to provide some additional
evidence to support our thesis. Stroetmann (1978),
for instance, shows in an analysis of SMEs that:
"For example, in leather production, imports and
substitutive materials, more than two-thirds of all
jobs have been lost from 1963 to 1973. At the same
time, companies having fewer than 200 employees
increased the relative percentage of working places
provided by about 70% (from 50% to more than 85%),
whereas out of six firms having more than 500
employees only one - a smaller one - survived". The
general coincidence of volume and size specific
changes in manufacturing employment suggests that,
in a sluggish or recessionary economic climate,

small businesses are more likely to maintain
certain levels of demand for labour than larger
ones.

Our analysis also suggests that the general
pattern of trends in service employment is largely
identical with the one observed in manufacturing.
At the level of individual industries the
employment growth of SMEs has occurred mostly in
those NACE groups which represent rather basic
services (for instance, wholesale trade in
furniture and household materials, retail trade in
footwear and leather goods, cleaning materials, and
the like). Most high-productivity services in their
turn (like banking and the non-food sector in
retail trade) exhibited increasing employment in
large enterprises.

Regional Patterns and Trends of SMEs

The following maps (see also Appendix 2) show the
present size structure of employment in
manufacturing industry in the regions of the EEC,
as well as the average annual variation in
employment in establishments with 1-9 and 10-49
employees during the seventies and early eighties.
While a certain proportion of these small or
medium-sized establishments are likely to be
branches or subsidiaries of larger multi-plant
enterprises, the great majority are undoubtedly
local, independent, single-plant firms. At this
size scale, 'firm' and 'establishment' are thus
broadly interchangeable. It should be noted that
average annual variation has been calculated using
the formula given in Appendix 1.

As can be seen, SMEs gained considerably in
importance virtually throughout Europe in terms of
their employment shares in the seventies and early
eighties. In some cases, they were able very
greatly to increase their share of employment. This
seems to have been particularly true for
establishments with 10-49 employees, either because
larger establishments have shrunk or smaller ones
have increased their employment share. By the early
1980s, 42% of EEC regions had at least one-fifth of
their manufacturing employment in firms of this
size.

Since in many regions with a strong growth in
the share of employment in medium-sized
establishments (10-49 employees) the share of
employment in small establishments (1-9 employees)

Fig. 3. Employment in % in Manufacturing Industries in Establishments with 1-9 Employees in the EEC Level II Regions (c. 1980).

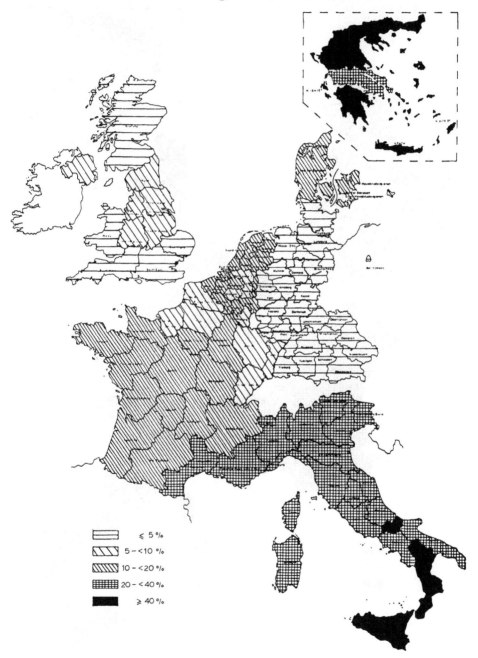

≤ 5 %
5 – <10 %
10 – <20 %
20 – <40 %
≥ 40 %

Fig. 4. Employment in % in Manufacturing Industries in Establishments with 10-49 Employees in the EEC Level II Regions (c. 1980).

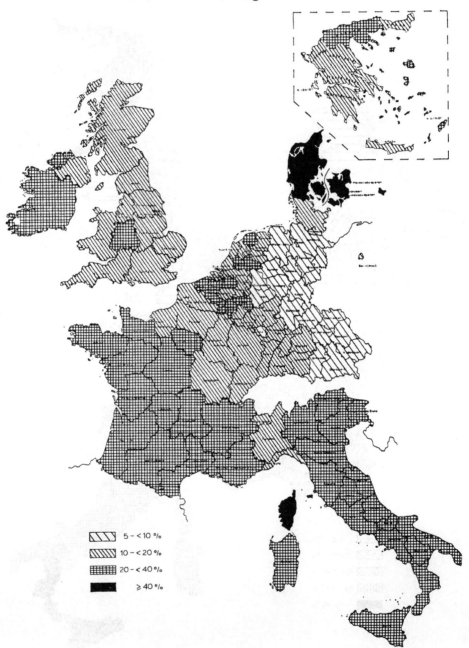

5 - < 10 %
10 - < 20 %
20 - < 40 %
≥ 40 %

Fig. 5. Average Annual Variation in Employment in %
in Manufacturing Industries in
Establishments with 1-9 Employees in the
EEC Level II Regions (c. 1970-1980).

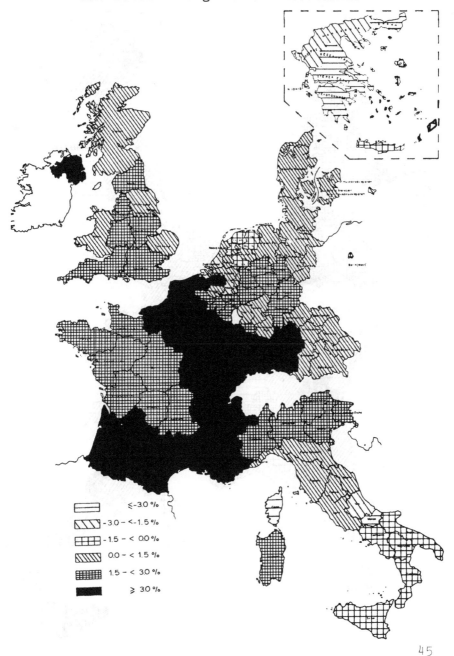

⊟	≤-3.0 %
◨	-3.0 - <-1.5%
⊞	-1.5 - < 0.0%
◩	0.0 - < 1.5%
▦	1.5 - < 3.0%
■	≥ 30 %

45

Fig. 6. Average Annual Variation in Employment in %
in Manufacturing Industries in
Establishments with 10-49 Employees in the
EEC Level II Regions (c. 1970-1980).

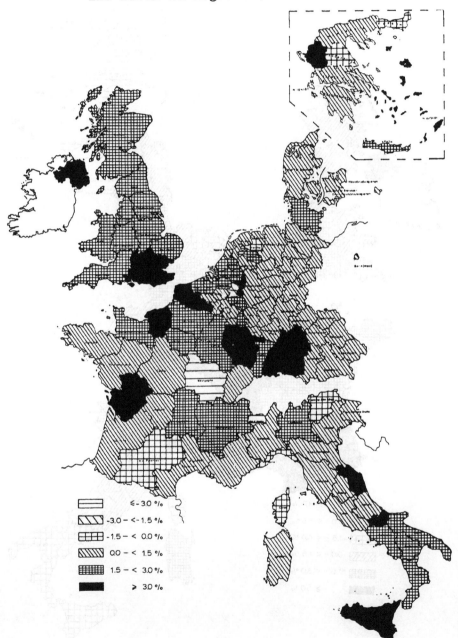

≤ -3.0 %
-3.0 - < -1.5 %
-1.5 - < 0.0 %
0.0 - < 1.5 %
1.5 - < 3.0 %
≥ 3.0 %

dropped strongly at the same time, it would appear that during the seventies there was a marked expansion of small establishments which then appear in the early eighties in the category of establishments with 10-49 employees. With the data available in this study, it is not possible to confirm this assumption, and hasty conclusions should not be drawn at this point. The growth in the employment share of medium-sized establishments could just as easily be due to the shrinkage of more large establishments to medium size and the liquidation of more small establishments (1-9 employees).

The share of employment in large establishments in the traditional industrial countries, such as the Federal Republic of Germany, the United Kingdom, the BENELUX countries and Northern France, is still predominant despite positive trends in employment shares in SMEs in the seventies and early eighties.

Only in the United Kindom, Belgium, Central and Southern Italy, in the French region Languedoc-Roussillon, the coastal regions of the Netherlands and Lower Saxony, Hamburg and the Saarland[3] does there seem to have been an increase in the share of employment in large establishments. However, data problems with respect to the first two countries (see notes) are such that this apparent finding is probably incorrect. Thus very recently published United Kindom statistics in fact reveal that large manufacturing establishments actually shed employment rapidly during the 1970s, whereas employment in small UK plants grew (Frank et al. 1984). This trend has continued in the 1980s (see Chapter 1).

In general, the less developed rural and peripheral regions of the EC are characterized by over-proportional shares of SMEs, while large establishments still predominate in the highly developed and densely populated regions. The relatively greater importance of SMEs in such regions as southern Italy, rural France, Ireland and Greece clearly reflects the limited historic extent and character of industrialization in these isolated areas. These rural and peripheral regions have not attracted large-scale industry, but have rather specialized in labour-intensive small-scale industries such as clothing, textiles, footwear and furniture[4]

SMEs in these regions are moreover probably disadvantaged because of their very location in structurally weak, peripheral areas. They do not enjoy the locational advantages of more central, densely populated areas (agglomeration economies), such as density of information, accessibility to customers, availability of highly-qualified manpower, access to finance and business services, and so on. Studies also suggest that technological innovation is concentrated in large establishments in densely populated central regions, and that any innovation diffusion which does occur takes place firstly in or between such centres. Peripheral rural areas, and with them the SMEs which are primarily located here, do not participate in this until much later (Nijkamp and Paelinck 1974). This may partly reflect the appreciably higher costs of information access by EC-wide telecommunication systems in peripheral as compared with central regions revealed by recent research (Goddard et al. 1983).

These location disadvantages together with the familiar deficits in management, labour quality, information, finance, exports, and research and development (see Hamke et al. 1976, Hunt et al. 1979 and Stroetmann 1978) mean that rural or peripheral region SMEs lack the prerequisites to be innovative in the local economy. Their contribution to job maintenance and creation is therefore very much more limited than might be desired. Peripheral regions thus derive little stimulus to economic growth from their concentration of SMEs, with a resultant widening of the gap in incomes and output between the centre (densely populated, highly developed regions) and periphery (rural, relatively inaccessible, problem regions). In concrete terms this means that within the countries of the European Community a further intensification of regional disparities is likely, or that at least the existing difference between the centre and periphery must be expected to continue.

Conclusions

Several general conclusions can be drawn from the results and they can be summarized as follows.
- Between 1973 and 1980 employment in manufacturing industry in the European Community fell by around 3.2 million. At the same time employment in establishments with a workforce of 500 and more dropped by about 3.6 million. Although the utmost caution must be exercised in comparing these

figures, since there are differences in definitions, it can broadly be said that the loss of employment in industry over recent years has been mainly in large establishments, while smaller establishments have at least been able to maintain the level of their employment, if not increase it.

- At the regional scale, large establishments have only been able to increase their employment shares in parts of the United Kingdom, Belgium, Central and Southern Italy, the French region of Languedoc-Roussillon, the coastal regions of the Netherlands and Lower Saxony, Hamburg and the Saarland. In the highly industrialized developed regions SMEs are historically less well represented; their shares of employment, however, have grown (with the exception of the German city states Hamburg, Bremen and Berlin) in the seventies and early eighties, often quite considerably.

- In certain highly industrialized regions which are specialized in such declining industries as coal-mining, steel, shipbuilding and textiles, medium-sized enterprises have been able to increase their share of employment greatly, especially in the Nord-Pas-de-Calais, Lorraine, Alsace and Haute-Normandie.

- Viewed from a European-wide perspective, SMEs are particularly characteristic of structurally-weak regions that exhibit low shares of employment in industry, low population density, an extremely low GDP and high unemployment, especially among young people. Examples include the regions of Greece, Ireland, southern Italy and rural France.

- The development of the share of employment in very small establishments (1-9 employees) in the peripheral regions of southern Italy and Greece, on the other hand, was the converse of the general global expansion in this category found in the rest of the EEC. In these extreme peripheral regions, and starting from an extremely high level of employment in this size category, the share of small establishments dropped in some cases drastically over the period under review. Whether this development is due to the liquidation of establishments with 1-9 employees and/or the expansion of establishments in this size category into that of establishments with 10-49 employees cannot be established within the framework of this study.

EEC

Notes

1. Most available analyses in the area of SMEs and regional development are case study based and thus are not suitable, for instance, for purposes of gaining an overall picture of regional patterns or trends or to select priority regions for policy intervention.
2. France 1978: EUROSTAT 7,213,000, regional statistics of DG XVI 7,625,000, "Bulletin de Liaison" de L'U.N.E.D.I.C., Institut National de la Statistique et des Etudes Economiques 6,968,589, unpublished data from the social statistics 5,830,079.
3. No data is available for Greece. The period examined for the Federal Republic of Germany is only from 1970 to 1975.
4. See findings on centre-periphery differences in regional manufacturing structures within the EC, 1973-81, in Keeble, D., P.L. Owens and C. Thompson (1982) Centrality, Peripherality and EEC Regional Development, HMSO, London: Keeble, D., R. Evans and C. Thompson (1983) Final Report on Updating of the Centrality, Peripherality and EEC Regional Development Study, Department of Geography, University of Cambridge.

References

DFG (1979) Regionale Arbeitslosigkeit
EEC Statistical Office in Luxemburg, Unpublished data in social statistics: Structure of wages and salaries in industry in 1972 and 1978
EUROSTAT (1981) 'Main Regional Indicators (Excerpts from the Yearbook of Regional Statistics)', Luxemburg, Structure of Earnings and Labour Cost (1972, 1978, 1981)
Federal Statistical Office, Statistical Yearbook 1981 for the Federal Republic of Germany
Frank, C.E.J., R.H.C. Miall and R.D. Rees (1984) 'Issues in Small Firms Research of Relevance to Policy-making' Regional Studies, 18, 3, pp. 257-266
Fürst D., P. Klemmer, P. Zimmermann (1976) Regionale Wirtschaftspolitik, Düsseldorf
Goddard, J.B., A.T. Thwaites, A.E. Gillespie, I.G. Smith (1983) Study of the Effects of New Information Technology on the Less Favoured Regions of the Community, Centre of Urban and Regional Development Studies, University of Newcastle upon Tyne

EEC

Hamke, F., K.A. Stroetmann (1976) Die Anpassung
kleiner und mittlerer Unternehmungen an den
technischen Wandel. Eine Analyse der
Innovationsprobleme kleiner und mittlerer
Unternehmungen unter dem Gesichtspunkt
möglicher staatlicher Fördermassnahmen. ISI
Diskussionspapier 22.11.1976
Hunt, D. (November 1979) Small Independent
Enterprise and Employment Creation. Main
Report for the Commission of the EEC
Kamp, M.E. (1981) 'Zum Zusammenhang von
regionaler und sektoraler Arbeitslosigkeit und
regionaler Unternehmensgrössenstruktur',
Beiträge zur Mittelstandsforschung, Heft 68,
Göttingen
Myrdal, G. (1959), Okonomische Theorie und
unterentwickelte Regionen, Stuttgart
Nijkamp, P., J.H.P. Paelinck (1974) Diffusion of
Development Processes in Regional and Urban
Systems, Rotterdam
Statistical Office of the European Communities in
Luxembourg (1971-1980), EUROSTAT Review
Stroetmann, K. (1978) 'Innovation in Small and
Medium Industrial Firms' in Gerstenfeld, A.
and R. Brainard (eds.) Technological
Innovation: Government-Industry Cooperation,
New York, pp. 93-103

EEC

Appendix 1

Sources of the Statistical Data

Belgium: O.N.S.S., Office national de securite sociale. Effectifs des employeurs et des travailleurs assujettis a la securite sociale au 30 juin 1973 et 30 juin 1982.

F.R.G.:   Statistisches Bundesamt. Statistisches Jahrbuch fuer die Bundesrepublik Deutschland 1972 und 1977.

United Kingdom: Department of Employment Gazette, January 1976. From Department of Employment displayed data: Census of Employment 1978.

Netherlands: From the 'Stichting Economisch Technologisch Instituut voor Gelderland' in Arnhem displayed data. Maandstatistiek van de industrie, Augustus 1982. Centraal Bureau voor de Statistiek, 's-Gravenhage.

Denmark: The Chamber of Danish Trades and Crafts. The Creation of New Jobs in Small and Medium Enterprises in Denmark, o.O., o.J.

Greece: E.O.M.M.E.X. 1983

France: 'Bulletin de Liaison' de L'U.N.E.D.I.C., Institut National de la Statistique et des Etudes Economique pour 1977 et 1981.

Italy: 6° censimento generale dell'industria, del commercio, dei servizi e dell'artigianato, 26 ottobre 1981. Volume 1 primi risultati sulle impresse e sulle unita locali (dati provvisori), Tomo 1 - Dati nazionali, regionali e provinziali, Instituto Centrale di Statistica, Roma 1983. Instituto Centrale Statistica, Annuario di Statistiche Provinciali, Volume XII, Edizione 1973, Roma 1973.

Luxembourg: Ministere d'Etat Service Central de la Statistique es des Etudes Economiques: Resultats de l'enquete 1975 et 1978.

Ireland: Small Firms Association. The Confederation of Irish Industry: Development Proposals for Small Firms 1983.

EUROSTAT: Main Regional Indicators (Excerpt from the Yearbook of Regional Statistics) 1981.

Change Rate Calculation

The average annual variation in percentage share of SME employment in manufacturing was calculated by the following formula, which reduces the impact of very large percentage change values based on small initial figures:

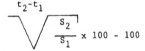

$$\sqrt[t_2-t_1]{\frac{S_2}{S_1}} \times 100 - 100$$

S_2 = percentage share value t_2
S_1 = percentage share value t_1
t_2 = (c. 1980)
t_1 = (c. 1970)

EEC

Appendix 2

Notes concerning the maps

Employment structure (1980)

- Federal Republic of Germany 1975
- Denmark 1980 (1-9 = 6-9)
- Netherlands 1981
- Greece 1978 (except ≥ 500)
- France 1981
- Italy 1981
- Luxemburg 1980 (except 1-9) (10-49 = 20-49)
- Ireland 1981 (except 1-9) (10-49 = 3-50)
- United Kingdom 1981 (Estimation by ABT Forschung)
- Belgium 1982 (Estimation by ABT Forschung)

Average Yearly Changes in Employment (1970-1980)

- Federal Republic of Germany 1970-1975
- Denmark 1970-1980
- Netherlands 1970-1981
- Greece 1973-1978
- France 1977-1981
- Italy 1971-1981
- Luxemburg 1975-1980
- Ireland (Data not available)
- United Kingdom 1973-1981 (Estimation by ABT Forschung)
- Belgium 1971-1982 (Estimation by ABT Forschung)

Chapter three

NEW FIRM FORMATION IN THE NETHERLANDS

Egbert Wever

Introduction

As was described in the introductory chapter, newly
created firms attract a lot of attention in the
Netherlands. The main reason for this has to do
with the employment function of new firms. Moreover
policy-makers in the problem regions now realize
that bigger companies will probably not be able to
create all the new jobs needed. From research
conducted in the (problem) provinces of Friesland
and Limburg it became immediately apparent that
there are large spatial differences in the number
of new firms founded even within a small country
like Holland. These differences excited the
interest of others and resulted in a research
project financed by our Ministry of Economic
Affairs. The main research questions investigated
in this project were:
- how many new firms have been founded in the
  various regions (districts of Chambers of
  Commerce) within the Netherlands?
- how many of these firms have survived?
- what are the regional differences in the type of
  new firms created?
    The results of this investigation were
published in 1984 (Wever 1984). Differences were
found in the number of births as well as in the
number of closures. As a result, a follow-up
research project was commissioned by the Ministry.
The main research in this second project, based on
questions directed to new entrepreneurs (including
those who had failed), were:
- do new entrepreneurs in different regions differ
  as far as personal characteristics are concerned?
- why are new firms in some regions doing better
  than in other regions?

Netherlands

From a policy point of view it is easier to prevent a new entrepeneur from failing than to persuade someone to start. Therefore attention was focussed on the way new entrepreneurs prepare and run their firms. Because of this emphasis it was decided to co-operate with the department of business-administration of the Technical University Twente. Such co-operation fits very well within the business oriented economic geography promoted in Nijmegen University (see Wever and Grit 1984). This research project was completed only recently. In this chapter the most interesting results of both projects will be presented. Emphasis will be laid on spatial aspects.

The basis for the research on new firms was a 'cohort analysis'. In this sort of analysis a record is made of all changes that occur in the lifetime of firms that were started or established in a region in a given year. In this project the chosen cohorts were 1970, 1975 and 1980. To these cohorts belong all firms that entered the business register of a Chamber of Commerce in that year for the first time and which had not been in existence for more than three years prior to that data. There are three types of new firms:
- newly created branch plants of already existing companies;
- plants relocated from another district;
- newly created independent firms.
The first two categories can be seen as external initiatives, though branches can also be created by a 'regional' company. The third category can be seen as internal or regional initiatives, although even this is not quite correct. Most plants established in the Netherlands by foreign companies are registered as independent firms in company law. However the number of such plants is small compared to the total number of new independent firms. It would therefore seem reasonable to use the term 'regional' initiatives.

It is not possible in a review chapter to consider in detail all the positive and negative aspects of the data used. However an important restriction is that not all openings which create employment are registered by the Chambers. So the research does not include public institutions, semi-public services, independent professions and most agricultural, mining and fishing activities. Another point is that the Chambers register purely administrative and 'hobby' (not run for the owners' livelihood) firms and although an attempt was made to exclude them not all will have been successfully excluded from the research. A third point is that new firm registration takes place in 38 centres throughout the Netherlands. Although it is considered important to have uniform procedures it is possible that some differences may exist. And, finally, data about the number of jobs in the new firms is incomplete. Only figures for recent years are available, so we were not able to follow, as David Birch did, the employment creation process.

However, the use of data from the Chambers also has positive aspects. The first is that data can be compared for 38 regions covering the whole of the Netherlands. Moreover, the data include small firms - even firms without employees - and nearly all industrial groupings.

Cohort analysis, being a record of change, is what Taylor (1984) calls descriptive monitoring. It can nevertheless be useful because explanation is difficult if the spatial pattern which is the object of investigation is unknown. Moreover descriptive monitoring mostly is not a goal in itself, but a first step in the longer process of fact-finding and explanation. In method, cohort analysis is similar to the more well-known components-of-change analysis. It is a components-of-change analysis for firms all of the same age.

Cohort analysis corresponds to the demographic cohort survival method, used for forecasting the population of regions. However in this contribution cohort analysis is not applied to forecasting the future number of firms, but to finding the spatial pattern in birth and death rates of new firms.

Dutch geographers live in a small country, yet they often make a distinction between different (production) environments. The research results presented here are restricted to a limited number of regions in different environments, located all over the country. Some of these regions are located in urban areas, such as the Randstad. This choice was based on the assumption often made that conditions in urban regions are favourable for new firm formation. Moreover the big cities in the Netherlands are rapidly becoming problem areas from an economic point of view. We opted for the Chamber districts of Amsterdam and Rotterdam, both consisting of the city and some immediately adjacent municipalities. In order to provide a contrast some peripheral regions were also selected. Here we opted for two problem regions: a predominantly rural one (district Leeuwarden), and

Netherlands

predominantly rural one (district Leeuwarden), and an old mining district (Heerlen). In addition the Amersfoort and Breda districts were chosen, both located in the 'intermediate' zone (Fig. 1). The results presented relate to these six districts.

Fig. 1. Chambers of Commerce districts in the Netherlands

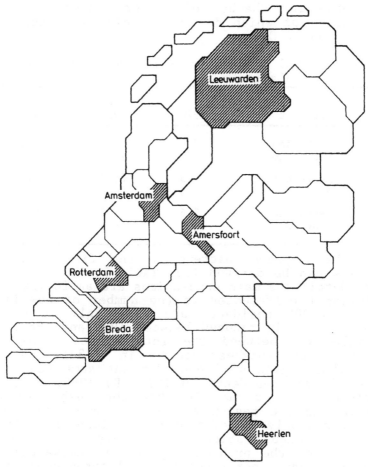

New Firm Formation

The rate of formation of new firms in the Netherlands increased between 1970 and 1980 from 13.8 to 22.6 (+ 64%) per 10,000 residents. Although a new firm is not the same as a new entrepreneur, there is reason to believe that entrepreneurship has become more popular in the Netherlands in the last ten years.

Of more interest to geographers is the spatial pattern. In order to compare the districts the number of new firms is mainly related to the number of residents. Of course a more appropriate basis would be the working population or even the male working population aged between 25 and 40 (the group with most new entrepreneurs). This was not attempted because such statistics are not easily available for Chamber of Commerce districts, the boundaries of which do not coincide with those of the Bureau of Census.

Table 1. Total number of new firms per 10,000 of population.

District	1970	Cohort 1975	1980
Amsterdam	22.8	23.8	30.0
Rotterdam	14.5	23.4	28.5
Amersfoort	17.5	26.7	31.0
Breda	17.8	20.2	26.6
Leeuwarden	7.6	9.8	14.7
Heerlen	13.1	14.2	17.9

The regional pattern in the firm formation process can be derived from Table 1. Without going into detail the main conclusions are as follows:
- Regional differences in the number of new firms per 10,000 residents are strikingly large and were scarcely reduced between 1970 and 1980. The difference between the intermediate region of Amersfoort (highest score in 1980) and the problem region of Leeuwarden was some ten firms per 10,000 residents in 1970. By 1980, this had risen to 16 firms. In 1980 the number of new firms in the region at the bottom of the whole list was only 36% of that of the leading region.
- Though league tables, fortunately, show changes over time the problem regions of Leeuwarden and Heerlen have poor results in all three cohorts.
- In general the number of new firms is relatively high in districts in the urbanized Randstad and the intermediate zone.

This general picture does not change a great deal as far as regional initiatives are concerned although external initiatives are most important for districts in the intermediate zone. In Amersfoort and Breda the number of external

Table 2. The number of regional initiatives (newly created independent firms) per 10,000 of population and per 1,000 firms in 1980.

	Per 10,000 of population	Per 1,000 firms
Amsterdam	28.1	5.5
Rotterdam	24.9	5.7
Amersfoort	26.1	7.5
Breda	22.1	6.3
Leeuwarden	13.1	4.6
Heerlen	17.5	5.6

initiatives for the three cohorts together is equal to 17.0 and 14.9% of the total number of initiatives. In the problem areas, in spite of regional policy, external initiatives account for only 10.5% in Leeuwarden, and 2.8% in Heerlen. In Table 2 the number of regional initiatives per 10,000 residents is given. The picture changes to some degree when the number of new regional initiatives is expressed per 1,000 existing (registered) firms. Then the position of the intermediate zone regions is strengthened.

Fig. 2. Number of new firms per 10,000 residents by category of municipality

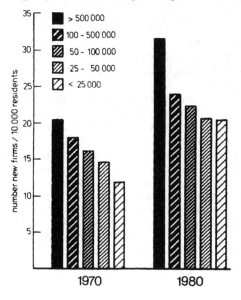

Looking at the number of new firms, not only are the differences between individual districts of interest, but also the variations between different sorts of municipality. Often there is an assumed link between the nature of an area (the production environment) and the number of new firms. A good example here is so-called incubation theory. A variant is the assumption that large cities offer more favourable conditions for new firms than do rural areas. One argument would be that activities in large municipalities are partly carried out for the benefit of surrounding areas. This reasoning seems to be correct (Fig. 2). However the increase between 1970 and 1980 was largest in the small (rural) municipalities. This suggests that rural areas too are increasingly functioning as a seedbed for new firms.

New Firms: Industrial Structure

Some firms are more important for the regional economy than others. A firm making products for export cannot be compared with a new bar or disco. In general there will be differences between the activities started in the various districts. Most entrepreneurs start activities with which they are already familiar. In that way a relationship arises between the industrial composition of new firms and the existing firms in a region. For two districts (Rotterdam and Heerlen) this relationship has been examined for the year 1980 and for 49 industrial groupings. The respective Pearson correlation coefficients were 0.90 and 0.91. This result implies that new firms do not contribute essentially to the diversification of the regional economy. 'Weak' regions in general will generate 'weak' activities.

It is quite understandable that the literature about new firms deals chiefly with activities that are considered (regionally) basic. However most new entrepreneurs start traditional and non-basic activities (shops, cafés, pubs, repair work, etc.). For the regional economy these are not the most interesting firms, because they often simply replace fellow-entrepreneurs. The net effect (employment, value added) for the regional economy will be small. Nevertheless in the Netherlands in 1970 some 49% of all new firms started in the retailing and personal service sector. In 1980 this was still 43%. Moreover there are also many non-basic activities in the building sector, in wholesale trading and even in the growing business services category (many banks, insurance and brokerage companies are non-basic in character). In general the basic component in regional new firm formation will be small. The manufacturing sector seems to be most important in this respect, but this sector accounts for only some 10% of all new firms. The popular, new and innovative firm will not constitute more than some three per cent of all new firms. This aspect of innovative new firms is dealt with elsewhere (Wever 1984).

Table 3. Sectorial composition of new firms in the 1980 cohort as a percentage of total new firms.

| District | Sector | | | | |
	Manufacturing	Building	Wholesale	Retailing	Business services
Amsterdam	7.3	6.4	17.5	25.6	27.6
Rotterdam	9.2	11.0	17.5	21.2	29.8
Amersfoort	8.5	5.7	16.0	27.3	28.0
Breda	10.1	8.7	17.6	24.4	24.9
Leeuwarden	8.9	11.0	11.4	29.3	19.0
Hengelo	11.0	7.2	14.6	31.6	23.2
Heerlen	8.0	14.0	8.6	26.5	15.1

For the six Chamber districts the sectoral composition of new firms is given in Table 3. Differences are largest in wholesaling, retailing and business services. Problem areas have more new firms in the retailing sector, but less in the wholesaling and business services sector. Though this does not necessarily imply a weak sectorial composition of new firms in problem areas, there is also no reason to assume that in these areas the low number of new firms is even partly compensated by a higher proportion of 'stronger' ones.

The Survival Of New Firms

Although it is economically advantageous to have many firms starting up in a particular region, if they disappear in the shortest possible time, the benefits are shortlived. For that reason the number of 'closures' is given (Table 4). This number includes firms that have left the district

Table 4. Closure-rates per cohort and district as a percentage of the total number of new firms.

District	1970	Cohort 1975	1980
Amsterdam	71.2	59.0	32.1
Rotterdam	71.0	60.6	39.5
Amersfoort	64.3	49.1	27.1
Breda	62.3	46.5	28.9
Leeuwarden	58.3	48.4	21.8
Heerlen	60.9	52.6	21.4

concerned (relocation).

It is well known that many new firms close within a short time. Of all new firms started in 1970 nearly 50% had already disappeared (closed or relocated) within five years. After 12 years, more than 60% were closed. In general the wholesale trading and building sectors are characterized by high closure rates. These are sectors with low entry barriers (capital, certificates, etc.), but low barriers certainly are no guarantee of success. On the contrary, they may simply give support to a badly prepared new firm. However, sectorial closure rates show only small differences, compared to the 'birth' rates. This is in line with the findings of Birch (1979).

On a regional scale there are some differences too. The urban districts (Amsterdam, Rotterdam) of the Randstad are characterized by high closure rates. Most problem areas show relatively low rates. This difference remains when differentiating

Table 5. The number of surviving new firms from the 1970, 1975 and 1980 cohorts per 10,000 of population.

District	1970	Cohort 1975	1980
Amsterdam	6.4	10.0	20.4
Rotterdam	4.2	9.2	17.2
Amersfoort	6.5	13.6	22.6
Breda	6.7	10.2	18.9
Leeuwarden	3.2	5.0	11.5
Heerlen	5.1	7.5	14.1

Netherlands

Fig. 3. The location of new firms (1970-80) and
    still surviving end-1980

Number of new
firms related to
existing stock

▦ high

▨ moderate

▧ low

▨ very low

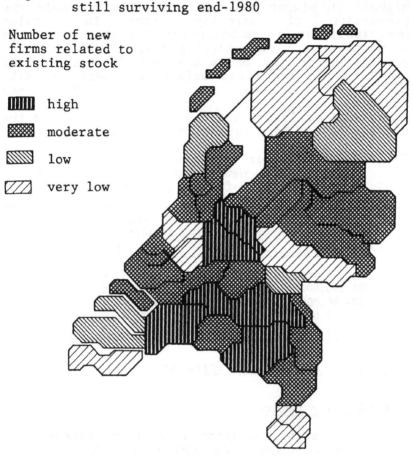

Source: Annual Report NMB 1980, 30

between sectors, suggesting that aspects of the
(production) environment do influence closure
rates.
    Though the differences in closure rates are
not as large as in birth rates, they do influence
the spatial pattern of surviving firms. The
relatively strong position of the Randstad
districts is weakened by high closure rates and the
weak position of most problem regions becomes
slightly more positive. The 'winners' definitely
are to be found in the intermediate zone (Table 5).
This is in line with the results of an
investigation of one of the Dutch banking companies
(Fig. 3).
    The same change can be observed in comparing

urban and rural municipalities. Closure rates are highest in bigger municipalities. As a result the proportion of existing firms in smaller municipalities is substantially higher than the proportion of firms starting there (Table 6). The reverse holds for Amsterdam and Rotterdam. Some 28.7% of all new firms originated there in 1970, but of the existing new firms only 22.5% are located there. This again illustrates the importance of less urbanized and rural areas in the process of new firm formation and development.

Table 6. The number of new firms (a) and of surviving new firms (b) in different categories of municipalities (share of total).

| | Cohort | | | | | |
| | 1970 | | 1975 | | 1980 | |
Category	a	b	a	b	a	b
> 500,000	28.7	22.5	26.3	19.4	24.4	22.5
100–500,000	14.6	13.0	13.2	13.0	11.8	11.4
50–100,000	12.3	12.6	14.4	14.4	13.9	13.4
25– 50,000	15.1	16.0	15.2	16.2	17.9	18.1
< 25,000	28.3	35.9	30.8	35.7	32.0	34.5

New Firms: Regional Performance

Introductory remarks

When considering the importance of the formation of new firms it might seem logical to try to explain the regional differences found. However, this will not be attempted in this article. Instead, this second part will concentrate on regional differences in the process of starting and running a new firm. The spatial dimension is introduced by presenting the results for three regions, each with a specific environment.

The project concerned was carried out in 1984 and was partly based on the data of the cohort analysis. Only the 1975 and 1980 cohorts were included. The information required could only be obtained by interviewing the founders of new firms, those who were succesful and also those who failed. It would be difficult to find the founders of firms in the 1970 cohort and in any case it would be almost impossible to reconstruct their starting process. An additional difficulty in the project presented itself with new firms that were not successful. The Chambers of Commerce only have the names and addresses of the persons who registered the closure. The further activities and addresses of these individuals afterwards are unknown. This is why only new firms belonging to the 1975 and 1980 cohorts that were closed after 1981 were included in the research. Even for these firms it was sometimes difficult to find the founder. A third restriction was based on the importance of new firms for the regional economy. It was decided to concentrate on new firms only in sectors that presumably are basic in character: manufacturing, wholesaling and business services. Within these sectors not all new firms were included, but only the independent ones, founded by one or more individuals. In total 319 founders filled in questionnaires, of which 72 were related to firms that had already been closed.

Success or failure

In the literature about new firms it is often assumed that specific characteristics of the entrepreneur influence, positively or negatively, the start of a firm. For example, it is well-known that many new firm founders had previously worked in small or medium-sized enterprises. In these enterprises employees gain the experience necessary for entrepreneurial training. This training may not only encourage an employee to start his own business but may also reduce the risk of failure. Let us just mention some other hypotheses. Starting young is sometimes considered to be less favourable, because a young entrepreneur might lack experience. The same holds for people with a limited educational background. They have often been confronted with only a small number of activities and this is less favourable from the point of view of entrepreneurial training. On the other hand people who have already started a new firm before and employees in management functions are presumed to be better prepared when starting. Firms founded by more than one person are sometimes supposed to have a better chance of survival, partly because the know-how of different founders can be complementary and partly because together they can possibly raise more starting-capital. Starting from an unemployment situation is considered to be less favourable, especially when

Netherlands

Table 7. Some characteristics of new entrepreneurs that succeeded or failed, as a percentage of total.

Characteristic	Success %	Failure %
Has been owner/manager of a firm before	25	31
Has worked with an employer		
1-10 employees	25	32
>500 employees	21	12
Starting capital		
< FL 25,000	57	74
≥ FL 25,000	43	26
Oriented to local/regional market	58	69
Hindered by conditions imposed by suppliers of outside capital	23	34
1-5 clients take 60% of turnover	8	23

the escape from unemployment is a more important starting motive than the actual wish to be an entrepreneur. Lack of capital can also create a less favourable starting situation.

By comparing the situation and characteristics of founders that were successful and those who failed, the hypotheses mentioned above can be tested. All new firms that had been closed, and firms that although still in existence in 1984 had no real future in the eyes of their owners, were considered to be 'failures'. This category of failures consisted of 94 entrepreneurs. Some results are presented in Table 7.

Generally it can be said that the measured personal characteristics (of course not the character itself) of entrepreneurs do not differ remarkably as between those who succeeded and those who failed. The same holds for the motives reported for starting up a business. Wishing to be one's own boss turned out to be the most important motive for both categories.

The circumstances at the launch did not differ very much for both categories of entrepreneurs. Less successful entrepreneurs had more often had experience in small firms and in production functions, they started with less capital and had more problems working with external capital. Contrary to our expectations entrepreneurs who had previously owned or managed a firm were somewhat less successful. The same result has been found by O'Farrell. That less successful entrepreneurs asked

Netherlands

for more help, though in general external advice
was seldom taken, was also an unexpected finding.
When they did seek advice it came more frequently
from accountants, banks and friends than from
governmental advice institutions.

Table 8. The preparation for the start of the firm
(as a percentage of all respondents
mentioning a factor).

Factor	Success	Failure
Definite idea of goods and services to be offered	88	82
Definite idea of potential clients	85	83
Careful choice of legal company status	68	59
Adequate knowledge of finance and administration	67	61
Taking people into employment	67	49
Budgeting for sales	65	56
Budgeting for running-in period	57	43
Budgeting for expected taxes	56	48
Budgeting for working capital	54	39
Budgeting for costs of loan repayment	53	36
Budgeting for depreciation costs	48	44
Sounding out prospects by talking with potential clients	47	60
Sounding out competition	44	36
Budgeting for fixed assets	43	28
Planning debt repayment period	42	27
Budgeting labour costs	41	31
Attempting to attract outside capital	35	30
Investigating grants and subsidies	31	29
Investigating business advisers	22	15
Made an advertising campaign beforehand	22	12
Preparation completed by drawing up a detailed business plan	22	16

The more important differences between
successful and less successful entrepreneurs have
to do with their behaviour as businessmen. The
successful ones prepare the launch much more
systematically and give special attention to market
orientation. Successful firm founders are more
oriented to external markets and to more clients
(Table 8).

The differences in the preparation of the
launch are reflected in the problems the
entrepreneurs are confronted with afterwards. Less
successful founders met more marketing problems,
because their commercial function was much less

developed. As a result of their better market
orientation successful founders are confronted with
financial problems, that is, problems arising from
the very fact of their success.

Of course the results of the analysis of
success or failure produced no great surprises. No
one will be a good entrepreneur simply as a result
of a higher level of education. But that does not
mean such factors do not influence the number of
new firms founded. Nevertheless we had previously
noticed regional differences in the number of firm
closures. Theoretically two explanations can be
given for this. The first one (popular in economic
geography) relates firm 'deaths' to (negative)
aspects of the environment. The second one poses
that some regions generate more 'good'
entrepreneurs than others.

The second possible explanation has been

Table 9. The characteristics of entrepreneurs in
the three districts investigated (as % of
total entrepreneurs).

Characteristics	Leeuwarden	Breda	Amsterdam
Age			
< 40	87	76	62
≥ 40	13	24	38
Educational level			
Low	40	33	22
Middle	50	47	40
High	10	20	38
Level of responsibility			
in previous job			
No previous job	8	6	9
Low	56	30	30
Middle	18	28	17
High	19	36	44
Has been manager or			
owner of plant	24	26	33
Number of employees			
at last employer			
Not been employee	8	6	9
0-20	39	30	39
>100	24	43	27
Was unemployed	26	16	10
Started alone	79	65	72
Starting capital			
< FL 25,000	53	58	61
> FL 100,000	18	9	15
No wish to use			
outside capital	32	19	20

investigated first. Translation of the concept of a
'good' entrepreneur into measurable characteristics
was based on the four well-known functions of an
enterprise: the financial, commercial, production
and social function. As new firms normally start on
a small scale no attention was given to the social
function. For the enquiry use was made of the
contents of evaluation models for firms used by
accountants. Firstly some of the characteristics of
the firm founders are presented (Table 9). Figures
for only three districts are given, one out of
each zone (Randstad, intermediate zone, periphery),
as examples.

Referring to the assumptions previously made,
the results of the analysis of success/failure, and
making allowance for the rather limited absolute
number of cases, there is no reason to assume a big
difference in the starting circumstances for firm
founders in these three regions. Perhaps the
situation in Amsterdam looks a little bit better
(older, higher educational background, higher
position as an employee, was not unemployed), while
the Leeuwarden pattern appears somewhat worse than
that for Breda.

Table 10. The preparation for the launch of the
firm (percentage of respondents
mentioning a factor).

	Leeuwarden	Breda	Amsterdam
Mean number of aspects considered	8.6	11.5	8.9
Considered (%):			
-legal status	47	74	70
-product mix	71	91	87
-client group	76	86	77
-market situation	42	58	55
-financial administration	58	86	60
-business advisers	18	47	18
-budgeting fixed assets	32	42	33
-budgeting working capital	42	61	30
-sales prognosis	45	58	67
-budgeting depreciation costs	37	56	33
-budgeting taxes	42	61	40
-budgeting for running-in period	40	63	40
Preparation was completed by drawing up a detailed business plan	13	30	15

Netherlands

Table 10 shows quite another picture. Although the circumstances in which the firm was started in Leeuwarden are reflected by a poor preparation for the launch, the better situation in the Amsterdam area is not explained by a good preparation. The situation for the Breda region is clearly the most favourable of the three areas. As a consequence the entrepreneurs in the Breda region have been confronted with fewer problems than those in Amsterdam and Leeuwarden.

The same favourable conclusion for Breda is evident in Table 11. More firms have been closed down in this region than in Leeuwarden, but the ones that remain show much better results. Their sales are higher, they have created more jobs and they have been confronted with fewer problems.

Table 11. The present (mid-1984) position of the new firms: some aspects.

	Leeuwarden	Breda	Amsterdam
Sales in 1983 (%)			
< FL 100,000	48	22	34
≥ FL 1.000,000	11	29	19
Fulltime employees (%)			
0	52	34	68
1-10	45	50	29
> 10	3	16	2
Number of problems in running the firm (mean)	6.2	4.4	4.4

The most interesting conclusion when the whole set of seven study districts is considered is that the two areas with the highest net rate of new firm formation (Breda and Amersfoort) are also characterized by relatively many 'good' entrepreneurs. The firms in the two urban districts of Amsterdam and Rotterdam seem to have started up under favourable conditions, but their results are nevertheless disappointing. This is particularly so for Amsterdam. The problem areas, especially Leeuwarden, have low net rates of new firm formation and also relatively few 'good' entrepreneurs.

These conclusions raise questions about the reasons for the differences. One possibility would be the different production environment in the regions investigated (the first theoretical explanation). Some questions asked of the respondents had to do with outside problems with which they were confronted during the preparation of the launch and afterwards (Table 12). Again data for only three districts is given.

Although there are clear differences in the environment for new firms in the three regions, Table 12 gives no reason to believe that the relatively many 'good' entrepreneurs in Breda can be attributed predominantly to a more favourable environment as measured by the factors mentioned.

Table 12. New firms and business environment: the influence of some external factors (percentage of respondents mentioning a factor).

Factors	Leeuwarden	Breda	Amsterdam
Had problems getting enough information	21	16	17
Lack of knowledge of possible assistance	32	19	18
Disappointed with help	29	21	12
Problems getting starting capital	18	19	27
Problems getting outside capital	37	23	33
Proportion outside capital at the start	32	28	43
Problems working with outside capital	32	19	20
Problems with finding: right employees	16	18	17
right premises	26	9	15
inexpensive premises	16	7	12
new clients	34	37	47
Asked for help solving problems	55	41	40
Enough people in same sector to talk with	60	33	65
Satisfied with suppliers in own region	82	80	83

Conclusions

There are considerable differences between districts in the birth rate of new firms within the Netherlands. There are also noticeable, although smaller, differences in the death rate of newly created firms. Starting from the assumption that the success of a newly founded firm is predominantly dependent on the characteristics of the entrepreneur, a survey of new firm founders was carried out, 72 of whom had already closed their firm by mid-1984.

In the comparisons it turned out that frequently-mentioned characteristics of the entrepreneur such as age, educational background, former job, and acquaintance with businessmen led to no obvious conclusions. The same holds true for the sectors, although the study was based on perhaps unduly-aggregated sectors, such as manufacturing, wholesaling and business services. The research results seem clearly to indicate that it was the preparation of the launch and the market orientation that made a new business a success or a failure. This implicitly means that regions in which new firms do better must either have more 'good' entrepreneurs or more favourable external conditions for starting and running new firms. This last factor, however, cannot explain the strong position of the Breda region compared to Amsterdam. Perhaps it may partly explain the poor results of Leeuwarden. This immediately gives rise to a further question, concerning the unexplained differences. Some hypotheses were rejected, but nevertheless an explanation still has to be found.

One factor which must be noted at this point is the question of research design. Though no less than 319 responses were received this was not enough to obtain statistically valid answers to all questions. It is possible that all variables together could statistically explain some part of the regional differences found. Even when working on an aggregated basis it was not possible to avoid small sub-populations and problematic generalizations arising in consequence. Nevertheless the scale of the regional differences in the number of 'good' entrepreneurs strongly suggests that other factors are important, which according to certain regional experts perhaps have to do with the 'credibility' factor of Shapero described in Chapter one.

In the problem areas of Leeuwarden and Heerlen, local experts judged the findings to be realistic. As an explanation for Leeuwarden was mentioned the Frisian characteristic of 'exporting' its 'best sons'! This area has experienced for many years selective outmigration of its most dynamic and creative people: "our entrepreneurs are located elsewhere". The Heerlen region had a long period of prosperity. At the same time there was an hierarchical structured society dominated by the Catholic church and the mining companies. This society did not stimulate the business initiative of people belonging to the 'working' class. Here too, dynamic people who felt unhappy with this situation often left the region. In both regions a social incubation climate existed wich is not stimulating to potential entrepreneurs. By a Myrdalian backwash outmigration this climate was strengthened and maintained. Explanations of this sort, although hypothetical, are appealing. They are certainly not by definition unrealistic. Perhaps economic geography research should attach less importance to the material aspects of the environment of firms (as did the incubation theory - see Jansen (1981) and de Ruijter (1984)) - and more to social elements. This seems especially recommendable in research about new and small firms. Such research will of course need co-operation between social psychologists, sociologists and perhaps historians.

Our research was disappointing because only regional experts for the problem areas raised appealing explanations as mentioned above. The experts of the 'good' areas could not offer any explanations when asked. However, in these regions an important role may well be played by the relatively large number of immigrants. Certainly some of the new entrepreneurs in the Breda and Amersfoort area have been recruited from these relatively higher educated and salaried in-migrants. A comparable situation was found by Gould and Keeble (1984) in the Cambridge area. It could be that these people have also fostered a less rigid and more dynamic society in which new initiatives are looked upon more positively. Aydalot (1984) has stressed the importance of this factor for the explanation of the striking economic development of traditional rural areas in France.

Whether these suggestions are valid or not, there is reason to consider follow-up research about the business-mindedness of regional populations. There may well be a case for international comparative research on this topic. A first attempt was made by Huisman and De Ridder (1984). Their interesting results were presented to the last Small Business Conference held in Amsterdam. Research of this kind, starting out from the residents of regions and not from entrepreneurs, may well generate new explanations.

Netherlands

The fact that such research will be of a rather different nature than that normally found in economic geography should be a challenge to all geographers active in this field.

References

Aydalot, Ph. (1984) 'Questions for Regional Economy', Tijdschrift voor Economische en Sociale Geografie, 1, 4-14

Ayodeji, O., A.Rolland and S.Hayes (1982) 'Components of Business Change as Objects of Job Redistribution Policy. A Pilot Study of the Dutch Growth Centre of Purmerend', Tijdschrift voor Economische en Sociale Geografie, 1, 43-50

Birch, D.L. (1979) The Job Generation Process, MIT, Cambridge Mass.

Cross, M. (1981) New firm formation and regional development, Gower, Aldershot

Gould, A. and D.Keeble (1984) 'New Firms and Rural Industrialization in East Anglia', Regional Studies, 3, 189-203

Huisman, D. and W.J. de Ridder (1984) Vernieuwend Ondernemen. Een analyse van de relatie tussen ondernemersklimaat en economische ontwikkeling, Scheveningen.

Jansen, A.C.M. (1981) 'Incubatie-milieu: analyse van een geografisch begrip', Geografisch Tijdschrift, 4, 306-316

Rothwell, R. and W.Zegveld (1982) Innovation and the small and medium sized firm, Frances Pinter, London

Ruijter, P.A. de (1984) 'De bruikbaarheid van het begrip 'incubatiemilieu'', Geografisch Tijdschrift, 2, 106-110

Storey, D.J. (1982) Entrepreneurship and the new firm, Croom Helm, London

Taylor, M. (1984) 'Industrial geography', Progress in Human Geography, 2, 262-275

Wever, E. (1983) 'Cohort analysis in economic geography', Tijdschrift voor Economische en Sociale Geografie, 3, 217-224

Wever, E. (1984), Nieuwe bedrijven in Nederland, Van Gorcum, Assen

Wever, E. and S. Grit (1984) 'Research Methods and Regional Policy', in M. de Smidt and E. Wever (eds), A Profile of Dutch Economic Geography, Van Gorcum, Assen, 39-63

Chapter four

NEW FIRMS AND HIGH-TECHNOLOGY INDUSTRY IN THE UNITED KINGDOM: THE CASE OF COMPUTER ELECTRONICS

David Keeble
Timothy Kelly

Introduction

Since the late 1960s, the United Kingdom, in common with most other countries of the European Community, has experienced a significant resurgence in the numbers of small manufacturing and service firms, both absolutely and relative to large corporations (Baroin and Fracheboud 1983, Greffe 1984, Keeble 1985a). This resurgence is undoubtedly due chiefly to a substantial increase during the 1970s and 1980s in the rate of new, independent business formation (Gudgin 1984). Thus the total number of UK new firm births in production industries (chiefly manufacturing) rose each year between 1980 and 1983, for example, from 14,487 to 18,962, or by 31% over this period alone (Ganguly 1984). Various explanatory theories which may account for this striking trend are currently under debate, including recession-push theory, technological change theory, and theories based on the impact of rising real incomes, rising energy costs, government initiatives, and even deliberate large firm fragmentation policies (Keeble 1985b, Storey 1982, 1984, Shutt and Whittington 1984). This paper concentrates on technological change theory, arguably one of the three most convincing explanations, the others being recession-push and income growth theory.

Technological Change Theory

Recent years have witnessed growing interest in explanations of the long-run historic evolution of advanced capitalist economies which characterise this evolution in terms of Kondratiev-type long waves of boom and slump (Mensch 1979, Freeman

1983). Central to most such explanations is the impact of bursts of radical technological innovation as hypothesised by Schumpeter (1939). In this context, workers such as Freeman (1984) argue that the 1970s and 1980s are witnessing a new 'technological revolution' based on radical innovations in micro-electronics and associated information technology industries which is generating a 'creative gale of destruction' along Schumpeterian lines. The significance of this micro-electronics revolution rests not only on the creation of entirely new products and industries - computer electronics and software, information technology equipment, satellite telecommunications, robotics - but even more on "the fact that this new technological system affects every other branch of the economy" (Freeman 1984, 18), through the adoption of micro-electronic based process technology in a very wide range of manufacturing, service and even household activities. While radical innovations in even newer biotechnologies may further reinforce this technological revolution, "the main elements of the new technological paradigm for the 5th Kondratiev" are in Freeman's view firmly and necessarily rooted in micro-electronics.

The empirical evidence assembled by workers such as Freeman is compelling in emphasising the radical nature of current technological change. From the present perspective, however, its particular interest lies in the argument that because of its _speed_ and _nature_, the micro-electronics revolution is creating a host of new production, process and market opportunities which are particularly suited to exploitation by small, flexible manufacturing firms established by entrepreneurs drawn from the ranks of skilled workers and research engineers and scientists. The rapidity of micro-electronics innovation since the 1950s is remarkable, epitomised by a doubling in integrated circuit miniaturisation levels every two years between 1965 and 1980, and the development since 1970 of RAM (Random Access Memory) semiconductor chips from 1K (1000) bits capacity to 64K in 1979 and 256K in 1984. Technological dynamism of this kind may well favour small, flexible firms which can perceive and adjust to new technologies and market possibilities more rapidly than large, organisationally and technologically more rigid, corporations. A crucial factor in this, of course, is the development of new mass markets and hence

very rapid demand growth for microprocessor-based
products, reflecting rapidly declining unit
production costs because of technological change
and economies of mass production. Equally, however,
the crucial role of highly-qualified research
engineers and scientists in these technological
changes, coupled with often relatively limited
financial barriers to entry, permits the breaking-
away of such individuals to establish their own
independent firms to exploit commercially-valuable
product and process innovations. In such high-
technology sectors as the semiconductor industry,
therefore, the 1970s have witnessed a dramatic boom
in numbers of new firms, illustrated by the seven-
fold increase in the number of semiconductor
establishments, most of them single-plant firms, in
the USA between 1964 and 1982 (from 98 to 701
establishments). Moreover, there is growing
evidence that the diffusion of microprocessor
techniques is also enhancing opportunities for
small firm and entrepreneurial development in many
other, apparently technologically-unsophisticated,
industries, such as food and drink, printing, and
mechanical engineering. While other factors are
undoubtedly involved in new firm growth since 1970,
therefore, technological change theory would seem
to be an essential component of any broader
explanation of this phenomenon.

The Location Of New Technology-Based Firms

One very important characteristic of new firms in
technologically-dynamic industries is their
markedly-uneven spatial distribution, which appears
to differ significantly from that of older,
declining manufacturing sectors (Hall 1981). Before
reviewing the specific case of the computer
electronics industry documented in later sections
of this chapter, some context for the later
analysis may be provided by consideration of the
general locational pattern of all new firms in
production industries in the UK, and possible
explanations for this. Particular attention will
also be paid to the development of marked local
concentrations of technologically-based new firms
in the form of what have been termed 'technology-
oriented complexes' (Steed and DeGenova 1983).
    The very recent publication of county data
(Ganguly 1985) on business formation as measured by
new VAT registrations permits for the first time

analysis of the detailed spatial pattern of new firm creation in the United Kingdom. The figures recorded in Table 1 and Fig. 1A and 1B refer to all new VAT registrations during the four years 1980 to 1983 inclusive in production industries (manufacturing, plus mining and quarrying and gas, electricity and water). In rate terms, expressed per one thousand employees in production industries in 1981, Table 1 reveals that in the 1980s, the geography of new production firm formation in the UK has been dominated by the South East, together with adjacent East Anglia and South West England. The lowest regional rates have been recorded by Northern England, Scotland and Yorkshire/ Humberside.

The county-level data (Fig. 1A) highlights very high rates in Greater London and surrounding counties, including those in East Anglia, together with three perhaps surprising rural/peripheral zones of high formation rates, in the far south-west, rural West Midlands and Wales, and the Scottish Highlands. With the exception of the Highlands, most of northern Britain is characterised by very low rates. The volume map (Fig. 1B) is dominated by Greater London (over 12,000 new firms, or 20% of the UK total), with much smaller clusters in other English conurbations.

Recently-developed theories of the geography of new firm formation in industrialised countries

Table 1. New Firm Formation Rates in the Production Industries, 1980-1983, by Region.

Region	New Firms 1980-83	Business Formation Rate[1]	Region	New Firms 1980-83	Business Formation Rate[1]
South East	24,473	13.8	North West	6,039	7.1
East Anglia	2,132	11.0	Wales	2,052	7.0
South West	4,412	10.3	Yorks/Humber	4,387	6.4
West Midlands	6,733	8.0	Scotland	2,869	5.1
North. Ireland	1,026	8.0	North	1,803	4.5
East Midlands	4,717	7.7	UK	60,643[2]	9.0[2]

1. New businesses per 1,000 production industry employees 1981
2. Excluding 4,207 new businesses unallocated by region: full UK rate 9.6

Source: Ganguly 1985, unpublished 1981 Census of Employment Statistics

United Kingdom - high-tech

Fig. 1. New firms (1B) and new firm formation rate
     (1A).

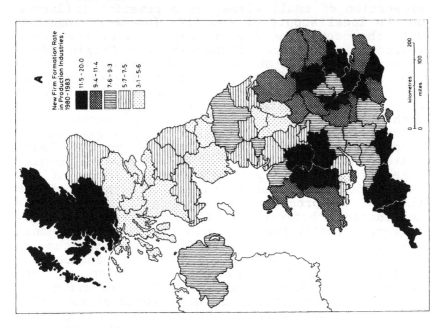

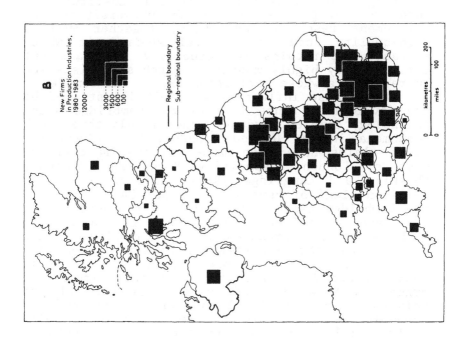

emphasise the role of spatial variations in the size of existing firms, and especially the proportion of small firms, as a powerful influence on the local supply of new firm founders, together with the occupational characteristics of the local resident work force (Fothergill and Gudgin 1982, Storey 1982, Lloyd and Mason 1983, Gould and Keeble 1984, Keeble 1985b). For technology-based new firms, however, it may be argued that two related but more fundamental underlying locational mechanisms or forces exist, which are perhaps most evident in the development of 'technology-oriented complexes'. The latter, epitomised by the Santa Clara county -'Silicon Valley' - of California, take the form of highly localised clusters of new high-technology firms which exhibit dynamic growth through a process of 'synergy', or intense interaction, between new firms and entrepreneurs, research institutions, local banks and finance agencies, and business service organisations. A variety of internal mechanisms undoubtedly contribute to the remarkable spawning of new independent firms, vertical disintegration of production, and general dynamism which characterise TOCs. But underpinning if not initiating this dynamism in most documented cases is the impact of existing major scientific research institutions, such as large science-based universities or government research facilities, together with a high-quality local residential environment which attracts and retains the crucially important but intrinsically highly mobile research scientists and entrepreneurs whose activities create the complex.

Both these influences are well illustrated by the development since 1975 of the Cambridge high-technology complex, arguably one of only three such phenomena in the United Kingdom. The others for which claims have been made are the M4 corridor west of London, especially Berkshire (Breheny, Cheshire and Langridge 1983), and the so-called 'Silicon Glen' of central Scotland (Faux 1984). In the Cambridge case, Segal Quince & Partners (1985, 23) have identified a remarkable growth of 322 high-technology companies in the Cambridge region at end-1984, three-quarters of them indigenous and independent, and 72% founded in only the last six years, since 1978. The growth of this complex is argued by Segal to reflect the key role of the university in providing both entrepreneurs and new technologies for small firm formation: while "only....17% of new company formation has been by

individuals coming straight from the University....
(the latter) has indirectly been the ultimate
origin of virtually all the other companies" (Segal
Quince & Partners 1985, 32) through a hiving-off
process from existing University-engendered firms.

In addition, however, it is clear that "the
most important ingredient in the area's success is
people" (Marsh 1985), reflecting the fact that "it
is the technical input of human design expertise
that contributes the bulk of value added to high
technology production in small firms" (Oakey 1984)
and the concentration in Cambridge of highly-
qualified researchers and entrepreneurs cannot be
explained without reference to the city's
exceptional residential environment, and the
quality of life - architectural, historic,
cultural, intellectual - it affords. "Cambridge
exercises an unusual hold over people who have
studied and worked there" (Segal Quince & Partners
1985, 59), such that no less than 80% of new
manufacturing firm founders in the county who have
migrated there (migrants accounting for 70% of all
founders) report that its "pleasant environment as
a place to live" was "of great importance" in their
migration decision (Keeble and Gould, 1985). The
role of environment-related migration of potential
entrepreneurs to attractive small-town and rural
locations is thus arguably a very important
influence in the 1980s on the location of new
technology-based enterprise as well as explaining
the high rates of new business formation generally
already noted in such high-amenity areas as south-
western England, rural Wales, and the Highlands of
Scotland (Jones, Caird and Ford 1984, see Fig. 1A).

Technology Based New Firms: The Case Of The Computer Electronics Industry

The remainder of this paper presents the first
results of a detailed original survey, carried out
at the Department of Geography, Cambridge
University, of what is arguably the UK's leading
high-technology industry, namely the computer
electronics sector. This was defined according to
the 1980 Standard Industrial Classification as
sectors MLH 3302 (Computer hardware) and MLH 8394
(Computer Services). A population of all
identifiable UK computer hardware and computer
services establishments (excluding computer bureaux
and personnel agencies) was used in the survey

accumulated from trade directories, journals and business registers. In all, 822 units were included in either a national postal questionnaire or a personal interview questionnaire in Cambridgeshire/ Hertfordshire and Scotland. During the course of the survey 72 (8.7%) units were found to have closed down or gone out of business while a further 52 (6.3%) units were found to have no UK manufacturing or software development facilities or were not involved in computer electronics. The remaining 698 units represent 572 separate firms of which 529 (92.4%) are UK-owned. The response rate to the survey is currently 61.9% or 432 units, though a basic range of data has been collected for the remaining 266 units using trade directories, and information from the Companies Registration Office supplemented by telephone enquiries.

Technological Change And New Computer Firm Formation

The computer electronics industry provides one of the clearest examples of a long-established industry which has been transformed over a relatively short period of time by technological change. The development of the microcomputer in the later 1970s was in many ways a logical progression from the process of miniaturisation in electronic components which had been associated with the space race and the development of the microprocessor. However, the first commercially available micros such as the Altair, the Apple, the PET and the ZX80 did not come from within the multi-million dollar R&D budgets of the large American multi-national computer manufacturers, but from spare time enthusiasts and disaffected graduate students. Small new firms played a major part in this technological change on both sides of the Atlantic, and firms such as Apple, Microsoft, Sinclair Research and Microvitec had already grown to a considerable size by the time the established multinationals began to move into this emerging market in the early 1980s. Behind these market leaders came a myriad of smaller firms exploiting new market niches in micros for small businesses, educational or scientific applications and in the home. In software too, the multiplicity of programming languages and operating systems used by manufacturers encouraged new firm formation as did the demand for a range of peripheral devices and data communications equipment. Fig. 2 shows the rate of new firm formation in the UK computer industry over the period 1965-1983. Within this time series, there appears to be a definite 'business cycle' effect leading to recession-induced decline in firm formation rates in the years 1971/2, 1975 and 1980. However, the most striking feature is the increasing rate of firm formation, particularly after 1975, which peaked in 1979 when almost 50 new and currently surviving firms were formed in the industry. It might be expected that the low rates of firm formation before 1975 signal a higher rate of failure amongst older firms. In fact the rising trend after 1975 is still apparent even when the time series is corrected to allow for the probable rate of firm failure (the dotted line in Fig. 2) which is calculated using firm failure rate probability tables derived from Ganguly's (1983) study of VAT registration data.

Fig. 2. New Computer Firms in the UK, 1965-1983

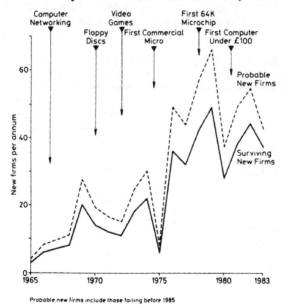

Probable new firms include those failing before 1985

The period since 1975 can therefore be taken to represent a phase of technological change and increased firm formation in the computer industry during which time 320 surviving new firms were born adding an extra 8,931 employees by 1984. The Census of Employment carried out in September 1981 enumerated 110,474 employees in the computer hardware and services industry and, according to these calculations, approximately 8.1% of this employment is in firms founded as independent units since 1975. Of the new firms in the survey, 28 (8.5%) have been subsequently acquired by other firms while a further 15 (4.7%) firms were established through management 'buy-outs' of firms from the receivers or from within larger organisations. However, this figure probably underestimates the role of management buy-outs as a route to new firm formation, as firms purchased as 'growing concerns' from their former owners have been excluded from this particular definition of new firms.

The Geographical Distribution Of New Firms

Table 2 shows the geographical distribution of new firms formed since 1975 in the computer electronics industry. Perhaps the most striking feature of the table is the high rate of new firm formation in East Anglia. This is partly explained by the low level of existing Information Technology Employment

Table 2. The Geographical Distribution of New Firms in the UK Computer Electronics Industry.

Region	New Firms	Employment 1984	Formation Rate[1]
Greater London	61	1,340	0.66
Rest of South East	92	2,307	0.63
All South East	153	3,647	0.64
East Anglia	67	1,630	6.23
South West	13	519	0.58
West Midlands	18	594	0.50
East Midlands	8	286	0.41
North West	16	392	0.42
Yorks/Humber	7	377	0.70
North	2	34	0.12
Wales	7	350	0.47
Scotland	29	1,102	0.81
Great Britain	320	8,931	0.74

1. New Firms 1975-84 per 1,000 information technology
   employees 1981
Source: Original Cambridge University survey data

in the county (10,756 - 2.6% of the GB total). But
it is mainly the result of the extraordinarily high
rate of new firm formation in Cambridgeshire (59
firms - NFF Rate = 14.6: see Fig. 3A and 3B). This
represents more than a sixth of all new firms
founded in the computer industry over the last ten
years. It might be argued that this reflects a
'study base' effect such that more smaller firms
have been indentified in the researcher's home
area. However, the average size of firms in East
Anglia (24.3) is not significantly smaller than the
UK average (27.9), while the survey results are
entirely in line with the independent work on the
Cambridge high-technology complex by Gould and
Keeble (1984) and Segal Quince (1985) discussed
earlier. Interestingly, the next highest county new
firm formation rate is Oxfordshire (6 firms - NFF
Rate = 4.4) which is similarly a predominantly
rural county with a premier university. In general,
Fig. 3A clearly supports the notion of a Bristol-
Norwich axis of computer industry - high technology
firm development. This is at least consistent with
the arguments concerning the impact of attractive
small-town or rural region residential
environments, and of existing research activity,
advanced in earlier sections of this paper.

Of the other regions, only Scotland has a new
firm formation rate higher than the national
average (29 firms - NFF=0.81). This is of course in
some contrast to Scotland's overall very low new
production firm formation rate (Table 1), and
reflects a concentration of new computer firms in
the central lowlands (Fig. 3A and 3B). Furthermore,
the Scottish new firms are bigger in size than the
national average (Scottish new firms average 38.0
employees per firm; GB = 27.9). Given that the
growth of the electronics sector in Scotland has
been largely induced by regional policy incentives
and the influx of branch plants of foreign-owned
multinationals, it might be reasonable to assume
that these firms had grown up because of the subcontracting opportunities offered by the
multinationals. This 'dependency' hypothesis is
examined in more detail below.

Initial tests of possible explanation of the
spatial pattern of new firm formation rates
revealed little correlation at the regional level
with Storey's index of entrepreneurship (Storey
1982, 196) (Spearman's Rank test r=0.35), or even
with the two indices used by Whittington (1984);
owner occupation and percentage of manual workers.

Fig. 3. New computer firm employees (1B) and formation rate (1A).

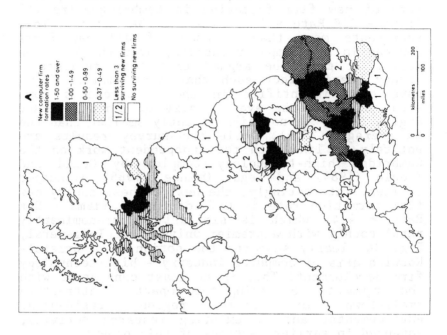

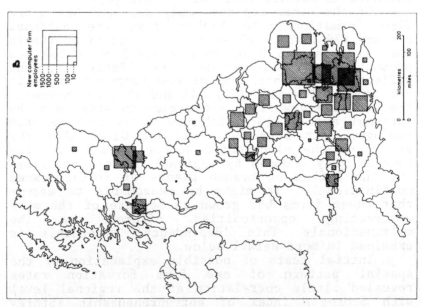

United Kingdom - high-tech

However, it is significantly correlated with one of the constituent indices which make up this entrepreneurship index, namely the regional index of percentage of employees in small (less than 10 employees) manufacturing plants (r=.70,$\alpha_{.05}$ =0.54). This lends some support to the hypothesis that the presence of small firms in an area gives rise to the birth of new firms. The new firm formation rate index does show something of a bias towards rural and small town areas. For instance, of the 13 counties with a firm formation rate, per 1,000 Information Technology Employees, greater than 1, only two (Avon and South Yorks) contain urban areas of any significant size (greater than 200,000 population 1981 Census).

Table 3. Urban-Rural Distribution of Computer Industry New Firms and Employment.

	Firms	Employment	1981 Manufacturing Employment ('000s)
Greater London	61	1,340	650
Conurbations	28	785	1,295
Free-standing cities	29	847	950
Large Towns	61	1,311	756
Small Towns	96	2,859	1,609
Rural Areas	45	1,799	655
Great Britain	320	8,941	5,915

Source: Original Cambridge University survey data
Note: The urban/rural classification adopted is derived from Fothergill and Gudgin (1982)

Conversely, Table 3 shows that, with the notable exception of Greater London, the conurbations and other free-standing cities (greater than 250,000 population) are relatively under-represented by new firm formation and employment. More than 50% of the new employment is in small towns and rural areas, while if Cambridge, with a non-student population of less than 100,000, were included in this category, it would exceed 57%. The Greater London case is interesting in having both a higher firm formation rate (0.66) than the rest of the South East (0.63), and a higher share of new firm employment (15.0%) than that which would be predicted by the 1981 share of manufacturing employment (11.0%). This is consistent both with the high rates of new production firm formation in Greater London noted earlier (Fig. 1A and 1B) and with the turnaround in the relative employment performance of Greater London since 1977 found by Keeble (1985a, Table 5). In the specific case of the computer electronics industry it would seem to be accounted for by the growth of software firms in the City and other small office automation firms which have their HQ in London but manufacturing facilities outside the metropolis, either in branch plants or through sub-contract. The unique role of London as the dominant UK market for high technology products may thus play a part in its above average firm formation rate, along with firm size, occupational characteristics, and volume of existing scientific research activity.

On the whole, new firm formation would appear to be further intensifying existing patterns of concentration of the electronics industry in the expanded South Eastern core at the expense of intermediate and peripheral areas. For instance, some 72.8% of all surviving new firms and 64.9% of new firms employment in the computer industry is in the regions of the South East, East Anglia, the South West. This compares with 47.7% of GB firms (1982) and 44.4% of GB employment in these regions (Regional Trends 1984 Tables 7.1 and 10.6). This finding is in accordance with other work on the location of high-technology firms (Oakey 1981, Rowlinson 1985), Research and Development establishments (Buswell and Lewis 1970, Howells 1984) and product innovation (Oakey, Thwaites and Nash 1980, Goddard and Thwaites 1984) which indicates a concentration of activity within the South East. Overlain on this inter-regional division is the poor performance of the conurbations (other than Greater London) and other large cities which have fared much less well than might have been expected from their industrial structure and volume of industrial employment, and a concentration of growth in outer, less-urbanised areas of Southern England. The latter, focussed especially on the Bristol-Norwich axis, arguably afford pleasant living environments for mobile entrepreneurs and highly-qualified workers, together in several cases with a research environment generated by a major university or other existing R&D establishments.

United Kingdom - high-tech

Firm Growth In The Computer Industry

Studies of new firm growth have characteristically shown that while new firms may contribute a large percentage of net new jobs in an area or in an industry, they have little short term effect on overall employment patterns. The same could be said to be true of the computer industry, where the UK jobs lost by a single company, ICL, over the period 1979-84 (-9,775) exceed the number of jobs created in all new firms over the period 1975-84 (+8,931).

Table 4. New Firm Numbers, Employment and Growth Rates in the UK Computer Industry, 1984[1].

Date	Firms	Employment	Average size
1983–84	44	651	14.8
1981–82	83	1,244	15.0
1979–80	79	2,655	33.6
1977–78	72	2,508	34.8
1975–76	42	1,873	44.6
1975–84	320	8,931	27.9

1 Figures relate to all surviving firms in 1984

Source: Original Cambridge University survey data

This initially pessimistic conclusion must, however, be tempered by the fact that many small firms subcontract much of the manufacture and distribution of their products and thus create additional indirect employment. As an extreme example, one leading new firm in Cambridgeshire, which has a turnover in excess of £75m, claims to have created indirect to direct employment in the ratio of more than 20:1 through its subcontracting arrangements. Furthermore, new technology-based firms do exhibit a much faster rate of growth in both employment and turnover than other new firms in more stable technologies. For instance, of the 320 new firms identified by this study, 15 (4.4%) exceeded 100 employees and 38 (11.9%) exceeded 50 by 1984. This compares with Storey's (1982, 22-23) estimate of only a 0.5-0.75% probability that new manufacturing firms in Cleveland would employ more than 100 workers by the end of a decade (based on a total sample of 159 firms, 1965-76). The average employment size of firms in this survey of 27.9 workers is also higher than that recorded in similar studies. For instance, Fothergill and Gudgin (1982, 117) find an average size of 15 for new manufacturing firms in Leicestershire at the end of an eight year period (728 firms, 1968-75); while Gould and Keeble (1984, 191) record an average size of only 12.1 in East Anglia at the end of a ten year period (703 firms, 1971-81). Only in Scotland does Cross (1981, 134; 504 firms, 1968-77) find a comparable average firm size of 24.2 for new manufacturing firms over ten years, and this is consistent with the higher average size of firms in Scotland of 38.0 recorded in this survey. While a straight comparison between these various studies is invalidated by the variation in the industrial sector, region and period, nevertheless it does serve to illustrate the high rates of growth within surviving new firms in the computer industry.

The Computer Industry In Cambridgeshire/ Hertfordshire And Scotland

In order to study the process of new firm formation in greater detail, two areas were chosen for interview surveys of entrepreneurs/managers; Cambridgeshire/Hertfordshire and Scotland. These two areas were chosen firstly because they contain an established base of computer industry employment, accounting together for 18% of national employment in the industry at the September 1981 Census of Employment. Secondly, they exhibit rates of new firm formation higher than the national average (Cambs = 14.6;Herts = 1.2; Scotland = 0.8; UK = 0.7). Thirdly, in regional policy terms, they present a contrast between a 'core' non-assisted area and a 'peripheral' assisted region. Information gathered from the survey was supplemented with data from the Scottish Development Agency, the Cambs County Council Research & Information Unit and from Hertfordshire Industrial Services Ltd (HERTIS).

The objectives of the survey were to focus on the relationship between the existing industrial and academic base in an area and the new firms sector, to see what light this might throw on the process of firm generation. One assumption of this methodology is that entrepreneurs tend to stay in the same geographical area and market sector in which they were previously employed. This assumption is supported by other studies of new firm founders (Beaumont 1982, Fothergill and Gudgin

1982, Keeble and Gould 1985) and corroborated by Table 8 which shows that only 9.6% of founders come from backgrounds other than in academic research, computer firms or other electronics firms. This particular subset of founders are generally people with a background in accountancy or financial services who have joined a 'team' of entrepreneurs, or who formerly worked in the data processing department of a non-electronics firm. Thus it seems reasonable to look at the existing structure of employment in the computer industry in an area in order to understand the quantity and quality of new firms formed.

Ownership Status of Establishments

The most striking contrast between the industry as a whole (old and new firms) in the two areas is in the level of foreign ownership and the means by which foreign capital has entered the local economy. Table 5 shows that almost three-quarters of the employment in the Scottish sector is overseas-controlled (mainly from the US) and that all 14 units were established directly as branch plant or regional offices. There seems to have been two distinct phases of branch plant formation in

Table 5. Legal Status of Establishments in the Computer Industry in Cambridgeshire/ Hertfordshire and Scotland.

| Status | Cambs-Herts | | | Scotland | | |
	Employ.	Units	Aver. Size	Employ.	Units	Aver. Size
Independent and HQ	3,413 (30.8%)	101 (73.3%)	33.8	888 (10.3%)	34 (48.6%)	26.1
Local Branches	186 (1.7%)	7 (5.1%)	26.7	787 (9.1%)	13 (18.6%)	60.5
UK-Owned Branches and Subsidiaries	5,014 (45.2%)	16 (11.8%)	313.4	589 (6.8%)	9 (12.9%)	65.4
Foreign Branches	37 (0.3%)	2 (1.5%)	18.5	6,344 (73.7%)	14 (20.0%)	453.1
Foreign Acquired	2,431 (21.9%)	10 (7.4%)	243.1	0 (0.0%)	0 (0.0%)	-
Total Establishments	11,081	136	81.5	8,608	70	123.0

Source: Original Cambridge University survey data

Scotland; the first dating from the post-war period to the early 1960s when several of the major US companies chose Scotland for their European manufacturing facilities (IBM, Honeywell, Burroughs, NCR). Fig. 4 shows that these plants continue to provide the bulk of employment despite job-shedding associated with technological shifts from electro-mechanical business machines to microprocessor based products. A second phase followed the entry of Britain into the European Community in 1973 and the formation of the Scottish Development Agency in 1975 since when the area has been consciously marketed as Europe's 'Silicon Glen'. This second phase has included new plants from IBM and Burroughs and new starts by DEC, Wang and SCI.

By contrast, in Cambs/Herts all but two of the units in the overseas sector were acquired by parents in North America rather than being established directly. In addition, there are a number of important minority shareholdings by foreign companies in local firms including Acorn (49.3% Olivetti, since February 1983), CADCentre (30% SIA) and ICL (26% ITT, exercised through STC).

Fig. 4. Employment/Age Profiles for Computer Industry Establishments in Scotland and Cambs/Herts.

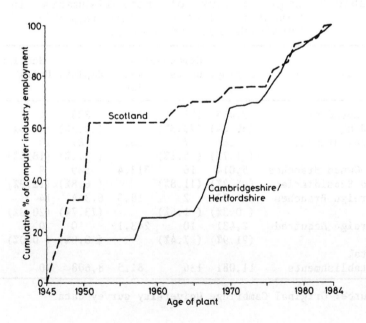

United Kingdom - high-tech

In employment terms, the foreign-owned sector is much less important than in Scotland (21.8%) though it has grown recently because most of the acquisitions have taken place since 1980 and have, on the whole, been associated with expansion rather than contraction of employment. The motives underlying the takeovers have often been the acquisition of local skills in Computer-Aided Design (Compeda, CIS, ARC, Shape Data) and have generally allowed the firms concerned to expand with greater financial backing while continuing as 'management companies' within the corporate structure.

In Cambs/Herts almost four-fifths of the establishments in the industry are independent firms and their local branch units, but these account for just under a third of total employment. The largest single employer, despite job-shedding since 1978, is STC-ICL which has five separate sites in Hertfordshire plus a 40% shareholding in CADCentre in Cambs. These operations, along with those of other long established employers such as GEC Computers, Peterborough Software and F International, raise the average size of units in Cambs/Herts to over 80 employees. But nevertheless Fig. 4 shows that 72.3% of employment in the industry in the area is in firms new to the area since 1965, and 30.6% is new since 1975. This gives the industry in Cambs/Herts a markedly younger age profile than Scotland.

Activity, Skill And Gender Divisions

Trends towards concentration in manufacturing industry and the growth of multinational corporations have allowed firms to implement a functional division of labour between establishments which are often geographically separated on national, and increasingly international scales. Thus it is argued that firms are attracted by, and in turn act to shape, differential labour market characteristics between areas. In simplistic terms therefore it has been argued that there is a division of labour in the UK between skilled, managerial and R&D, male-oriented jobs in the 'core' regions and semi-skilled and unskilled, automated production line, female-oriented jobs in the 'periphery' (Massey 1984, Cooke et al. 1984). In the computer industry specifically, this might be reflected in a spatial

United Kingdom - high-tech

Table 6. Activity Codes for Computer Industry
Establishments in Cambridgeshire/
Hertfordshire and Scotland.

Activity	Cambs/Herts		Scotland	
	All Units %	New Firms %	All Units %	New Firms %
Hardware	56.3	40.5	86.6	70.6
Software	28.9	52.3	10.9	22.7
Distribution	14.8	7.2	2.5	6.7
Accessories a.o. and Other				
TOTAL	100.0	100.0	100.0	100.0

Source:Original Cambridge University survey data
Note: The activity codes are calculated from the market
sector divide of each firm (according to a twelve-fold
classification) weighted by the employment size of each
firm.

division between software in the 'core' and
hardware in the 'periphery'.

The figures for the computer industry in
Cambs/Herts and Scotland offer some support for
this hypothesis in activity and skill divisions
(Tables 6 and 7). However, this is not true of
gender differences (Cambs 34.4% female; Scotland
30.1%), which are the opposite of those expected
from the 'spatial division of labour' hypothesis,
nor of job-tenure where part-time working, of
little importance in either area, is marginally
higher in Cambs/Herts. This should act as a caution
against overgeneralised stereotyping of regional
labour markets. In activity-type and skill
divisions there are, however, clear differences
between the industry in the two areas, but
interestingly this is, if anything, emphasised
rather than lessened in the character of new firms
in the two areas, suggesting that differences run
deeper than just reflecting the locational
preferences of multi-nationals.

In the Scottish industry there has always been
an orientation towards hardware manufacture which
may perhaps have been reinforced by the eligibility
of manufacturing but not services for regional
policy aid. The high barriers to entry in the
hardware market are likely to contribute to a lower
rate of new firm formation, and in both Cambs/Herts
and Scotland the subset of new firms is more biased
towards the software sector than the existing

Table 7. Skill-Type Divisions for Computer Industry
Establishments in Cambridgeshire/
Hertfordshire and Scotland (percentage of
total employment).

Job Type	Cambs/Herts		Scotland	
	All Units	New Firms	All Units	New Firms
Managerial, Sales and Clerical	39.6	34.1	19.3	18.5
Research and Development	20.7	35.7	8.6	12.0
Skilled Employees	21.9	22.7	31.7	16.2
Semi-Skilled and Unskilled Employees	17.8	7.5	40.4	53.3
TOTAL	100.0	100.0	100.0	100.0
Sample Employment	7,919	1,278	8,306	869
% Sample Coverage	71.5	72.7	96.5	78.9

Source: Original Cambridge University survey data

industry base. Within the hardware sector, the new
firms in Cambs/Herts are concentrated in
microcomputer design and marketing (57.4% of
hardware sales), with actual manufacture often
subcontracted elsewhere; while in Scotland the
concentration is directed towards peripherals
manufacture (77.4% of hardware sales). Within the
software sector the ratio of package software to
the more research-intensive custom software is
30:70 in Cambs/Herts compared with 40:60 in
Scotland among new firms.

Activity divisions between the two areas are
reflected in skill divisions between computer
industry employment in the two areas (Table 7).
Perhaps the clearest contrast lies in the ratio of
white-collar to blue-collar jobs in the two areas:
in Cambs/Herts the ratio is 60:40 for all units and
70:30 for new firms while in Scotland the ratio is
approximately 30:70 in both sectors with a
particular concentration of semi-skilled and
unskilled employment in Scottish new firms, which
is relatively unimportant in Cambs/Herts. The
Scottish example is probably biased by the presence
of a few new firms which have grown very rapidly
and have inhouse manufacturing facilities, rather
than using subcontractors, in particular Rodime and
Future Technology Systems. Nevertheless,
differences between the two areas are quite clear.

United Kingdom - high-tech

A wealth of literature suggests that Research and Development levels are likely to be low in a 'branch plant' economy (for instance Haug et al. 1983, McDermott 1979). The evidence of this survey suggests however, that differentials are even greater among new firms where the level of R&D employment in Cambs/Herts (35.7%) is virtually three times that of Scotland. The level of R&D in Scottish new firms (12.0%) is, however, almost twice as high as in the foreign-owned sector (6.6%), and it is likely that this is closer to the industry average than the abnormally high levels of R&D in Cambs (43.5%).

The Firm Formation Process

The study of the nature of the computer industry in the two areas has highlighted several factors which are likely to affect the rate and nature of firm formation: external control, size of plants, age profile of establishments, activity divisions and skill divisions. To study the effects that these have, it is necessary to look in more detail at the characteristics of founders, and here it becomes pertinent to separate the groups of firms in Cambs and Herts in order to 'unpack' the distinctions which exist. Tables 8 to 11 deal with the previous employment of founders by type, size and ownership/location of firm/university and their technical qualifications. One feature immediately apparent in these tables is the 'university effect' in Cambs and to a lesser extent in Scotland. This is shown in the number of founders coming directly from academic research (Cambs: 24 founders, 13 firms); the number of founders with Ph.Ds (Cambs: 39 founders, 24 firms); and it is implied by the young average age of founders (Cambs: 76.7% of founders under 35; 16.4% under 25). Examples of firms which have been started up from ex-University connections in Cambridge include Applied Research of Cambridge (Architecture Dept.), Shape Data (Computer Science Lab) and Laserscan Laboratories (High Energy Physics). These statistics fully corroborate the argument over the crucial role of major science-based universities in the initiation and development of technology-oriented complexes advanced earlier. Moreover, in addition to the direct role of the University in generating entrepreneurs there is an equally important secondary effect as a provider of skilled

Table 8. Previous Employment of Founders by Type of Firm.

Previous Employment	Cambs No.	Herts No.	Scotland No.
Academic Research	24	2	12
Computer Firm	41	26	37
Electronics Firm	7	7	4
Other Type of Firm	6	2	9
TOTAL	78	37	62

Source: Original Cambridge University survey data

graduates. Acorn Computers, for example, calculate that at least 50% of their 100+ graduates come from Cambridge University.

In Scotland, university-industry relationships are not quite as evident as around Cambridge (12 founders; 8 firms). Nevertheless, several firms owe their origins directly to ex-university personnel; for instance Raannd and CAS (Heriot-Watt); Intelligent Terminals and Memex (Edinburgh University). The Scottish Development Agency also quotes the high number of technically oriented research and teaching establishments (8 universities and 55 technical colleges) as one of the selling points of the area to potential investors. Thus while other researchers have found few formal or direct links between university and industry in terms of research collaboration of information flows (Oakey 1981, 39-46: the scientific instruments industry), or have been unable to show any locational pull exerted by universities (Howells 1984, 24-25: the pharmaceuticals industry), nevertheless in the computer industry there is a clear university influence as a source of entrepreneurs and skilled personnel. Interestingly, Hertfordshire, which has few direct university links except through the spillover from Cambridge and London, has the lowest percentage of founders coming from university and the highest percentage of in-migrant founders (42.9%).

Table 9, showing the size of 'incubator plants' for entrepreneurs, again indicates the distinctive nature of the firm formation process in Cambs which has acted through 'splitting' and spin-off of entrepreneurs from small and medium-sized firms rather than from larger establishments as in Herts and Scotland. This correlates with the findings of Table 10 which shows that founders in

United Kingdom - high-tech

Table 9. Previous Employment of Founders by Size of Firm.

Size of Firm (employees)	Cambs	Herts	Scotland
Under 25	6	1	2
25-99	11	2	5
100-499	17	4	2
500 and over	6	17	29
University	24	2	12
TOTAL	64	26	50

Source: Original Cambridge University survey data

Cambs have come principally from local firms and the University, whereas in Herts and Scotland the externally-owned sectors account for almost 50% of all founders. These figures undoubtedly reflect underlying differences in the size distribution of plants in the two regions. Fothergill and Gudgin (1982, 125-126), in their study of new firm formation in the East Midlands, show that firms employing less than 25 people provide over a quarter of all founders. It is likely therefore that the smaller average size of firms in the industry in Cambridge (25.3) in comparison to Herts (161.7) or Scotland (123.0) contributes to the higher rate of firm formation observed there.

Table 10. Previous Employment of Founders by Ownership/Location of Firm.

Ownership/Location	Cambs	Herts	Scotland
In-Migrant Founders	12	12	10
Locally-Owned Firms	52	3	17
UK-Owned Firms	2	11	16
Foreign-Owned Firms	1	2	11
TOTAL	67	28	54

Source: Original Cambridge University survey data

The role of the foreign-owned sector, often attracted by regional policy, in stimulating or alternatively suppressing an indigenous industry, has been much debated in the literature. McDermott (1979) in his study of the electronics industry in Scotland in 1975 has shown that only one indigenous firm owed its origin to a major externally-controlled establishment. By contrast, this study shows that 11 founders (8 firms) in Scotland came from backgrounds in the foreign-owned sector and' 16 founders (9 firms) from firms owned in the rest of the UK. It appears therefore that almost 40 years after the first foreign-owned electronics company came to Scotland, and ten years after McDermott's study, a spin-off effect from the foreign-owned sector is becoming apparent, in what the Scottish Development Agency (1982, 3-4) has termed a 'third generation' of indigenous enterprise. By contrast the decision by the Ministry of Technology in the Labour Government of 1969 to locate the Computer Aided Design Centre in Cambridge has had a rapid effect and it has been instrumental in the formation of at least 14 software/consultancy firms in the Cambridge area. This would appear to have clear implications for a technology-oriented regional policy (Ewers and Wettman 1980).

McDermott's article goes on to argue that the indigenous sector in Scotland plays a subsidiary 'satellite' role as suppliers and subcontractors to the multinationals. IBM at Greenock for instance claim to support indirectly some 4,000 jobs through such arrangements. This study, however, finds little support for the 'dependency' hypothesis: for instance, the average percentage of sales/billings of the Scottish new firms within the region (58.3%) is actually lower than that for all computer industry establishments in Scotland (61.5%), and while the percentage of sales exported abroad is slightly lower for Scottish new firms (18.1%) than for all establishments (20.0%), it is nevertheless much higher than that recorded by McDermott (6.5%) and the same as that for new firms in Cambs (18.5%) and Herts (18.0%). Thus while the indigenous new firms sector has certainly benefited from sub-contracting and supply arrangements it does not appear to be any more dependent on local markets than the rest of the industry in Scotland, or new firms elsewhere.

Finally, Table 11 shows almost 90% of all new firm founders surveyed have some form of higher education, and 80% have at least one degree indicating that the unqualified inventor genius is important more in the mythology than in the reality of high technology industry entrepreneurship. Since only 16% of adults in the UK go on to higher education (Social Trends 1985, Chart 3.19), rates of entrepreneurship in the computer industry are likely to be highly sensitive to sub-regional

Table 11. Technical Qualifications of Founders.

Qualifications	Cambs	Herts	Scotland
Ph.D.	39	2	16
Computing/Electronics Degree	16	12	17
Other Degree	9	9	11
Other Technical Qualifications	8	2	7
No Qualifications	3	7	8
TOTAL	75	32	59

Source: Original Cambridge University survey data

variations in the qualifications of the resident population (Gould and Keeble 1984). When this is compounded with the variations in the composition of the R&D and managerial sectors of the industry in the two areas (Table 7), it fully corroborates Marsh's view (1985) quoted in the introduction, that "the most important ingredient in the area's success is people".

Conclusion

The original results presented above provide considerable evidence of the importance of technological change, scientific research and innovation, in generating a surge of new small companies in the UK computer industry since the early 1970s. These high technology companies are moreover appreciably larger and have grown faster than new firms generally. Our chapter also shows that the geography of new computer firms formation is biased towards Southern England, with a particular emphasis upon Greater London, Cambridge and the Norwich-Bristol axis. Central Scotland is an exception to this pattern. The evidence indicates that new computer firms in Cambridgeshire and Hertfordshire differ in significant ways from their counterparts in Scotland, notably in terms of products, skill requirements, and level of Reseach and Development activity. But both groups of firms appear to reflect a relatively substantial spin-off process from local universities, and exhibit similar levels of female employment and of local market orientation, contrary to the dependency arguments in the Scottish case. From a local or regional perspective, the findings suggest that new high technology firms do tend to cluster in particular locations, and that while in the long term (30 years) regional policy-induced branch plants in Scotland have generated new firm spin-off, the most striking clusters, other than London, have evolved in residentially attractive areas possessing existing major research facilities.

Note

The authors would like to acknowledge the support of the Economic and Social Research Council in funding this research project.

References

Baroin, D. and P. Fracheboud (1983) 'Les PME en Europe: et Leur Contribution a l'Emploi', Notes et Etudes Documentaires, La Documentation Francaise, Nos. 4715-6

Beaumont, J. (1982) The location, mobility and finance of new high-technology companies in the UK electronics industry, unpublished MSS, Dept. Trade and Industry, South East Regional Office

Breheny, M., P. Cheshire and R. Langridge (1983) 'The Anatomy of Job Creation? Industrial Change in Britain's M4 Corridor', Built Environment, 9,1, 61-71

Buswell, R.J. and E.W. Lewis (1970) 'The geographical distribution of industrial research activity in the UK', Regional Studies, 4, 297-306

Central Statistical Office (1984) Regional Trends, HMSO, London

Central Statistical Office (1985) Social Trends Vol. 15, HMSO, London

Cooke, P., K. Morgan and D. Jackson (1984) 'New technology and regional development in austerity Britain: the case of the semiconductor industry', Regional Studies, 18,4, 277-289

Cross, M. (1981) New firm formation and regional development, Gower, Farnborough, Hants.

Dept. of Employment Gazette (1983) 'Final report on the September 1981 Census of Employment' Dept. of Employment Gazette (Dec 1983) Occasional Supplement No.2

Ewers, H-J., and R.W. Wettman (1980) 'Innovation-oriented regional policy' Regional Studies, 14, 161-179

Faux, R. (1984) 'How the SDA Nurtured High Technology in Silicon Glen', The Times, April 27, 1984

Fothergill, S. and G. Gudgin (1982) Unequal growth: Urban and regional employment change in the UK, Heinemann, London

Fothergill, S., M. Kitson and S. Monk (1984) Urban industrial decline: The causes of the urban-rural contrast in manufacturing employment change, Final Report - June 1984, Cambridge University, Dept. of Land Economy

Freeman, C. (1983) Long Waves in the World Economy, Butterworths, London

Freeman, C. (1984) The Role of Technical Change in National Economic Development, Science Policy Research Unit, University of Sussex

Ganguly, A. (1983) 'Lifespan analysis of businesses in the UK 1973-82' British Business 12-18 Aug. 1983, 838-845

Ganguly, A. (1984) 'Business Starts and Stops: Regional Analyses by Turnover Size and Sector 1980-83', British Business, 15,9, 350-353

Ganguly, A. (1985) 'Business starts and stops: UK county analysis 1980-83', British Business 18-24 Jan. 1985, 106-110

Goddard, J.B. and A.T. Thwaites (1984) 'Unemployment in the North; Jobs in the South - the regional dimensions to the introduction of new technology', Centre for Urban and Regional Development Studies, Discussion Paper, No.54, University of Newcastle upon Tyne

Gould, A.J. and D.E. Keeble (1984) 'New firms and rural industrialisation in East Anglia', Regional Studies, 18,3, 189-201

Greffe, X. (1984) Les P.M.E. Creent-Elles Des Emplois?, Economica, Paris

Gudgin, G. (1984) Employment Creation by Small and Medium Sized Firms in the UK, Department of Applied Economics, University of Cambridge

Hall, P. (1981) 'The Geography of the Fifth Kondratieff Cycle', New Society, March 26, 535-537

Haug, P., N. Hood and S. Young (1983) 'R&D intensity in the affiliates of US owned electronics companies manufacturing in Scotland', Regional Studies, 17,6, 383-392

Howells, J.R.L. (1984) 'The location of Research & Development: some observations and evidence from Britain', Regional Studies, 18,1, 13-29

Jones, H., J. Caird and N. Ford (1984) 'A Home in the Highlands', Town and Country Planning, 53,11, 326-327

Keeble, D. (1985a) 'Industrial Change in the United Kingdom' Chapter 1 in Lever, W.F. (ed.) Industrial Change in the United Kingdom Longman, Harlow

Keeble, D. (1985b) 'The Changing Spatial Structure of Economic Activity and Metropolitan Decline in the United Kingdom' in Ewers, H.J. (ed.), The Future of the Metropolis, De Gruyter, Berlin

Keeble, D. and A. Gould (1985) 'Entrepreneurship and manufacturing firm formation in rural regions: the East Anglian case' in Healey M.J. and B.W. Ilbery (eds.), Industrialization of the Countryside, Geobooks, Norwich

Lloyd, P. and C. Mason (1983) 'New Firm Formation in the UK', Social Science Research Council Newsletter, 49, 23-24

Marsh, P. (1985) 'Hi-tech Growth Companies: City Where Dreams Come True', Financial Times, January 5, 1985

Massey, D. (1984) Spatial divisions of labour: social structures and the geography of production, Macmillan, London

McDermott, P.J. (1979) 'Multinational manufacturing firms and regional development: external control in the Scottish electronics industry', Scottish Journal of Political Economy, 26,3, 287-306

Mensch, G. (1979) Stalemate in Technology: Innovations Overcome the Depression, Ballinger, New York

Oakey, R.P. (1981) High Technology Industry and Industrial Location, Gower, Aldershot

Oakey, R.P. (1984) High technology small firms: regional development in Britain and the United States, Frances Pinter, London

Oakey, R.P., A.T. Thwaites and P.A.Nash (1980) 'The regional distribution of innovative manufacturing establishments in Britain', Regional Studies, 14, 3, 235-253

Rowlinson, F. (1985) A Geographical investigation into the Unlisted Securities Market, Unpublished B.A. Dissertation, University of Cambridge, Dept. of Geography

Schumpeter, J.A. (1939) Business cycles: a theoretical, historical and statistical analysis of the capitalist process, McGraw-

Hill, New York

Scottish Development Agency (1982) Electronics in Scotland: Industry profile, Scottish Development Agency, Glasgow

Segal Quince & Partners, (1985) The Cambridge Phenomenon: the growth of high-technology industry in a university town, Segal Quince & Partners, Cambridge

Shutt, J. and R. Whittington (1984) 'Large firm strategies and the rise of small units: the illusion of small firm job generation', University of Manchester, School of Geography, Working Paper 15.

Steed, G.P.F. and D. DeGenova (1983) 'Ottawa's technology-oriented complex', Canadian Geographer, 27, 263-278

Storey, D.J. (1982) Entrepreneurship and the new firm, Croom Helm, Beckenham

Storey, D.J. (1984) Business competitiveness: the role of small firms, University of Newcastle-upon-Tyne, Centre for Urban and Regional Development Studies

Whittington, R.C. (1984) 'Regional bias in new firm formation in the UK' Regional Studies, 18,3, 253-256

Chapter five

THE LOCATION OF NEW FIRM CREATION: THE FRENCH CASE

Philippe Aydalot

Together with the economic slump and the reversal
of trends noticed since the beginning of the
seventies, regional economists are faced with new
problems. The issue at stake is the understanding
of regional dynamism in industrialized countries.
Two phenomena are now becoming increasingly
important as a result of the obsolescence of old
industrial regions. These are technological
innovation and firm creation. Nowadays, regions
with a capacity for innovation and for enterprise
seem to have a greater potential for a better
future than those situated in old industrial areas.
This provides a valid basis for the reorganization
of spatial structures which is taking now place.
Industries of tomorrow are not being established in
industrial regions of the past.
    Until the seventies the major preoccupation
was that of firm location and large firms in
particular provided the basis for the region's
growth. Now large firms are on the defensive and
are frequently cutting down their labour-force; as
a result, these areas can only rely on their
endogenous capacity to expand, this becoming
increasingly the driving force for regional
development. In other words, it is no longer the
firm and its performance which constitute the
determining factors. It is the environment and its
vitality which is subject to primary analysis, all
the more so because the economic slump is
responsible for the rise in the mortality rate of
firms which in turn adds more weight to the setting
up of firms.
    The rate of firms established owes its
importance not only to the fact that new firms are
a source of new employment or that they promote
technological innovation but also because it is one

of the most telling indicators of the local
environment dynamism. The weakening of the impetus
given by large firms which act as a dead point or
even a negative pole, tends to increase the
importance of initiative from the local
environment. Thus, the apparent return of regional
dynamisms to the detriment of areas originally in
the vanguard of the industrial revolution, and in
favour of areas until now cut off from all forms of
modern industrialization, creates a major problem.
When Gudgin (1978) makes the observation that, in
the main, zones which are least urbanized and least
industrialized tend to profit by the highest rate
of firm creation, he raises a dual question:
1. Is the rate of firm creation a valid indicator
   of economic vitality?
2. Why then, if that should be the case, is the
   rural environment more dynamic than others?

Answers most often suggested are related to
the problem of optimal location. Some believe that
faster development of rural areas can be explained
by differences in the profitability of
manufacturing investment; the countryside nowadays
is more likely to have profit prospects than is the
case with urban areas. As regards the latter,
Fothergill and Gudgin (1982) have argued that it is
the lack of free space in cities necessary for the
development of already existing firms which
accounts for the urban-rural shift. These two
hypotheses are based on the optimal-location
viewpoint. But if we assume that the majority of
new employment reflects the rate of firm creation
and that the majority of firms are set up near the
homes of their founders, the problem changes. It is
no longer necessary to question the fact that
founders do not consider in what surroundings the
prospects for development and profit are best. It
is however useful to learn why such a large
proportion of firm founders live and work in small
towns near the rural areas.

Let us also consider the controversy about the
respective roles of small and large firms as
regards their ability to act as the breeding ground
for new firms. While several arguments have been
put forward in order to explain the greater
capacity of small firms to act as an incubator, it
is not always true that this assumption can be
backed up by facts. One should, however, bear in
mind that the average size of firms is much smaller
in rural areas. This would tend to suggest an
explanation for the fact that the latter are areas

France

that are proportionately more favourable for firm
creation.
     The difficulty of any analysis is due to the
fact that firm creation (like the introduction of
new technologies) is only a visible aspect of a
more general trend which is difficult to
distinguish, namely economic dynamism. There is a
tendency to value the forces defining regional
development using only fragmentary evidence which
points to mere aspects of the whole. The object of
this paper is not to answer all the questions
raised here. The French case is interesting insofar
as the country's environmental structure has
changed in the last 15 years. It is also difficult
to analyse owing to the shortage of satisfactory
statistical information. It would, therefore, be
more convenient to limit this discussion to
outlining the situation in France regarding the
location of firm creation before offering any
explanatory elements.

The French Industrial Landscape

Fig. 1. Regional   manufacturing   network
        (manufacturing/   regional   employment
        1/1/1982).

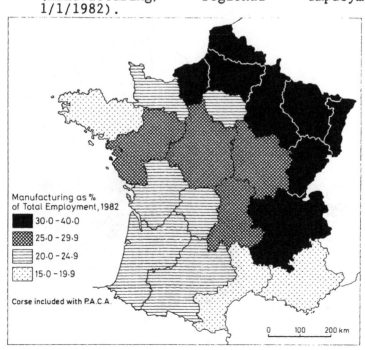

France

The level of manufacturing employment in France decreases gradually as one progresses from the North and North-Eastern regions which are the most industrialized to the South and South Western regions (Fig. 1). Notwithstanding the 30 year long industrial decentralization program and the slump of old industrial areas, employment in manufacturing remains relatively concentrated in the North and North East. But the map showing the number of firms related to the regional population gives an inverted picture of reality (Fig. 2); this shows that the largest numbers of manufacturing firms per 10,000 inhabitants are to be found in the South West. The paradox is however only an apparent one, its existence being due to the fact that the average size of firms is much greater in industrial regions than elsewhere (Fig. 3).

Industrial development over the last 20 years is characterized by a sharp drop in employment in large industrial areas (i.e. the North, Lorraine and Paris region) in favour of areas in the West.

Fig. 2. Number of firms per 10,000 inhabitants (manufacturing + construction, 1982).

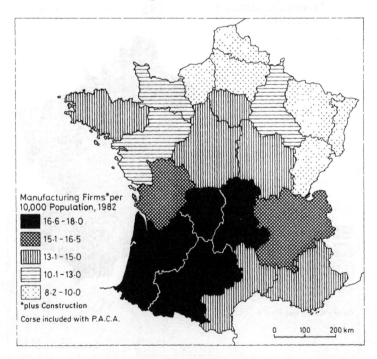

France

Fig. 3. Average Size of Firms (Manufacturing and Construction, 1982).

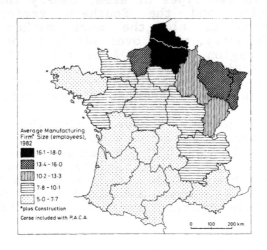

Average Manufacturing
Firm* Size (employees),
1982

16·1 - 18·0
13·4 - 16·0
10·2 - 13·3
7·8 - 10·1
5·0 - 7·7
*plus Construction
Corse included with P.A.C.A.

0   100   200 km

However, it is necessary to draw the distinction between the industrial decline of the North and in Lorraine related to the decline of old industries (such as coal-mining, steel and textiles) and the decline of the Paris region, with its more diversified industrial pattern and more modern industrial materials, which is related to the spatial expansion of the firm's functions. This means that production plants and assembly shops shift from Paris to the West whereas the management and research staff stay in Paris.

If, during the Golden Age of decentralization (1950-1975), the West benefited by industrial development, since the beginning of the seventies it has rather been the poor and peripheral regions which have maintained a satisfactory level of industrial performance, namely Bretagne, Languedoc and Poitou. Areas of production decentralization have shown signs of sharp regression during this recent period. The aforementioned development is not connected with any change of orientation in the decentralization program but with the fact that the latter has considerably lost its impetus. Thus it is the endogenous performance of different areas which now, to a large extent, determines the overall results.

Of some interest in this respect is the location of new manufacturing sectors which incorporate advanced technological devices (such as data processing equipment, electronic equipment and the aeronautic industry). These activities are clustered in two types of area, namely the Greater Paris region and the Southern regions. This concentration is all the more marked in the research industry, where over 50% is to be found in the Paris region, while 40% of the entire French research activity in manufacturing sectors is centred around the Southern Paris outskirts. The remainder is concentrated in a few cities in the South.

It is important to bear in mind that the South of France has, for over a century, been a zone of emigration. It has been perceived as a backward region possessing little manufacturing and doomed to irreversible decline. Such a reversal is not exceptional, at least not in Europe, for other countries have undergone a similar development.

Firm Location In French Regions

Over the last ten years, the annual number of firm creations in manufacturing and construction has increased by almost 30%. This trend conceals a contrast in development. A sharp drop occurred between 1976-1978 followed by a marked revival (Fig. 4). Such dramatic changes can be found in every region. The new firms which have been created are however relatively concentrated in the Paris region and in the Sunbelt (Fig. 5). The statistics available allow for the following observations.

Fig. 4. New Firm Creations in Manufacturing and Construction 1974-1983.

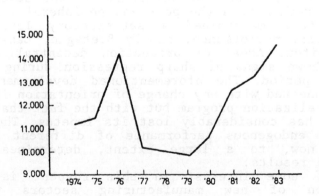

France

In terms of sectors, there is no visible relation between the rhythm of firm creation in a particular sector and the rapid development of that sector at large, this being the case even if this sector includes advanced technology. Sectors with a high rate of firm creation are often those in which employment is declining. This is clear both from correlation analysis for sectors at the national level ($r=0.11$) and at the interregional scale ($r=0.23$), representing the relation between the rate of development of regional manufacturing employment and the regional firm creation rate).

Table 1. New firm creation: correlations.

(1)	creation rate per sector (54 sectors), France, 1983. Manufacturing without food industry.
(2)	creation rate (per 10,000 inhabitants), Manufacturing, 21 regions, 1983
(3)	creation rate (per 10,000 inhabitants), Construction, 21 regions, 1983
(4)	creation rate (per 10,000 inhabitants), Business Services, 21 regions
(5)	rate of change of the number of manufacturing establishments, 1978-1982, 21 regions
(6)	migratory balance, 1975-1982, 21 regions
(7)	proportion of executives in the active population, 1982, 21 regions
(8)	Idem (7), excluding Ile de France
(9)	creation rate, Manufacturing + Construction, 21 regions, 1974-1982
(10)	migratory balance of active working population, 1975-1982
(11)	rate of employment change, per industrial sector, 1974-1981
(12)	rate of employment change per region, 1974-1981, 21 regions
(13)	creation rate (per 1,000 jobs) in Manufacturing, 1983
(14)	manufacturing employment 1980 (per 100 regional jobs)
(15)	creation rate (per 1,000 related jobs) in Manufacturing and Construction, 1974
(16)	business services (related to active population) 1982, 21 regions.

Results

(1)-(11)	r=0.11	(4)-(7)	r=0.93	(9)-(10)	r=0.54
(2)-(3)	0.72	(4)-(8)	0.63	(13)-(14)	-0.78
(3)-(4)	0.65	(2)-(12)	-0.23	(12)-(15)	0.22
(2)-(5)	-0.09	(9)-(16)	0.81	(13)-(16)	0.60

France

In the Greater Paris region, for instance, the high aggregate rate of industrial establishment is an expression of the powerful firm creation trend in the textile and printing industries, which accounted for two-thirds of all firm creations in the Ile de France in 1983. However, these two sectors only comprise 12% of total employment in the region, and 13% of their labour-force was lost between 1975 and 1982. In other sectors, firm setting-up rates in the Ile de France region are, on the whole, negligible. The only sectors which offer actual employment prospects account for a very small proportion of firm creations. Thus the three sectors of office and data processing equipment, electronic equipment, and aeronautic industry, which represent 19.7% of manufacturing employment in the Paris region (excluding food processing industries), only account for 5.3% of the overall firm creation in the area.

Fig. 5. Firm Creation (/1,000 manufacturing jobs) 1983.

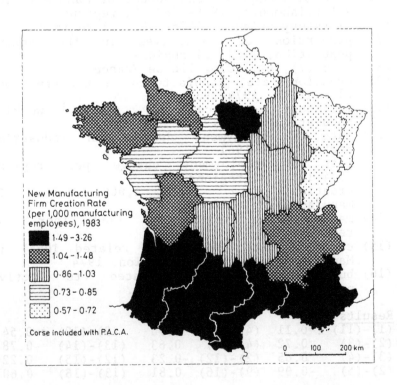

New Manufacturing
Firm Creation Rate
(per 1,000 manufacturing
employees), 1983

1·49 - 3·26
1·04 - 1·48
0·86 - 1·03
0·73 - 0·85
0·57 - 0·72

Corse included with P.A.C.A.

0   100   200 km

The formation of new manufacturing firms in France is centred around areas with little manufacturing, which often combine a rural environment with the proximity of a big isolated town. Thus, the correlation between the ratio of manufacturing employment/ active population and the new firm creation rate in manufacturing is clearly negative (r=-0.78).

The rate of manufacturing firm formation seems to embody, if only partially, the general regional dynamism. It is strongly correlated with other manifestations of the dynamism, even if there is no logical connection between them. Thus there is a close regional relationship between the rate of firm creation and the relative development of new technology (r=0.67) as well as with the regional migratory balance (r=0.81). The creation of firms in manufacturing, in the construction industry and in services are tightly bound together. Firm creation is an indirect and slightly obscure indicator of local dynamism. There is no clear link between the different manifestations of this dynamism. Examples of the contrary are numerous. Greater Paris, although extremely animated in terms of setting up of firms, has a negative migratory balance. New technology develops in areas with a high rate of firm creation even if, as we have seen above, creations often take place in sectors undergoing recession. The high level of creation in the clothing sector is a symptom of vitality which is also seen in the development of research and electronics.

Is the regional distribution of firm creation a result of the recession which began in 1974? A strong link can be observed between the two maps of firm creation in 1974 and 1983. The difference between the two is due to the fact that the time that has elapsed seems to have accentuated the initial disparities, so that the present structure is far from being the result of the crisis. It was, on the contrary, the initial structure that conditioned the ability of regions either to overcome the crisis or to succumb to it. Regions which were already dynamic before the crisis have become more active thus being able to overcome it -at least partly- while old industrial areas which were developing only slowly before the crisis, have felt its impact with redoubled strength. The fact that the level of firm creation in those regions has been stagnant contributed to this too. Thus, the Ile de France region accounts for no less than

Fig. 6. Firm Creation Change 1974-1983 (% of national increase).

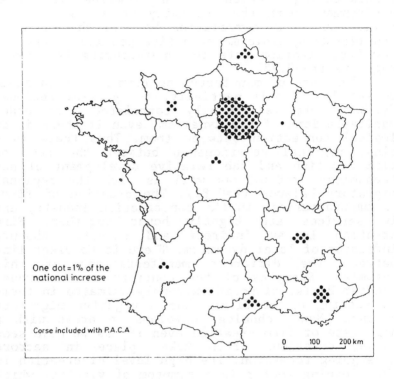

One dot = 1% of the national increase

Corse included with P.A.C.A

0   100   200 km

62% of the national increase in the annual volume of new firms (Fig. 6) established between 1974 and 1983 (for the secondary sector) while the four southern regions account for a further 20% of the total increase.

Firm creation in most advanced service sectors yields a similar picture. The leading role of Paris is again emphasized (45% of the national figure) while southern regions are also highly placed. Yet again we are confronted with the familiar bi-polar structure (with Paris on one side, and the sunbelt on the other) which is becoming almost a traditional feature in the regional analysis of French economic structures presented in this chapter.

In considering the significant negative correlation (r=-0.78) between the proportion of regional employment in manufacturing and the regional rate of manufacturing firm creation (related to manufacturing employment (1)), we should note that it is not industrial workers who create the firms. Secondly, if we recall the fact that the most industrialized areas, with the highest level of employment in manufacturing, also contain the largest firms, one is led to wonder about the possible positive correlation between firm creation rates and the number of firms in different regions. There is no point in saying that workers in areas where 26% of the labour force is employed in manufacturing are three times less creative than those who are working in areas where they represent only 18% of the active population, and seven times less than those in regions which have only eleven per cent of the total number in manufacturing.

Size Of Firms

The earliest year for which statistics are available on a regional level is 1974, the year in which the crisis broke out but one which is expressive of its earliest features. Economic indicators for France only began to show signs of deterioration in the summer of 1974 and it is likely that, on the whole, the decision to set up firms was not significantly affected by this turn of events as the process of taking it into account was a gradual one.

Analysis of the processes of firm creation for this year reveals some interesting findings. There is a marked negative correlation between the rate of firm creation in a particular region (in relation to local employment) and the average size of firms ($r=-0.76$), which indicates that the number of manufacturing creations, for a given number of workers, is an inverse function of the average size of firms in the region. Moreover, it can be shown that the rate of creation (related to the number of firms) is closely correlated with the average size of firms ($r=0.49$), according to an equation $y = 11.8 + 0.34$ x (where y is the number of annual new firms for every 1,000 firms already existing, and x measures the average number of workers per firm). Thus the following equation can be derived:

$$\text{Firm creations per 1,000 workers} = \frac{\text{number of firms} \times (11.8 + 0.34 \text{ T})}{\text{employment}}$$

(where T is the average size of firms)

We obtain $y = 0.53 + 0.67$ x   with $r=0.82$

France

All the same, firm creation is neither connected with the population size, nor with the number of workers employed, but with the number of firms, if we take into account the fact that large firms are on average more generative of new firms than small ones. For a given number of employees, however, they are much less generative. The following table indicates the theoretical value of firm creation in one year according to the model (and to the French 1974 figures).

average employment	annual rate of firm creation per 1,000 firms	creation rate for 10,000 workers
5	13.5	27.0
10	15.2	15.2
20	18.6	9.3
50	28.8	5.8

It is noteworthy that this pattern, however general it may be, provides the right approximation of firm creation in 1974. Let us apply it to two regions: the Nord-Pas de Calais which is very industrial, and the Languedoc-Roussillon, the least industrial region in France.

	manuf. empl./ tot. pop.	average size firms	firms/ 10,000 inh.	theoretical per 10,000 inh.	no. of firms per 1,000 workers
Nord-PC	16.3%	20.1	8.1	1.50	0.92
Lang.-R.	7.9%	5.7	14.3	1.97	2.49

A hypothesis emerges that it is the firms (and not the active working population, or workers in manufacturing, or members of a particular category of the population) that constitute the incubator for firm creation. It is equally interesting that the same equations examined using the data for 1983 show that the correlations which form the basis of this model have more or less disappeared. The correlation between creation rate (related to employment) and average firm size drops to 0.5 (against 0.76). The correlation between the creation rate (related to the number of firms) and the average size of firms drops to 0.15. This is

Table 2. New Firm Creation Statistics. France

France

	1974 New firm creation rate sec. sector /employment (1000)	/number of firms	1983 New firms	New firm creation rate 1983 /10 000 inhabitants manuf.	constr.	bus. serv.	/1000 jobs sec. sector	manuf.	1983 average size of firms, sec. sec.
Ile de France	1.42	16.8	4383	2.89	1.48	2.14	3.03	2.50	9.85
Champagne Ard.	1.20	15.7	296	1.23	0.98	0.34	1.49	0.99	11.3
Picardie	0.97	19.5	267	0.78	0.75	0.44	1.05	0.63	17.6
Haute Normandie	0.92	16.6	210	0.87	0.55	0.39	0.83	0.57	15.8
Centre	1.01	10.3	395	0.91	0.83	0.38	1.24	0.82	9.7
Basse Normandie	2.09	22.0	500	1.44	2.27	0.46	2.33	1.48	9.8
Bourgogne	1.40	13.7	346	1.10	1.07	0.51	1.64	1.03	8.8
Nord P.d.Calais	0.75	15.1	667	0.82	0.88	0.39	2.01	0.68	17.0
Lorraine	1.14	22.5	424	0.84	0.99	0.37	1.97	0.69	16.0
Alsace	1.06	17.8	301	0.95	0.99	0.72	1.22	0.72	15.1
Franche Comté	1.10	16.0	188	0.92	0.78	0.27	0.95	0.60	13.3
Pays d.la Loire	1.07	13.0	471	0.85	0.75	0.48	1.24	0.85	10.1
Bretagne	2.01	13.9	497	0.93	0.91	0.42	1.96	1.46	6.7
Poitou Charentes	1.84	12.4	306	0.99	0.96	0.41	1.18	1.23	6.4
Aquitaine	2.05	12.8	674	1.31	1.23	0.59	2.58	1.82	5.7
Midi-Pyrénées	2.34	13.6	606	1.49	1.14	0.55	2.87	2.07	5.0
Limousin	1.42	8.9	123	0.90	0.77	0.27	1.44	1.03	5.9
Rhône Alpes	1.40	15.5	1393	1.64	1.14	0.89	1.86	1.34	9.5
Auvergne	2.03	16.5	243	0.97	0.86	0.37	1.39	0.92	7.7
Languedoc-Rous.	2.92	16.2	612	1.51	1.66	0.92			
P.A.C.D'Azur	2.83	20.5	1464	1.55	2.18	1.09	4.27	3.26	5.3
Corse	-	-	100	1.42	2.75	0.75	4.06	2.71	6.3
France			14470	1,46	1,20	0,86			

due to the fact that many regions have "abandoned" the model, i.e. Ile de France, Basse Normandie and the four regions of the South. These six regions have taken off and risen above the norm so that in these regions we find more new firms than expected. Similarly, some other manufacturing regions, i.e. Franche Comté and Haute Normandie have been subject to a fall in their creation capacity. This perhaps suggests that a new pattern has emerged, one which favours the two dominant types: the large metropolis and the sun belt.

Size Of Firms And Industrial Dynamism

The recent emphasis placed on small firms seems to be all the more justified as the average size of firms is nowadays an indicator closely linked with all the manifestations of manufacturing dynamism. The increase in the firm's work-force, their propagatory role, and their ability to indicate the dynamism of the local environment are closely connected with one another as the following correlations show.

Table 3. Correlations between size of firms and manufacturing development

(1) average size of firms, France, 1982, 21 regions, manufacturing and construction.
(2) average rate of growth of manufacturing employment, 1978-1982.
(3) average rate of growth of regional employment, effect of size structure, 1978-1982.
(4) regional proportion of establishments, related to their size, 1979.
(5) rate of change of employment in establishments, according to their size, 1979-1982.

(1)-(2)	$r = -0.63$		
(2)-(3)	$r = 0.69$		
(4)-(5)			
establishment size:		1-10	0.60
		10-50	0.58
		...	...
		200-500	-0.57
		+500	-0.72

The first two correlations show the role of the small size of firms (and establishments) in the manufacturing performance of regions. The third set of correlations shows how the size structure of establishments in the regions is strongly associated with the performance of the establishments themselves. Large establishments which are located in regions with a considerable number of small establishments develop better than they do in regions where they dominate the scene. It is also worthwhile noting that recent developments have tended to even out the average size of firms from one region to another as the crisis hits large-sized firms and large-sized establishments as well as the regions which contain them.

This leads to the tentative formulation of a hypothesis: every firm, independently of the sector in which it is found, of its size or of the region which is its host, carries with it a certain capacity for industrial initiative. It acts as both the indicator and the origin of industrial dynamism. Regions which were able to retain their firms as indigenous organisations (while avoiding the process of concentration of capital) are nowadays better equipped than others for either reconversion or innovation. A firm represents a combination of the capacity for creation, the power of local decision-making, the ability to control the environment to its own ends; it works like a school for firm founders. Conversely, industrial concentration deprives the environment, it detracts from the spirit of enterprise while it decreases the number of firms, increasing the distance between the workers and the management. It moreover transforms the necessity to take risks inherent in every form of firm creation into a planned procedure of risk minimization.

Areas characterized by a high density of small firms can be defined by the following features:
- a complex manufacturing structure, as opposed to specialization in one particular industry;
- limited scale of manufacturing, such that firms were never able to attain a large size;
- social relations and management policy less affected by the institutionalized and paralysing 'rules of the game'.

As a hypothesis, it is possible to suggest some processes which form the basis of a regional typology examined from the point of view of firm creation and of the ability to generate

technological change. Factors likely to enhance a region's vitality include:
- the technical and educational standards (including qualifications and training);
- the existence of a lively industrial environment based on small and medium-sized firms which do not act as obstacles for new firms; they form an environment which is conducive to the creation of new firms, provoking collective initiative and training future firm founders;
- feeble sectorial specialization; a diversified environment facilitates new specialization and the introduction of new technology.

Regional decline would seem to be connected not so much with the presence of sectors in crisis (as there are plenty of examples of successful changes) but with the presence of a close industrial network controlled by large firms which master the development, block the arrival of new firms and make local development depend on decisions taken sometimes far from the firm's premises.

This process leads us to suggest the beginning of a regional typology which can be sketched in the following manner:
1. The metropolitan pattern, characterized by three features: technological superiority, a high rate of firm creation, but slow growth due to the reconversion rhythm entailing a rapid reduction of employment in activities in decline.
2. The 'Sun Belt' pattern including regions which often have no manufacturing tradition but which offer a high educational standard, a high capacity for the introduction of new technology which does not come up against resistance found elsewhere, a high rate of firm creation (undertaken partly by immigrants) and a noticeable rate of manufacturing development (as the absence of a strong manufacturing base almost entirely eliminates reconversion).
3. The old manufacturing region pattern which involves the concentration of industrial decision-making in a small number of declining large firms, as well as a considerable specialization in declining activities, a management adopting a defensive attitude and refusing to share power and to innovate unless the crisis incapacitates them from maintaining former practices. Under these circumstances new firm creation is highly unlikely.
4. The type representative of regions which have

benefited from industrial decentralization. It includes regions which in recent years have acted as a host for a great number of branch plants and firms established by external initiative, but which have a small account of firm creation. Such regions exhibit a high level of dependence, a low level of qualifications, a mediocre training system and a mediocre capacity for technological progress. However, these regions maintain a satisfactory level of manufacturing performance thanks to a set of modern industrial establishments.

5. The manufacturing region pattern representing a complex network which is often rooted in a mechanical engineering tradition, possessing a considerable technological vigour, a high capacity for adopting innovation but only a medium-level firm creation rate.

6. The industrial and scientific city pattern (for example, Grenoble in France) with a complex modern manufacturing structure, a high standard of education, a close connection between manufacturing and research, a great vitality and considerable technological dynamism.

Conclusion

This short survey of regional aspects of firm creation in France raises several problems which cannot be definitely resolved.

Regarding the distinction between urban and rural and the existence of an urban-rural shift, it would be wrong to assume that the city is in a state of decline in favour of rural areas. It is also by no means necessarily true that large firms are, by and large, doomed to decline. Neither large cities in the Western states of the USA, nor those in the South of France, are declining. Similarly, many large firms are conducive to development and may spread numerous positive effects, namely by means of subcontracting.

Decline hits old industrial areas whose vitality depends on a limited number of very large firms, while exclusively rural areas which are isolated and lack a serious manufacturing base also exhibit decline. It is, perhaps, necessary to analyse the industrial dynamics of today in terms of environment. A century of strongly variegated manufacturing has engendered areas which are nowadays incapable of a resurgence in development.

Areas which embody giant agglomerations, which depend on large firms and have conditioned generations of workers cannot undertake a new development. This is also the case in isolated agricultural and rural areas. In contrast, areas which combine large and medium-size cities and a rural environment as well as the redistribution of varied activities and possess a supple structure are in a better position to-day. The fact, however that they offer pleasant surroundings is not essential. The surroundings coincide with, rather than create, the new dynamism. Thus, the urban-rural shift is perhaps a measure of moving the development from totally urbanized and industralized areas towards a mixed environment where the manufacturing firm becomes rural for the most part but continues to get support from urban centres. As such, the constrained location thesis has a certain empirical validity even though it, no doubt, presents a somewhat mechanical vision. Strongly urbanized areas in decline are characterized by the absence of free spaces, but this does not mean that to offer space would be the major factor to stop the rot.

The above remarks can, moreover, help us to interpret the Sun Belt phenomenon which is currently emerging in various different parts of the world. It is clear that zones that are otherwise defined by their attractive climate and a high quality of life seem to possess particular advantages. However it may be argued that it is neither the sun nor the pleasant conditions which operate. Rather, part of the answer can be suggested by a historical approach. The regions in question are those that stayed out of the reach of the industrial urban trend of the 19th and 20th century. This absence of development preserved the environment and it offers today positive conditions: powerful conducive factors for firm creation, more open-spaced areas. These are also features explaining the good quality of life and not their present vitality alone. In the French case, it would seem that among regions excluded from previous industrial development, zones which are undergoing the most radical transformation, quantitative and structural, are those which are supported by large cities i.e. the south, whereas western regions tend to follow a development pattern dependent on external factors, the so-called peripheral type.

France

Note

1. Industrial creation is often measured in terms of regional manufacturing employment. It is not unlikely that this leads to the distortion of conclusions. Such a measure is based on the assumption that setting up could be attributed to those who work in manufacturing. The result of these measures is to show that major manufacturing regions are relatively uncreative as regards the setting up of new firms. If we consider the firm as the sign of the vitality of a local society and the springboard for its development, it would be necessary to measure firm creation in relation to the whole population (or to the whole adult population). The problem here is to find the breeding ground from which new firm founders are born.

References

Aydalot, P. (1984) 'The Reversal of Spatial Trends in French Industry since 1974' in Lambooy, J. (ed.), Spatial Dynamics and Economic Crisis, Finnpublishers

Aydalot, P. (1985) 'L'aptitude des milieux locaux à promouvoir l'innovation technologique', in Federwish J., H. Zoller (ed.), Technologies nouvelles et renouveau régional, Economica, forthcoming

Fothergill, S. and G. Gudgin (1982) Unequal Growth: Urban and Regional Employment Change in the UK, Heinemann, London

Gould, A. and D. Keeble (1984) 'New Firms and Rural Industrialization in East Anglia', Regional Studies, 18, 3, pp. 189-203

Gudgin, G. (1978), Industrial Location Processes and Regional Employment Growth, Saxon House, Farnborough

Chapter six

NEW FIRMS IN THE LOCAL ECONOMY: THE CASE OF BELGIUM

Rik Donckels
Christiane Bert

Some Theoretical Considerations

Local economy and new firms: an interdependent system

Our basic idea can be summarized as follows: there is a set of interdependent influences between the socio-economic characteristics of a micro-region on the one hand and the creation of new firms on the other hand. The system is presented in Fig. 1.

Fig. 1. The interdependent system.

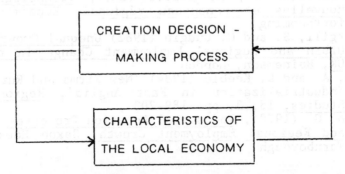

This basic idea implies two very important statements. First, new firm creation must be considered as a spatially defined dynamic process; while secondly, new firm creation can have a significant influence on the profile of the local economy. These two contentions will be developed further in the next two sections. It should also be noted that in describing the profile of the local economy, indicators such as population dynamics, supply of labour or factor endowments in general, sectoral structure, number and size of firms, infrastructural components, and local initiatives are all important considerations. For characterizing new firms, variables such as entrepreneurial profile, sector of activity and location can be very useful.

New firm creation: a multidimensional phenomenon

Role of the individual.
In our opinion certain traditional concepts from portfolio-analysis can be used in order to describe the individual decision-making process which is involved in new firm formation. This can be done in the following way:

- Let $A_{1'}$, ..., $A_{i'}$, ...,$A_{k'}$, be a set of possible actions.

  One of them can be the creation of a new firm in a particular sector at a specific location.

- All the A_i imply a certain number of "revenues" and "risks":

$$
\begin{array}{lll}
A_1 & (R_{11'}, \ldots, R_{1n}) & (= \text{vector of returns}) \\
    & (r_{11'}, \ldots, r_{1n}) & (= \text{vector of risks}) \\
A_i & (R_{i1'}, \ldots, R_{in}) & (= \text{vector of returns}) \\
    & (r_{i1'}, \ldots, r_{in}) & (= \text{vector of risks}) \\
A_k & (R_{k1'}, \ldots, R_{kn}) & (= \text{vector of returns}) \\
    & (r_{k1'}, \ldots, r_{kn}) & (= \text{vector of risks})
\end{array}
$$

It should be noted that the possible "revenues" can be of a different nature, such as financial earnings, selfrealisation, or independence from superior managers.

- $\forall$ i j : $R_{ij} = f_{ij}$ (individual characteristics)
  $$i = 1, \ldots, k$$
  $$j = 1, \ldots, n$$

  $r_{ij} = g_{ij}$ (individual characteristics)
  $$i = 1, \ldots, k$$
  $$j = 1, \ldots, n$$

- For the objective function we have:
  $u = u(R_{ij'}, r_{ij})$ where u = utility = scalar or vectoral function of the R_{ij} and r_{ij}.

The ultimate aim of the individual is to maximize his utility by choosing a particular action, taking into account a certain number of constraints.

Dependence on the socio-economic profile of the micro-area. In considering the socio-economic profile of a particular locality and its significance for new firm formation, at least four characteristics - factor endowments, sectoral structure, business organization, and entrepreneurial structure - merit attention. These are discussed more fully in Donckels (1981).

Factor endowments and availability of infrastructural components in particular seem to be necessary but not sufficient conditions for the emergence of new firms. Physical, educational, technical, legal and financial infrastructures should be available (see Sweeney, 1981). However, there is always the danger of a lack of entrepreneurial spirit and entrepreneurial initiatives. Out-migration of creative individuals can result in a kind of supply constraint. This is why the nature of the local business climate is arguably of such importance (Johannisson, 1984). Moreover, Gibb and Ritchie's work (1982) shows how the process of starting small businesses is highly influenced by the socio-economic dynamics of the area, such that a favourable general momentum and a stimulating environment can be of decisive importance.

According to Paraskevopoulos (1974) the two major growth components for regional employment change are the industrial mix on the one hand and the regional share on the other. Paraphrasing this approach, the creative potential for new firm formation of a particular area can be said to depend on the sectoral mix in the region concerned and on the creative capacity of a sector. The last concept deals with the probability of creating new firms as a function of sectoral characteristics. As an example we can refer to the theory of social marginality as proposed by Stanworth and Curran (1977). Their work provides empirical evidence that a significant number of new technology based firms have been created by people formerly living in a position of social marginality within a big firm.

Business organization is another element to be taken into account. We limit ourselves to mentioning one very particular item, namely the potential existence of barriers to entry, resulting from legal prescriptions or from a very specific market environment. It may also be worthwhile to draw attention to possible barriers caused by the existence of an information and communication gap between potential starters and public authorities. In recent years, impressive efforts have been made in various European countries to stimulate the creation of new firms. Empirical research shows, however, that potential users are not aware enough of the available support and incentives (Donckels and Degadt, 1985).

With respect to the entrepreneurial structure use can be made of a kind of "centre-periphery" model. Existing firms, and more particularly big firms, can play the role of a centre, encouraging peripheral activities such as the creation of new firms. Within this context it is important to stress that much depends on the extent to which the centre plays a dominant role and on whether or not spatial diffusion is possible. Local initiatives can be highly effective and efficient in stimulating the diffusion process, and in promoting the creation of new entities.

From new firms to the local economy: the feed-back

Creation multipliers. A very wide range of multipliers can be used to measure the real impact of the creation of new firms on the profile of the local economy. These are related to variables such as employment, value added, income, investments, and structural change. One should realize that the numerical value of these multipliers to a large extent depends on the specific characteristics of the newly created firms. More particularly, the potential for growth of the new firms, together with the business philosophy of the new entrepreneurs, will be of a fundamental importance for the impact on the region, within which the new firms have started. In this respect, one should take into account the fact that growth potentials can differ markedly from sector to sector and from area to area, as a function for example of specific market conditions. In addition it should be mentioned that growth cannot be considered as an essential objective for all new firms: no-growth can in some cases be the most appropriate strategy, as for example in order to avoid the very dangerous management gap.

Incentives to firm creation. In our opinion special attention should be paid to what we want to call the creation rate, that is the ratio of the number of new firms created in a particular period to the total number of firms in the foregoing period. The idea behind the creation rate is related to the stock adjustment principle in investment theory. The number of new firms created in a certain period, can be considered as a step in the direction of bridging the gap between the existing "stock" on the one hand, and the optimal stock on the other. The latter may be regarded as a function, for example, of specific market conditions in a particular area. Intersectoral and interregional comparison of these creation rates can be used to identify new potentialities for the creation of new firms. An analytical model should be built in order to explain these intersectoral and interregional divergencies. The reduced form of such a model can enable us to find the most appropriate instruments to be used as incentives for stimulating the creation of new firms.

Empirical Evidence For Belgium

Profile of the new firms

From Table 1 we can see that in 1984 in Belgium 53,490 new firms were created, according to the inscriptions into the commercial register.

For the distribution over the regions we refer to Table 2. In Fig. 2 the regional division is presented.

From Table 2 it is clear that the majority of the new firms have been created in Flanders (54.16%), while Wallonia accounts for 32.47% and Brussels for 13.37%. Some of the figures in Table 2 are simply the result of the differing physical geography of the three regions. Thus 79% of new businesses in the fishing sector are located in Flanders, while 90% of firms created in sylviculture are in Wallonia. For all other sectors excluding mining, electricity and home decoration, however, Flanders has the largest share.

The sectoral picture for the different regions is given in Table 3. For Belgium as a whole, the most important sectors are commercial activities (42.62%) and tourism (15.25%). It is perhaps noteworthy that even when combined as a single sector, manufacturing industries account for only 12.07% of total new firms created. This reflects the very marked predominance of service activities (80% of the total) in the generation of new

Belgium

Table 1. New inscriptions into the commercial
register in 1984 (absolute figures, per
region and per sector).

| Sector | Region | | | |
	Flanders	Wallonia	Brussels	Belgium
Agriculture	672	474	47	1,193
Sylviculture	38	374	5	417
Fishing	42	9	2	53
Mining	1	2	2	5
Manufacturing	3,616	1,861	978	6,455
- Food, Beverage,				
Tobacco	476	363	87	926
- Textiles	241	95	69	405
- Clothing	326	194	116	636
- Wood and Furniture	483	159	76	718
- Paper	596	322	355	1,273
- Chemicals	193	108	60	361
- Clay and Glass	98	53	27	178
- Basic Metals	263	92	25	380
- Non Ferrous Metals	4	2	2	8
- Metallic Fabrications	243	131	41	415
- Garages	546	290	99	935
- Residual	147	52	21	220
Construction	612	382	119	1,113
Electricity	578	652	209	1,439
Commercial Activities	12,492	7,287	3,021	22,800
Financial Activities	1,754	752	589	3,095
Insurance Activities	619	289	98	1,006
Home Decoration	774	814	234	1,822
Transport	545	285	223	1,053
Medical Services	191	114	34	339
Other Services	2,337	1,559	645	4,541
Tourism	4,701	2,515	943	8,159
Total	28,972	17,369	7,149	53,490

Source: Extracts of the commercial register, 1984.

businesses in Belgium in the 1980s. The findings
for the three regions are very similar. In each,
there is a predominance of commercial activities
and tourism, while the share of manufacturing
varies only between 10.72% (Wallonia) and 13.68%
(Brussels). In terms of broad categories,
therefore, there are no very marked differences in
the sectoral distribution of new firms between the
three Belgian regions. Only with a few individual
sectors, such as financial services and paper, can

Belgium

Table 2. Regional share of the new inscriptions per sector

Sector	Region			
	Flanders	Wallonia	Brussels	Belgium
Agriculture	56.33	39.73	3.94	100
Sylviculture	9.11	89.69	1.20	100
Fishing	79.25	16.98	40.00	100
Mining	20.00	40.00	40.00	100
Manufacturing				
- Food, Beverage, Tobacco	51.40	39.20	9.40	100
- Textiles	59.51	23.46	17.03	100
- Clothing	51.26	30.50	18.24	100
- Wood and Furniture	67.27	22.15	10.58	100
- Paper	46.82	25.29	27.89	100
- Chemicals	53.46	29.92	16.62	100
- Clay and Glass	55.06	29.77	15.17	100
- Basic Metals	69.21	24.21	6.58	100
- Non Ferrous Metals	50.00	25.00	25.00	100
- Metallic Fabrication	58.55	31.57	9.88	100
- Garages	58.40	31.01	10.59	100
- Residual	66.82	23.64	9.54	100
Construction	54.99	34.32	10.69	100
Electricity	40.17	45.31	14.52	100
Commercial Activities	54.79	31.96	13.25	100
Financial Activities	56.67	24.30	19.03	100
Insurance Activities	61.53	28.73	9.74	100
Home Decoration	42.48	44.68	12.84	100
Transport	51.76	27.06	21.18	100
Medical Services	56.34	33.63	10.03	100
Other Services	51.46	34.33	14.21	100
Tourism	57.62	30.82	11.56	100
Total	54.16	32.47	13.37	100

Source: see Table 1.

some degree of regional structural specialization be identified.

Profile of the regional economy

In order to provide a context for regional variations in new firm formation in Belgium, Table 4 records the total number or stock of all firms in existence at the end of 1983, by sector and by region.

Belgium

Table 3. Sectoral distribution of the new firms in
the three regions.

| Sector | Region | | | |
	Flanders	Wallonia	Brussels	Belgium
Agriculture	2.32	2.73	0.66	2.23
Sylviculture	0.13	2.15	0.07	0.78
Fishing	0.14	0.05	0.03	0.10
Mining	0.00	0.01	0.03	0.01
Manufacturing	12.49	10.72	13.68	12.07
- Food, Beverage, Tobacco	1.64	2.09	1.22	1.73
- Textiles	0.83	0.55	0.97	0.76
- Clothing	1.13	1.12	1.62	1.19
- Wood and Furniture	1.67	0.92	1.06	1.34
- Paper	2.06	1.85	4.97	2.38
- Chemicals	0.67	0.62	0.84	0.68
- Clay and Glass	0.34	0.31	0.38	0.33
- Basic Metals	0.91	0.53	0.35	0.71
- Non Ferrous Metals	0.01	0.01	0.03	0.01
- Metallic Fabrication	0.84	0.75	0.57	0.78
- Garages	1.88	1.67	1.38	1.75
- Residual	0.51	0.30	0.29	0.41
Construction	2.11	2.20	1.66	2.08
Electricity	1.99	3.75	2.92	2.69
Commercial Activities	43.12	41.95	42.26	42.62
Financial Activities	6.05	4.33	8.24	5.79
Insurance Activities	2.14	1.66	1.37	1.88
Home Decoration	2.67	4.69	3.27	3.41
Transport	1.88	1.64	3.12	1.97
Medical Services	0.66	0.66	0.48	0.63
Other Services	8.07	8.98	9.02	8.49
Tourism	16.23	14.48	13.19	15.25
Total	100.00	100.00	100.00	100.00

Source: see Table 1

From these figures it follows that 58.39% of the
firms are in Flanders, 30.67% in Wallonia and
10.94% in Brussels. In terms of sectoral structure,
the largest number of existing businesses in all
regions of Belgium are in the commercial activities
category. Commercial firms account for 32.04% of
the total stock in Flanders, 30.54% in Wallonia,
and 39.09% in Brussels. The share of the
manufacturing sector is 10.52% in Flanders, 10.27%
in Wallonia and 13.45% in Brussels. For the country
as a whole, the share is 10.77%.

Belgium

Table 4. Total number of firms by the end of 1983.

| Sector | Region | | | |
	Flanders	Wallonia	Brussels	Belgium
Agriculture	66,776	33,059	262	100,097
Sylviculture	214	1,860	42	2,116
Fishing	230	64	7	301
Mining	33	51	27	111
Manufacturing	33,941	17,410	8,127	59,478
– Food, Beverage, Tobacco	7,702	3,271	790	11,763
– Textiles	1,727	300	127	2,154
– Clothing	2,658	978	863	4,499
– Wood and Furniture	2,820	1,315	503	4,638
– Paper	2,936	1,393	1,508	5,837
– Chemicals	666	258	287	1,211
– Clay and Glass	1,330	946	170	2,446
– Basic Metals	271	188	153	612
– Non Ferrous Metals	272	133	101	506
– Metallic Fabrication	5,818	3,548	1,628	10,994
– Garages	6,754	4,776	1,621	13,151
– Residual	987	304	376	1,667
Construction	18,456	11,639	2,760	32,855
Electricity	899	865	206	1,970
Commercial Activities	103,359	51,756	23,627	178,742
Financial Activities	12,846	7,602	4,875	25,323
Insurance Activities	904	723	169	1,796
Home Decoration	11,995	6,617	2,304	20,916
Transport	8,543	3,980	1,496	14,019
Medical Services	325	209	45	579
Other Services	31,757	17,009	9,972	58,738
Tourism	32,339	16,605	6,518	55,462
Total	322,617	169,449	60,437	552,503

Source: N.I.S.

On the basis of Table 1 and Table 4, creation rates have been calculated in terms of new firms per 100 existing firms. These are recorded in Table 5. Of the three regions, it is Flanders, the region with the biggest "stock of firms" by the end of 1983, which records the lowest creation rate. The highest rate is found in Brussels, where the "stock of firms" is lowest. These findings coincide with the theoretical pattern which might be expected on the basis of the stock adjustment model.

Table 5 also shows that there are impressive differences in creation rates between different

Belgium

Table 5. Creation rate per sector and per region.

| Sector | Region | | | |
	Flanders	Wallonia	Brussels	Belgium
Agriculture	1.01	1.43	17.94	1.19
Sylviculture	17.76	20.11	11.90	19.71
Fishing	18.26	14.06	28.57	17.61
Mining	3.03	3.92	7.41	4.50
Manufacturing				
- Food, Beverage, Tobacco	6.18	11.10	11.01	7.87
- Textiles	13.95	31.67	54.33	18.80
- Clothing	12.26	19.84	13.44	14.14
- Wood and Furniture	17.13	12.09	15.11	15.48
- Paper	20.30	23.12	23.54	21.81
- Chemicals	28.98	41.86	20.91	29.81
- Clay and Glass	7.37	5.60	15.88	7.28
- Basic Metals	97.05	48.94	22.12	62.09
- Non Ferrous Metals	1.47	1.50	1.98	1.58
- Metallic Fabrication	4.18	3.69	2.52	3.77
- Garages	8.08	6.07	6.11	7.11
- Residual	14.89	17.11	5.59	13.20
Construction	3.32	3.28	4.31	3.39
Electricity	64.29	75.38	98.56	73.05
Commercial Activities	12.09	14.08	12.79	12.76
Financial Activities	13.65	9.89	12.08	12.22
Insurance Activities	68.47	39.97	57.99	56.01
Home Decoration	9.06	12.30	10.16	8.71
Transport	6.38	7.16	14.91	7.51
Medical Services	58.77	54.55	75.56	58.55
Other Services	7.36	9.17	2.84	7.73
Tourism	14.54	15.15	14.47	14.71
Total	8.98	10.25	11.84	9.68

Source: see Table 1 and Table 4.

sectors. These differences suggest the existence of marked sectoral variations in opportunities for new firm formation in Belgium, perhaps because of differences in market demand or barriers to entry. The highest rates are to be found in the electrical, basic metals, medical services and insurance sectors, while very low rates characterize agriculture, non-ferrous metals, construction and metallic fabrication. It is also clear that for a number of industries, sectoral formation rates vary significantly between the regions. While this may partly reflect random variation associated with small samples

Belgium

Fig. 2. Situation of the selected regions.

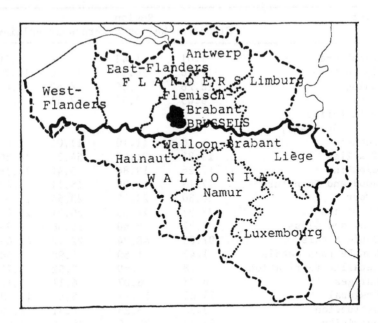

(agriculture and fishing, for example), differences also may be linked to sectorally-specific regional conditions and stimuli to new business formation.

Public Policy And New Firm Formation: The Case Of Flanders

Over the last decade, there has been a substantial increase in public policy concern with new business formation in Belgium, as one response to deepening recession, the closure of large companies, and steeply rising unemployment. The nature and impact of national, regional and local government initiatives with respect to new firms can be illustrated by specific reference to the case of Flanders, the region with the lowest overall firm formation rate in Belgium.

Physical infrastructure

During the last decade, specific zones for small and medium-sized enterprises (SME's) have been created throughout Flanders, as a special aspect of a more general regional development policy. A closer analysis shows that the occupation rate varies from 0 to 100%. Our impression is that political considerations were more important than economic ones in the decision-making process concerning the location of these zones. The marked variation in occupation rates furthermore proves that physical infrastructure itself is a necessary but not a sufficient condition for the emergence of new firms. In 1983 the first Business Centre was created in Flanders. It was so successful that for the moment the ambition is to create 20 Business Centres, providing support for about 400 new firms. These centres will offer a number of advantages to the participants: availability of premises, supply of common services (secretaries, telephone service, provision of conference space), and the provision of management assistance. It should be added that these centres do not satisfy those entrepreneurs needing rather larger premises for their activities. Recently a new initiative has been taken in order to provide this type of physical infrastructure.

Technological infrastructure

Public authorities at the national, regional and local level have created a wide range of incentives aimed at stimulating the diffusion of technological innovation. A special effort has been made by the 5 SRD's (Society for Regional Development) in order to encourage technological innovation in small and medium-sized firms. On a decentralized basis and at the local level information sessions and seminars have been organized in collaboration with professional bodies. Moreover, experts of the SRD's are visiting the SME's to assist them while introducing new technologies. These initiatives undoubtedly contribute to the realization of a favourable technological climate, within which new technology-based firms can emerge.

A further very recent initiative was the setting-up in 1983 of T.I.V. (Technological Innovation and Renewal Cell for Flanders). This institute, created by the SRD's, has been established to promote technology transfer in the region. Since 1982, the so-called DIRV-action (Third Industrial Revolution in Flanders) has also been of great importance. Through DIRV the Flemish government is attempting to generate a general momentum towards the development and adoption of new technologies. In February 1985 the technology fair "Flanders Technology International" took place in Ghent.

Educational infrastructure

A particularly interesting initiative with respect to education and training for entrepreneurship in Flanders is the Institute for Permanent Education of the Middle Class. The institute is responsible for twenty-one training centres spread throughout the region. In these centres young people wanting to start their own business can acquire the techniques, abilities and skills necessary to manage their business. It should be emphasized that in Belgium there are a large number of so called regulated businesses: by law, these businesses cannot be established without a certificate granted by the institute. This is the case amongst others for the following professions: motor vehicle repairer, dealer in fuel, miller, plumber, butcher, insurance broker, and central heating engineer. Within the training programme attention is paid to the technical aspects of the business, as well as to the development of managerial know-how.

Given the importance of the institute it seemed to be worthwhile to try to identify whether it has had any measurable impact on the new firm creation process in Flanders. In Table 6 information is provided on the number of successful candidates in 1982 per sector and per province. About 38% of the candidates were from West Flanders, while Limburg accounted for 21% and East-Flanders for 20%. These figures have been compared with the number of new firms created in 1984. There was no significant correlation. Our interpretation is that there exists a substantial start-up lag.

The institute also plays a considerable role in organizing lectures and seminars for people already in business, within the framework of a permanent education programme.

Specific initiatives

Specific private and public sector initiatives have also been taken to stimulate entrepreneurship. Some examples are:

Belgium

Table 6. Number of successful IPEMC candidates in
       1982.

Sector	Antw.	Flem. Brab.	Limb.	East Fland.	West Fland.	Total Fland.
Agriculture	11	5	13	15	7	51
Manufacturing						
- Food, Beverage,						
Tobacco	29	30	56	79	118	312
- Textiles	9	5	9	-	1	24
- Clothing	-	-	6	-	3	9
- Wood and Furniture	16	2	14	5	46	83
- Paper	3	-	15	9	16	43
- Chemicals	-	-	-	-	-	-
- Clay and Glass	-	-	3	-	-	3
- Basic Metals	-	-	-	-	-	-
- Non Ferrous Metals	-	-	-	-	-	-
- Metallic Fabrication	37	18	25	55	86	221
- Garages	25	14	48	33	41	161
- Residual	1	-	-	5	-	6
Construction	19	26	35	29	50	159
Electricity	4	10	32	29	32	107
Commercial Activities	16	4	40	48	99	207
Financial Activities	35	10	42	22	163	272
Insurance Activities	47	24	32	29	52	184
Home Decoration	9	8	14	10	11	52
Transport	-	-	-	-	-	-
Medical Services	16	7	2	19	-	44
Other Services	28	41	131	95	197	492
Tourism	2	-	4	18	26	50
Total	307	204	521	500	948	2,480

Source: Institute for Permanent Education of the Middle
       Class, Annual report 1982.

- Jaycees Antwerp have started a training programme
  called "Become your own boss".
- Within the context of Janssen Pharmaceutical, Mr.
  B. Stouthuysen has established a "school for
  entrepreneurs".
- The Belgian Association of Banks has undertaken
  an initiative entitled "Dare to start your own
  business". Projects introduced by people wanting
  to start new firms are evaluated by
  representatives of banks and universities.
  Evaluation criteria include the originality of
  the project, its export-orientation, and the
  employment and value-added creation to be

expected. Selected projects receive a financial premium and the managerial support of a banker as well. No less than 703 projects have so far been submitted, most of them by people younger than 30 years old. About 50% of the selected projects were introduced by unemployed people. From the evaluation it appears that for most of the potential entrepreneurs there was a lack of insight into the market opportunities, and technical aspects of the production process.
- In several high schools mini-enterprises have been created. The aim is to make young people familiar with real business life.
- In order to be able to organize in an efficient way a secondment system, the elaboration of a "brains-bank" has started at the regional level.

Conclusions

The birth of new firms can profitably be studied within an interdependent framework describing the interactions between the new firms on the one hand and the characteristics of the local economy on the other hand. Moreover, new firm creation by definition is a multidimensional phenomenon, the most important components of which are the individual profile of the new entrepreneur and the socio-economic structure of the micro-area he is living in.

In studying new firms, attention should be paid to the feed back in the direction of the local economy. The use of creation multipliers such as employment and value added may be of help here. It should be realized, however, that growth cannot be considered as an essential objective for all new firms, and that growth potentials can differ markedly from sector to sector and from region to region, for example as a function of specific market conditions.

In explaining the creation of new firms a kind of stock-adjustment model can be used. In this context, the creation rate measure, calculated as the number of new firms created in a given period divided by the total number of firms existing by the end of the foregoing period, is a key index of regional propensities to new firm formation.

The empirical evidence for Belgium shows that 53,490 new firms were created in 1984: 54.16% of them were located in Flanders, 32.47% in Wallonia and 13.37% in Brussels. With respect to the sectoral picture, very similar patterns are evident in the three regions : a net predominance of commercial activities and tourism, together with a limited share of manufacturing varying between 10.72% in Wallonia and 13.68% in Brussels. Because of this sectoral profile, creation multipliers are likely to be rather limited. Efficient collaboration between new and existing firms, and between SME's and big firms, could arguably increase these multipliers in a substantial way. The creation of new firms may also lead to an important auto-employment effect.

The findings for Belgium coincide with theoretical expectations developed on the basis of the stock-adjustment model: the lowest creation rate is found for the region with the highest "stock of firms" (Flanders), while the highest one is in Brussels, the region with the smallest stock.

One factor influencing new firm creation in Flanders has been the physical infrastructure. From the occupation rate of zones for SME's, however, it would appear that this type of infrastructure is a necessary but not a sufficient condition for the emergence of new firms. New business centres have been established recently and these seem to be very successful. Special efforts have been made to improve the region's technological infrastructure. More particularly, the diffusion of technological innovation has been stimulated, resulting in the establishment of a more favourable "technological climate". The Flemish government and its President, Mr. G. Geens should be congratulated on the success which has so far been achieved.

The institute for Permanent Education of the Middle Class is the keystone of the region's educational infrastructure with respect to entrepreneurship and new firms. Through a network of twenty-one training centres the institute can contribute in a substantial way to prepare young people for managing their own business. However, comparison of the number of successful candidates in 1982 with the number of new firms created revealed no significant correlation. This suggests the existence of a rather long start-up lag. As a general conclusion with respect to education, it is important to stress that in fact existing programmes only reach a somewhat limited number of persons. It is necessary to develop further the insight that education and training are very important: entrepreneurs in SME's have to become better managers. Furthermore, efforts need to be

made in order to bridge the information and
communication gap between SME's and their external
environment. Initiatives will be needed to decrease
the physical and psychological distance. In this
context local initiatives can be of a vital
importance.

During the last two years in Flanders several
specific initiatives have been undertaken in order
to stimulate entrepreneurship. It is our conviction
that this is a fruitful direction for further
private and public sector policy action, since the
creation of new firms is strongly influenced by the
"local business climate".

References

Donckels, R. (1981)'Theory of regional stagnation',
    in W. Buhr and P. Friedrich, Lectures on
    regional stagnation, Nomos Verlagsgesell-
    schaft, Baden-Baden, pp. 70-108.
Donckels, R. and J. Degadt (1985) 'SME's and public
    authorities on the information and
    communication gap', International small
    business journal, (forthcoming).
Gibb, A. and J.R. Ritchie (1982) 'Understanding
    the process of starting small business',
    European small business journal, 1, 26-45.
Johannisson, B. (1984) 'A cultural perspective on
    small business - Local business climate',
    International small business journal, 4,
    32-43.
Paraskevopoulos, C.C. (1974) 'Patterns of regional
    economic growth', Regional and urban
    economics, 4, 77-105.
Stanworth, M.J.K. and J. Curran (1977)
    Management motivation in the smaller business,
    Gower, Farnborough.
Sweeney, G.P. (1981), New entrepreneurship and the
    smaller firm, Institute for Industrial
    Research and Standards, Dublin.

Chapter seven

NEW FIRM CREATION IN DENMARK: THE IMPORTANCE OF THE
CULTURAL BACKGROUND

Sven Illeris

This chapter briefly describes some recent
geographical differences in new firm creation in
Denmark. In analysing the causes of these
variations, it stresses the importance of cultural
factors, which are receiving increasing attention
in studies of location. Finally, it considers what
kind of new firm policies may be efficient in
different cultural environments, in the context of
the Danish experience.

Where Are New Firms Created?

Knowledge about new firm creation in Denmark is
mainly due to recent research by Jane Wickmann
(1984), who sent questionnaires to a large sample
of manufacturing, construction and certain service
firms started in the years 1977-80. She received
1325 answers which should be sufficient for a
cautious geographical analysis.

The frequency of new firm creation is mapped
in Fig. 1, where the new firms are related to the
number of men aged 30-39 - the group from which
most new firm founders are recruited. It should be
noted that by using this denominator, the effects
of selective migration are eliminated. In
particular, allowance is thus made for the larger
number of potential founders to be found in outer
metropolitan immigration counties, such as those
surrounding Copenhagen, where the share of men aged
30-39 in the total population is above-average. The
data refer to the three above-mentioned sectors
combined, but figures for manufacturing firms alone
would have given a similar picture.

The pattern emerging from Fig. 1 is clear
enough: the frequency of new firm creation is

Denmark

Fig. 1. New firms 1977-80 per 1000 men aged 30-39.

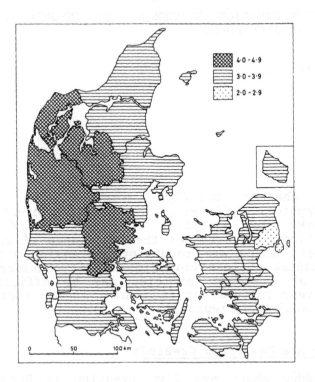

below-average in the Copenhagen area - by far the most important city in the country. On the other hand, it is above-average in parts of Jutland, the traditionally less developed part of Denmark.

The consequences of these variations for the total development of manufacturing employment are illustrated by Table 1, which shows a 'demographic' analysis for the central municipality of Copenhagen, compared to the rural communes (no town over 5000 inhabitants) of the five counties of Southern, Western and Northern Jutland. The national average is somewhere between these two areas.

The data refer to manufacturing establishments with more than 5 persons employed (not to firms, thus branch plants are regarded as individual establishments). The total employment development 1972-80 of each establishment is entered in one row, depending on whether the establishment started, closed down, expanded or reduced its employment, immigrated or emigrated, between 1972 and 1980 in the area in question.

Denmark

Table 1. Employment development in manufacturing
        establishments 1972-80.

Percentage of 1972 Employment	Municipality of Copenhagen	Rural Jutland (excl. East)
Starts	+ 7%	+ 33%
Closures	- 31%	- 10%
Expansions	+ 4%	+ 26%
Reductions	- 21%	- 9%
Immigrations	+ 1%	+ 3%
Emigrations	- 3%	- 1%
Total Net Development	- 43%	+ 42%

Source: Peter Maskell (1984), Table 3

Table 1 clearly shows that variations in start
and closure rates as well as expansion and
reduction rates are far more important than
enterprise removals, with which so much of the
location literature deals. And out of the former
four components, the start rates show larger
geographical differences than any other. While the
latter do include some branch plants, Maskell's
work supports the view that differences in new firm
formation are important for current regional
employment change in Denmark, especially between
urban and rural areas. It is not known whether
Copenhagen has ever had a higher incubation
'frequency' than other parts of Denmark. If so,
this is very clearly not the case any more.

Jane Wickmann's sample does not allow any
detailed analysis of geographical differences in
new firm creation. There can hardly be any doubt,
however, that such differences exist, some areas
being traditionally known as 'starter areas'. One
example is the southern part of the county of
Ringkøbing in Western Jutland. With its origin in
the hosiery production of poor heathland farmers, a
textile industry had developed here, characterised
by frequent starts of new, small firms. In recent
years many firm creations have also been observed
in other branches, such as engineering and computer
software.

External Factors And Personal Factors

In location studies, research normally attempts to
analyse a number of external factors or forces

which in different geographical environments influence the development of economic activities in positive or negative ways. This may also be done with respect to new firm creation in Denmark, on the basis of answers by new firm founders to Jane Wickmann's questions about major start problems. It should be noted that the number of answers in each category is small, and that problems which revealed no geographical variation have been omitted.

Finding premises is clearly easier in a peripheral region than in the Copenhagen area. The problem is connected with the fact that most new firms - about 70% - start in existing, cheap buildings. This is particularly the case in the central municipality of Copenhagen, where 92% of the new firms were created in existing buildings. The obvious implication is that a slum clearance policy which eliminates such buildings may be detrimental to the creation of new firms. The higher cost of urban premises is probably also a factor in this respect.

Finding staff has rarely been a problem in recent years, but it seems most likely to be so in the metropolitan area where unemployment is lower than in peripheral areas.

It is often a problem to finance a new firm. However, Table 2 seems to indicate that it may be easier to raise capital in a peripheral area than in a metropolitan area - a finding which is supported by other Danish evidence. One explanation has something to do with different styles of relationships between people. In a small community, bank managers are more likely to know potential starters personally, or at least to know somebody who knows them, than in a metropolitan area. Applications for bank finance therefore tend to receive a less formal consideration. Another part of the explanation is that small town starters are more likely than metropolitan starters to own a house which may serve as security for a loan.

Certain external factors thus do seem to favour new firm creation in peripheral and more rural areas of Denmark, compared with the Copenhagen metropolitan region. But these are not the only factors which influence the creation of new firms. There are also personal factors. How likely are people in different parts of the country to create their own firm? Where do the persons, who create firms, live?

As already mentioned, most firm starters are men, aged 30-39. Jane Wickmann therefore

Denmark

Table 2. Major start problems mentioned by new firms.

Percent of new firms in the area	Municipality of Copenhagen[1]	County of Copenhagen[2]	County of Ringkøbing (West Jutland)	County of North Jutland
Finding suitable premises	19%	24%	10%	9%
Finding suitable staff	17%	15%	5%	15%
Obtaining finance	47%	41%	41%	19%

1) Including Frederiksberg 2) Suburban
Source: Jane Wickmann (1983), Table 14.

interviewed 750 men, aged 13-39 in 1982, about their wishes to establish and run their own firm. No less than 30 per cent of those men who were not already self-employed expressed a wish to become so. However, the share varied from 22 per cent in the Copenhagen area to 43 per cent in rural areas.

How may this geographical variation in the occurrence of potential starters be explained? Among the characteristics of firm creators, one reveals a very clear occupational - and hence in turn geographical - bias. Wickmann's research shows that roughly 50% of the starters were sons of self-employed fathers (usually farmers, fishermen, artisans or retailers), whereas a much smaller share of all fathers were self-employed. On the other hand, very few fathers of starters were white collar workers. This must, of course, be seen in connection with the fact that rural and peripheral areas have an above-average share of self-employed fathers, and metropolitan areas an above-average share of white collar fathers.

Life-Modes And New Firm Creation

It may therefore be argued that the occurrence of a certain group of persons in a particular area is a factor in new firm creation, and that this factor can be traced back to the father's occupation. Thus it is not an individualistic factor, but a factor that has to do with the social environment, whether there is an 'entrepreneurial climate' or 'industrial dynamism'. It is difficult to characterise it in any precise way. Let us call it the cultural factor. But we need to understand the mechanism better, especially if we want, for reasons of government regional or national economic policy, to influence the creation of new firms. We cannot just sit down and wait for a number of suitable fathers to turn up.

When looking for theories which could help in this respect, Hjalager and Lindgaard (1984) found the concept of life-modes, used by ethnologists, the most fruitful one. In particular they used Højrup's distinction (1983) between three life-modes which he identified in a peripheral region of Denmark:

a) the life-mode of self-employment. In this life-mode, the dominant job-related motivation is to be self-employed, to own the means of production, and to control the production process. For the individuals concerned, what they produce - whether they are farmers, fishermen, artisans, or have small factories, transport firms or shops - is less important than the fact of economic self-determination. People who adhere to this life-mode may shift from one branch to another, or may in periods be wage-earners - but always with the aim of becoming independent some day. On the other hand, they rarely wish the firm to grow so much that they lose close control over it. So job creation per firm is limited, but 'self-employment' entrepreneurs are important by their sheer numbers and by the cultural tradition they carry on to the next generation. They do not distinguish between working hours and leisure. Often the whole family is involved in the firm, and similar-minded friends from the local area will help in difficult periods. Thus the cultural factor does not only influence the upbringing of young people, it also brings with it a pattern of mutual help. In a way reminiscent of the traditional agglomeration advantages of metropolitan areas, rural areas thus afford co-operation advantages for new business formation. This life-mode is in fact clearly over-represented in rural areas and under-represented in metropolitan areas. Of course, adherents to this life-mode are great starters of new firms. And their firms are inevitably created where they live. One should also be careful n,ᴜ to underestimate the technical level and viability of their firms. They are very willing to acquire a good education and invest in advanced technology if the survival of the firm makes it necessary. The competitiveness of both farming and manufacturing products from small firms in Denmark prove that they often have succeeded.

b) The <u>career</u> life-mode. The dominating value in this life-mode is to advance in one's career. This means that a good education is of primary importance as a tool to obtain both satisfactory jobs and satisfactory salaries. The careers of individuals adhering to this value system mainly take place inside private corporations or public hierarchies. But these individuals may also start their own firms, if that happens to be the best way to profit from their expertise and production ideas, so they are also important for firm creation. Typically, the firms they create are technologically advanced, innovative, well organised and with good marketing capabilities. Their firms will often grow quite rapidly, to a significant size. However, the entrepreneurs involved do not mind moving at a later stage to other firms, while they may also let their firms be taken over by large corporations. According to Hjalager and Lindgaard, this life-mode is overrepresented in the metropolitan areas. Thus the new firm creators from this group - and the firms they establish - are geographically concentrated in a pattern which is the opposite of that for entrepreneurs with the self-employment life-mode.

c) The life-mode of <u>wage-earners</u>. The dominant value here is to sell one's labour at the highest possible price, in order to have as much and as rich a leisure time as possible. Thus, the adherents to this life-mode are not very likely to create new firms. In some countries, however they have started co-operative firms. In Denmark there have been some cases where they have taken over firms from bankrupt owners, thus

Højrup's three life-modes hardly exhaust the social landscape. Possibly one could talk of a life-mode of public field-workers (teachers, nurses, social workers, etc.), but it is very unlikely to give rise to new firms. It might also be possible to define a youth life-mode, which in the 1970's created some co-operative firms in the rural hinterlands of the biggest Danish cities.

It has been possible here only very briefly to outline the life-mode concept. But it can be argued that it does go some way to deepen understanding of the cultural and hence geographical differences in people's propensity to create new firms. More detailed investigation might well uncover still further dimensions of this approach. For instance, it may be that in Denmark, the life-mode of self-employment is better developed in regions where family farms have dominated (e.g. Western Jutland) than in regions with big estates (e.g. Lolland-Falster). There may also be a religious dimension (as Max Weber suggested). Some areas with very strong starter traditions - such as the county of Ringkøbing (Denmark), Smaaland (Sweden), and Surnmøre (Norway) - are also characterised by strong puritan traditions. Of course in other countries, other cultural components may be more important.

How Can We Use This Understanding?

We cannot create new life-modes or cultural patterns overnight. Then how can this understanding help policy-makers who may wish to speed up the creation of new firms? The answer of Hjalager and Lindgaard is clear: we must adapt our policy measures to the life-modes. We have been too ready to think that policy measures which are appropriate in one cultural setting are also appropriate in all other settings.

We may be able to control some external influences, but their effects depend on the people they are directed towards. There are many examples of more or less 'counter-productive' measures, in particular in areas where most potential starters adhere to the life-mode of self-employment. The reason is that we - the public administrators and experts who designed the measures - usually belong to another life-mode with different values, motivations and languages, who therefore respond to other kinds of incentives.

In rural or peripheral areas where the life-mode of self-employment prevails, there is a cultural gap to overcome, and it is especially important that:
- incentives should be given with an absolute minimum of written administration and time-losing

formalities;
- advisory and educational support should be offered very close to the location of the firm, by people who are well acquainted with local production conditions, and it should be closely geared to the concrete needs of the firm;
- premises that are offered should be cheap (in most cases old buildings can be adapted);
- cooperation between small firms should be encouraged, but never enforced by external parties.

Such a policy is very different from a policy aiming at the promotion of firms based on the career life-mode. The latter make use of most traditional incentives, which is not surprising, since their creators share the same values and language as the people who designed the policies. Thus support for technological development, provision of well-equipped industrial estates, incentives to removals, a high-quality infrastructure, creation of good educational facilities and an attractive physical environment, are the measures which seem to be effective.

As already mentioned, potential firm starters adhering to the career life-mode seem to be more numerous in big metropolitan areas than in rural or peripheral regions. In particular in suburban areas, where increasing unemployment is encouraging local governments to start thinking about a firm creation policy, it might be natural to direct measures towards this kind of new firm founder. This may also be appropriate for medium-sized towns in regions throughout the different European Community countries. Unfortunately, however, those areas which appear to exhibit the lowest rates of new firm creation, namely the inner city areas of large metropolitan regions, are precisely the locations in which neither self-employment nor career life-modes are widespread today. There thus seems to be a need to encourage them in some way. Or could the old wage-earner life-mode or new youth life-modes give rise to the creation of new firms in inner areas?

References

Hjalager, A.M and G. Lindgaard (1984)
    Livsformer og lokale erhvervspolitiske initiativer, Nord REFO, Oslo

Denmark

Højrup, Th. (1983) Det glemte folk, Livsformer og centraldirigering, Institut for europaeisk folkelivsforskning and Statens Byggeforsknigsinstitut, København

Maskell, P. (1984) 'Industriens lokalisering 1972-1982', in Illeris, S. and P.O. Pedersen (eds): Industrien-koncentration eller spredning. AKF, København, pp. 80-107

Wickmann, J. (1983) Ungskoven i dansk erhvervsliv, ivaerksaettere 1977-80, Haandvaerksraadt, København

Wickmann, J. (1984) 'Ivaerksaetterne og deres virksomheder' in: Illeris, S. and P.O. Pedersen (eds), Industrien-koncentration eller spredning. AKF, København, pp. 182-201

Chapter eight

THE NATURE OF NEW FIRMS IN IRELAND: EMPIRICAL
EVIDENCE AND POLICY IMPLICATIONS

Patrick N. O'Farrell

Introduction

Unemployment has been a persistent feature of the
Irish economy since independence and the recent
recession has exacerbated the scale of this crisis.
The persistence of the unemployment problem coupled
with the drain of actual and potential
entrepreneurs during the long period of large scale
net emigration indicates that the adaptiveness to
economic change is slow and points to the need to
address entrepreneurial capability as a key
limiting resource. Is the business climate
insufficiently rewarding? Do Irish people lack
entrepreneurial capacity or does society not
legitimise entrepreneurial behaviour by according a
low social status to the entrepreneur? Is the
structure of industrial incentives and fiscal
allowances optimal for stimulating manufacturing
entrepreneurship? This paper reviews temporal,
spatial and sectoral trends in indigenous new firm
formation and presents some evidence on new firm
founders and the characteristics of their firms.
The role of public agencies in the delivery of
policy is briefly assessed and the nature of the
Irish socio-cultural background as a seed-bed for
entrepreneurship is discussed. Finally, State
policy measures for the small firm sector are
critically evaluated.
    It is well known that the proportion of
manufacturing employment accounted for by small
establishments employing fewer than 50 people
varies considerably across countries from as low as
9 per cent in West Germany to as high as 47 per
cent in Japan. The Irish Republic with 24 per cent
employed in small plants, occupies a central
position in a list of twenty major developed

countries with a lower share than other small economies such as Switzerland (38%), and Norway (29%); but higher than the UK (13.5%), and the Netherlands (18%)(Kennedy et al. 1983, 34). In Ireland, there is a relatively high concentration of manufacturing employment (56%) in the establishments employing between 50 and 500 and a very low proportion (18.6%) in the large establishments of over 500 employees. Hence, there is a tendency for manufacturing employment in Ireland to be relatively concentrated in establishments between 50 and 500 employees. Furthermore, the share of manufacturing employment accounted for by plants with less than 50 persons engaged has fallen from 34 per cent in 1929 to less than one quarter in 1981 (Kennedy et al. 1983, 26).

Temporal Trends In New Firm Formation

Some researchers have identified a relationship between national economic performance and levels of firm formation[1] such that downturns in the economic cycle and rising unemployment stimulate entrepreneurship by forcing people to set up their own business following or in anticipation of redundancy (Binks and Coyne 1983, 38). Conversely, Gould and Keeble (1984, 183-184) observed that no recent recession related increase in firm formation is apparent in East Anglia. Our evidence corroborates that of Gould and Keeble with the recession years of 1974-75 witnessing the lowest levels of new firm formation; the rate of entry rose rapidly in response to the recovery from 1976 to peak in 1978 and then fell back slightly with the onset of the recession in 1979-80 (Table 1). Consequently, it is the periods of upswing in the economic cycle which have stimulated the highest levels of new firm formation in Ireland while troughs have depressed entry rates.

Table 1. Annual Number of New Indigenous Single Plant Firms 1973-1980 (inclusive).

	1973	1974	1975	1976	1977	1978	1979	1980	Total
Total Openings[1]	153	127	123	178	215	226	198	162	1,382
Survivors[2]	142	109	119	169	238	273	247	185	1,482

1. Dublin is excluded; total incorporates survivors and new entries which subsequently closed.
2. Dublin is included
Source: O'Farrell and Crouchley (1984)

Ireland

Spatial Variations in Formation Rates

Fig. 1 shows that there are substantial spatial variations in new firm formation rates between 1973 and 1981, even when the denominator includes a proportion of non-manufacturing employees the exclusion of which would bias the rates in rural areas (Gudgin and Fothergill, 1984, 205). The highest rate is in Roscommon - some 75 per cent above the national average - and Fig. 1 shows that new firm formation rates are most buoyant in a block of predominantly rural counties running

Fig. 1. Annual Number of New Firms per 1,000 manufacturing employees plus one-fifth non-manufacturing employees (1973).

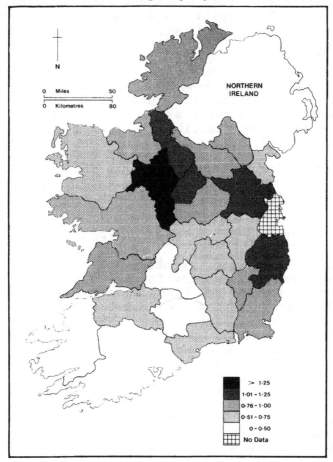

north-west to south-east from Sligo and Leitrim to Meath and Wicklow. By contrast, the counties of the South East, South West and Mid West, with the exception of Clare, have recorded below average rates of indigenous new business formation in manufacturing - with the rate in the South West, for example, being only one-third of that achieved in Roscommon. The lowest rates of all were recorded in Dublin (for where only data on survivors is available). In an econometric analysis O'Farrell and Crouchley (1984) have shown that the number of new enterprises emerging is related to several features of the local area including the sectoral mix, degree of urbanisation and occupational mix (the proportion of gainfully employed males classified as employers, managers and professionals). This contrasts with the findings of Gudgin and Fothergill (1984, 204) for both the East Midlands of England and East Anglia where the proportion of non-manual workers is not significantly associated with new firm formation rates when the urban/rural effect is controlled. There is a need, however, to unravel the causal factors underlying the rural/urban variable. Are higher rates in rural areas, having controlled for the plant size distribution, due to cheaper land prices, the wider availability of suitable premises, the lack of many alternative employment opportunities including those in the black economy, or some other process? At present, there is no complete explanation of this phenomenon.

Sectoral Variation Formation Rates

There are very considerable between-sector differences in new firm formation rates around the national average of 1.27 new firms per annum per 1,000 manufacturing employees (Table 2). The highest entry rate occurs in furniture (4.6) followed by metal trades, wood, cork and brushes, and plastics - all industries with relatively low entry barriers especially in the form of low start-up capital requirements. The lowest rates of entry were recorded by butter and milk products, drink and tobacco, boots and shoes, bacon and slaughtering, and hosiery. These figures demonstrate that between industry variation in new firm formation is very high: the rate of entry in furniture, for example, is twenty-five times greater than in either drink and tobacco or boots

Ireland

Table 2. Number of new indigenous single plant firms by sector, 1973-1981.

Sector[2]	Number new ISPs	Number ISP survivors	Manufact. employment 1973	Number new ISP annum/ 1,000 manufact. employees (1973)	Number new ISP survivors annum/ 1,000 manufact. employees (1973)
1. Bacon and slaughtering (4,5)	13	12	8,027	0.202	0.187
2. Creamery butter and milk products (6)	5	4	7,001	0.089	0.071
3. Grain milling and animal feed (8)	12	9	4,274	0.351	0.263
4. Bread, biscuits (9)	24	23	4,884	0.614	0.589
5. Jam, canned food, sugar, cocoa, chocolate, margarine, miscellaneous food (7,10,11,12,13)	51	41	6,525	0.977	0.785
6. Drink and tobacco (14-18)	7	6	4,930	0.178	0.152
7. Woollen and worsted, linen, cotton, jute, nylon etc. (19-21)	30	23	8,411	0.446	0.342
8. Hosiery (22)	14	8	5,317	0.329	0.188
9. Boot and shoe (23)	7	4	4,911	0.178	0.102
10. Clothing (24)	68	54	9,183	0.926	0.735
11. Made-up textiles (25)	17	15	4,815	0.441	0.389
12. Wood, cork, brushes (26,28)	78	72	3,056	3.190	2.945
13. Furniture (27)	214	197	5,813	4.602	4.236
14. Paper/paper products (29)	13	12	1,348	1.205	1.113
15. Printing and publishing (30)	42	34	3,334	1.575	1.275
16. Miscellaneous including fellmongery and leather (31,32,47)	85	68	9,516	1.117	0.893
17. Fertilizers, paints, chemicals, soap, pharmaceuticals (33-36)	33	29	4,069	1.014	0.891
18. Glass, pottery (37)	34	30	4,138	1.027	0.906
19. Cement, structural clay (38,39)	70	63	7,410	1.181	1.063
20. Metal trades (40)	359	330	12,490	3.593	3.302
21. Machinery manufacture (41)	42	34	3,290	1.596	1.292
22. Electrical machinery (42)	62	51	5,315	1.458	1.199
23. Shipbuilding and repairs, railroad equipment, roads and other vehicles (43-46)	38	33	4,383	1.084	0.941
24. Plastics (48)	41	33	1,970	2.602	2.094
25. Construction, agriculture, services (60,65,70)	23	18	2,062	1.394	1.091
Total	1,382	1,203	136,473	1.266	1.101

1. Table excludes Dublin; there were 279 new ISPs in Dublin which survived until 1981. The national rate of new firm formation for survivors including Dublin is 0.813 compared with 1.101 for the country outside Dublin.

2. Numbers in parentheses are IDA Product Codes.
Source: O'Farrell and Crouchley (1984).

155

and shoes.

A regression analysis, with the number of new indigenous firms per annum per 1,000 employees in sector i (1973) as the dependent variable, indicated that there are three variables associated with it: (i) the proportion of plants in the sector employing fewer than twenty people which, as hypothesised, is positively related to entry rates; (ii) the median age of the sector's plant stock which is negativelly associated with entries; and (iii) the percentage of sectoral employment controlled by multi-plant enterprises which is also inversely related to the rate of formation (O'Farrell and Crouchley 1984). An interpretation of standardised residuals from an equation including the three significant independent variables suggests that the sectors where indigenous new firm formation rates have been higher than those predicted by the regression equation are furniture, metal trades, plastics and wood, cork and brushes. This implies that there are other factors, in addition to those included in the model, which explain the pattern of formation. One such factor is that most new firms in these industries produce products with high bulk or weight to value ratio which for logistic reasons are subjected to little or no competition from imports (i.e. the new enterprises produce predominantly non-traded goods).

The employment growth record of indigenous single plant firms has been disappointing. Examination of the survivors of all cohorts (i.e. net of closures) opening since 1967 shows that of the 2,300 openings since 1967 and still operating in 1981, 96 per cent employed fewer than 51 people at the end of the period. Only 1.1 per cent of new firms employed over 100, while 4.3 per cent had expanded to above 50 employees (O'Farrell 1984). Few small firms, therefore, have displayed substantial employment growth, and growth arises primarily from small companies supplying local and regional markets with low technology non-traded goods, such as farmyard gates, plastic mouldings and low quality furniture in which transport costs limit the scope of external competition.

Employment Trends in the Indigenous and Overseas Sectors

In order to comprehend the nature and scale of the structural changes which were occurring in the

Table 3. Manufacturing Employment Change between 1973-81, by Sector and Nationality.

Sector	1973	Overseas 1981	% net Change	Irish 1973	1981	% net Change
Food	5,967	6,379	6.9	40,889	40,939	0.1
Drink/ Tobacco	4,226	4,052	-4.1	6,564	6,808	3.7
Textiles	5,369	8,815	64.2	17,516	10,573	-39.6
Clothing/ Footwear	5,270	4,742	-10.0	19,617	13,584	-30.8
Wood/ Furniture	811	958	18.1	9,977	10,741	7.7
Paper/ Printing	1,790	2,194	22.5	12,708	14,771	16.2
Chemicals/ Plastics	5,987	9,081	51.7	5,266	4,898	-6.9
Glass/ Cement	1,378	2,305	67.2	14,154	15,430	9.0
Metals/ Engineering	19,844	29,437	48.3	22,660	28,265	24.7
Other	8,459	12,982	53.4	8,668	8,300	4.2
Grant Aided	178	1,168	556.2	2,366	2,634	11.3
Total	59,279	82,113	+38.5	160,385	156,943	-2.1

1. There were approximately 8,000 job losses in Dublin due to closures of plants ‹50 which were never surveyed. There is no data concerning the sectoral and nationality distribution of these jobs - the reason for their exclusion from the table - although the majority are likely to have been Irish-owned plants.

Source: IDA Employment Survey

Irish manufacturing system during the 1970s, it is necessary to disaggregate the employment change data by sector and nationality. Table 3 shows that multinational branches recorded a net employment increase of 38.5 per cent between 1973 and 1981 largely due to over 32 thousand jobs generated by new openings, with particularly large absolute gains in metals and engineering (principally electronics), textiles, chemicals and plastics and other manufacturing. The relatively small decline of 2 per cent in Irish manufacturing employment between 1973 and 1981 conceals much larger falls of over 30 per cent in textiles, clothing and footwear only partly compensated for by increases in metals and engineering, wood and furniture, glass and cement, paper and printing.

Hence, a fundamental dualism has become increasingly apparent whereby the impressive performance of industrial output and exports has been heavily concentrated in a limited number of sectors, notably chemicals and electronics, which are dominated by foreign-owned subsidiaries. The products of the indigenous net employment loss sectors are primarily internationally traded goods and their rapid decline implies an inability to compete internationally following the phasing out of EEC tariffs. Examination of competing imports data published by Blackwell, Danaher and O'Malley (1983) suggests that the increasing share of competing imports in the domestic market was particularly marked in the predominantly traded sectors. This evidence is further substantiated by the finding that in the larger plants (employing over 200) in metals and engineering, wood and furniture and other manufacturing - which are more likely to produce traded goods - employment fell by 30 per cent between 1973 and 1980; while employment in indigenous firms with under 200 workers in these sectors increased by 32 per cent in the same period (Blackwell and O'Malley 1984, 131). The relatively buoyant employment growth of the smaller enterprises in metals and engineering, wood and furniture and other manufacturing; and in the paper and printing, glass and cement sectors as a whole was based largely upon products sheltered to a substantial degree in the home market against imports by high bulk or weight to value ratios including metal fabrication, furniture, structural steel, packaging, and plastic mouldings. Hence, the gross job gains - more than half of which came from new plants - were due primarily to the growth of domestic demand. This was boosted after 1974 by certain exceptional factors notably expansionary government policies funded partly by heavy foreign borrowing and by the boom in food export earnings and agricultural incomes during the transition to full EEC membership (O'Malley, 1983, 3). Cuts in government borrowing and spending and the slowing down in price rises for food exports have produced more difficult conditions for either growth of existing indigenous non-traded businesses or the spawning of new firms. In those industries where labour costs are an important competitive cost element, firms are only likely to survive if they

Ireland

restructure production towards segments that have
some other competitive advantage such as
applications engineering, design, or market
accessibility.

Characteristics of New Firm Founders and their Companies: Some Comparative Evidence

A survey of a stratified random sample of 173 new
indigenous single plant firms (ISPs) which
commenced production between January 1st, 1977 and
January 1st, 1981 was conducted in the Spring of
1983 (O'Farrell, 1985). It is appropriate before
examining the performance of the firms, to
summarise very briefly some of the major founder
characteristics. First, establishing a new firm is
a youthful phenomenon: the median age at foundation
is 32 with 84 per cent of the entrepreneurs being
younger than 40. Three-quarters of the founders,
despite their relative youth, have had two or more
full-time jobs before setting up their own
enterprise and 84 per cent were married at the time
of foundation. Most have also achieved a fairly
high level of educational attainment: one fifth
have university degrees or the equivalent, while
only 10 per cent have received solely primary level
education. Some 45.6 per cent had a father who was
self-employed compared with 27.3 per cent of the
male workforce in 1973 (13.5% outside agriculture),
suggesting that an entrepreneurial father is an
important element in the range of influences upon
the potential entrepreneur. Does entrepreneurship
facilitate occupational mobility? The data on first
job and last job prior to foundation suggests that
there is considerable upward mobility from clerical
secretarial, skilled and semi-skilled occupations
in the entrepreneur's first job to managerial
positions in their last job prior to founding
(O'Farrell 1985). The process of new firm formation
is a means of achieving social mobility especially
for people from skilled manual working backgrounds.
The occupational mix of employment within
establishments influences the supply of
entrepreneurs independent of the size distribution
of plants. If the share of new founders arising
from various socio-economic categories in their
last job is compared with the equivalent proportion
of the gainfully employed population in 1971, some
distinct trends emerge (O'Farrell 1985). First, the
probability of a person of managerial/

professional status setting up a new firm is more than four times greater than their frequency in the population would suggest. Second, the chance of someone from a skilled manual job starting a firm is almost double the expected number according to their population share. Third, there are only one-third the number of semi-skilled, and one-seventh the number of unskilled founders relative to their numbers in the population. Also, farmers and agricultural workers recorded only one-fifteenth the number of manufacturing entrepreneurs which would be expected according to their frequency in the population.

Financing the New Firm

The question of finance for the new firm has been a subject of controversial debate for many years focusing upon the degree to which small firms experience a finance gap. New founders in Ireland have used bank loans (79%) as a source of start-up capital to a greater extent than in either Greater Manchester (15%) or South Hampshire (42%)(Lloyd and Mason, 1984, 215). The other major difference is that 57 per cent of new founders in Ireland received grants in order to commence production whereas Cross (1981) reported that no firms in Scotland started up with the aid of a grant.

Lack of home ownership constitutes a significant barrier to entry for some potential entrepreneurs, especially manual workers, since the banks require security against loans. Some firms which were refused loans at the start succeeded in raising one after being in production for a couple of years. This highlights a major dilemma for many new small firms: they need to demonstrate a track record in order to be able to obtain a loan, but they cannot achieve a track record without one. Not only did skilled manual entrepreneurs have difficulty raising bank loans, but they were also less successful in obtaining a grant to start production: only 35 per cent of skilled manual founders recorded a grant as a component of their initial capital investment compared with 70 per cent of managers (O'Farrell 1985). This suggests either bias by the grant awarding agencies or lack of awareness of the grants system or inability on the part of founders from manual backgrounds to present convincing project proposals to the development agencies. The implication of bias by the grant agencies is largely disproved by the evidence that the percentage of firms founded by managers in receipt of some form of grant-aid had risen from 70 per cent at start-up to 92 per cent at the time of the survey but the percentage of manual founders with grant-aid had increased from 35 per cent to 81 per cent.

Clearly there is a learning process by founders from manual backgrounds whereby during the early years of their firm's life they become more aware of the role of some public agencies and most eventually apply for and receive grant-aid. Some 37 per cent of grant-aided firms stated that they would have founded a manufacturing enterprise even if they had not received a grant. However, all of these founders confirmed that the size and scope of their business would have been smaller and their machinery more dated had they not been awarded a grant, so although grant-aid was not decisive in the decision to start, it did have an important influence upon the nature and scale of the enterprise. A further one-quarter of the firms interviewed commenced operating without grant assistance but applied for and received grants in the post-start-up phase, having first established a track record. Finally, 37 per cent of firms in receipt of grants stated that grant assistance was crucial to their decision to found a manufacturing enterprise; these firms would not have started were it not for the existence of grants. This suggests that grant-aid substantially lowers one important entry barrier, namely access to capital.

New Firm Performance

The median turnover in 1983 of the 173 new firms started between 1977 and 1981 was IR£245.6 thousand and the median employment size was ten with the inter-quartile range lying between six and 21. Most firms started up on an extremely small scale: 15 per cent provided work for only the founder in the first year and 47 per cent employed fewer than four people.

As expected in the case of new firms, there is a high degree of orientation towards local and regional markets: 41 per cent of the output from the sampled companies was sold to customers within a 20 mile radius of the plant; 41 per cent was marketed in the rest of the Republic, while 18 per cent was exported. However, exporting is a highly concentrated activity with only 6 per cent of the new enterprises accounting for 90 per cent of all export sales.

Econometric models have been fitted to account for between firm variation in several important dimensions of new manufacturing firm performance including employment size, turnover, export propensity, percentage of sales to local area and productivity (O'Farrell, 1985). The direction of the relationships between the independent variables specified and the various dependents are generally as predicted and the econometric models indicate that there are some interesting and unexpected results to which I shall make only brief reference in this paper (see O'Farrell, 1985).

Both the age of the firm and that of the entrepreneur at the time of foundation, are unrelated to all five of the dependent variables of new firm performance. Similarly, the percentage of output consisting of components for other manufacturers, whether the founder had worked abroad during his previous career, the major source of initial capital, the firm structure (i.e. owner-managed or partnership), and whether the entrepreneur was self-employed prior to founding, are all unrelated to each of the dimensions of new enterprise performance. It is interesting from a policy perspective that firms established by entrepreneurs with previous experience of self-employment are not larger, more productive and more export orientated than those set up by first time founders. Also, it was contrary to expectations that the alleged advantages of a partnership over an owner-managed enterprise were not reflected in a better record by firms founded as partnerships in terms of the variables studied, with the exception of the propensity to sell in the local area. Owner managed enterprises displayed a greater degree of local market orientation.

As expected, total sales are positively related to both the propensity to export and productivity while grant-aided firms, as postulated, are significantly larger in terms of employment and turnover. Food industry establishments sell significantly more to the local area economy than those of other sectors, while wood and furniture plants exhibit lower productivity than other industries. The models revealed that entrepreneurs from manual working backgrounds controlled firms with lower levels of turnover and a greater dependence upon the local area market, while enterprises run by technical and clerical founders also sold significantly more to the local economy. As predicted, entrepreneurs with a university education or equivalent created more employment and, together with founders with regional technical college education, they were also more export orientated than firms run by people with other types of educational background.

New enterprises employing large batch or mass production technology are significantly larger than those using other production systems; they have a greater export propensity and sell a lower proportion of their output to the local area economy. A series of regional effects are associated with various aspects of new firm performance: firms in the West region are larger and generate greater turnover; while East, Mid-West, and South East region enterprises, apart from recording higher turnover, also sell more within their local area economies. Firms within three regions - the Midlands, the North East and Donegal/North West - generated significantly higher exports than those located elsewhere (O'Farrell, 1985). This may be attributed in part, to their proximity to the Northern Ireland border thereby facilitating export sales.

The Role of Public Agencies in Assisting Small Industries

There are a wide range of agencies, usually supported wholly or in part by public funds, whose task it is to assist industry in a variety of ways including job creation, training, research and development, exporting, financial assistance, and industrial relations. However, the survey results suggest that a proportion of small businessmen are either unaware of public institutions or, in many cases if they are aware, they have little knowledge of the detailed services provided and therefore do not avail of them. Low take up of aid and advice systems is partly a symptom of the relatively weak and unspecialised management structure of most small firms. This suggests that there are special problems with the marketing and delivery of policy to small firms. When the founders were classified, on the basis of several criteria, into three categories - graduates, opportunists and craftsmen - it was hypothesised that graduates would use a greater range of advisory services. The results confirmed that the probability of a graduate founder using an agency is about double that of a craftsman (some of whom operate completely outside the aid systems of the agencies) with the opportunists occupying an intermediate position (O'Farrell 1985). This confirms the existence of a major information and communications gap between many craftsmen and some opportunist entrepreneurs, on the one hand, and the major public agencies, on the other. Graduate founders who require the least aid have the ability to extract the maximum benefits from the system; while those who need it most cannot (or will not) derive the full range of grants and advice to which they are entitled. Approximately one-fifth of founders operate predominantly or exclusively without seeking aid or advice, a proportion which rises to a half in the case of craftsmen. Some founders are even unaware of the existence of several agencies; while others, although able to identify the agency, could not specify the forms of aid provided by individual bodies. There was a fairly widespread criticism of the marketing and delivery of services emphasising the need for a locally based signposting and counselling system and a more positive delivery policy involving more frequent visits to firms by agency personnel.

It is important that agencies assisting new business start-ups recognise the dynamics of the process emphasising the requirement for on-going support both during the start-up phase and beyond: what appears to be missing are links between sources of assistance/ideas and the firms themselves. The basic principle is to start from the small firm itself and to find the means to assist it in overcoming the bottlenecks encountered in establishing and developing a business venture. It is, however, important to query whether such an intensive 'hands on' approach would produce a substantial improvement in small firm performance and job creation? What would be the opportunity costs in terms of resources withdrawn from higher grant awards, large firms or other programmes? There is no doubt that delivery of policy is a major problem and a more intensive hands on approach involving regular factory visits would produce benefits. It is impossible to establish ex ante whether these would exceed the costs involved and indeed it is doubtful if they would be sufficiently well identified and measured ex post.

The Irish Cultural Background: Values, Norms and Entrepreneurship

Murray (1981, 46) considers that there is at best a modest legitimacy for entrepreneurial behaviour in Ireland given the values of the traditional farm family system to which the country is still culturally close, and the effect of the educational system with its persistent emphasis upon training for the professions and the liberal arts. It is not clear, however, whether the bias of the educational system is a cause or a consequence of social attitudes towards entrepreneurship, but there is no doubt that Irish society accords a higher status to occupations such as the law, medicine and teaching than it does to mechanical engineering and technologists. Fogarty (1973, 128) observed that, although the climate of opinion in the early seventies was not hostile to entrepreneurship, it was not particularly encouraging, Successive governments have consistently supported the concept of entrepreneurship, although their rhetoric has not often been matched by an appropriate framework of policy measures.

Many of the founders interviewed in a survey in 1983 were strongly of the opinion that Irish culture and society was not a fertile seed-bed for industrial entrepreneurship (O'Farrell 1985). Fogarty (1973, 28-29) observed, through the comments of his interviewees, that Ireland emerged as a "country where too many people still fail to acquire in their families, in the schools and colleges, in the Church or in work itself the qualities needed for initiative and enterprise ... the achievement motivation, the practical abilities, the awareness of world standards and of the possibilities of enterprise".

Hawkes (1982, 13) suggested that some of the most important constraints on economic development and growth are indigenous to Irish society including the servile mentality inherent in Irish culture, born of a colonial past and perpetuated in the authoritarian traditions of Church and State. The origins of the feelings of low self-esteem are to be found in centuries of colonial rule which fostered a mentality born of being rewarded not for individual achievement, but for dependent compliance; and Hawkes (1981, 54) observed that while changes are occurring, the low self-esteem stereotype fits the national character more closely than the high self-esteem one. It is reflected in the obsession with security, with permanent and pensionable jobs and in a stronger fear of failure than in desire for achievement. Kennedy et al. (1983, 121) suggest that this characteristic has carried over into the twentieth century and that it is prevalent in the professions, the public service and a considerable part of agriculture. A fear of failure as a significant factor inhibiting entrepreneurship is not something which is peculiar to Irish culture, since it is also a feature of British societal attitudes. While many social scientists familiar with Irish culture would accept these propositions, testing the effect of factors such as low self-esteem upon the expression of entrepreneurship poses formidable conceptual and analytical problems.

Hawkes (1981, 56) has also argued that the Church, the educational system (largely controlled by the Church) and the family have transmitted a cultural ethos characterised by authoritarianism, inducing conformity, stifling initiative, enterprise and risk-taking. However, during the past two decades the values and attitudes of Irish society have been influenced to a greater extent than ever before by external factors. The authoritarian and conservative tradition which was detrimental to entrepreneurship is exercising less influence but it is unclear whether it is being replaced by a set of values more conducive to the emergence of entrepreneurial behaviour. Hawkes (1981, 59) has argued that the Roman Catholic Church has been an "important factor in reinforcing and perpetuating the authoritarian tone of Irish society and in moulding an outlook on life characterised by conservatism, fatalism and a disinclination to tempt providence". He then goes further and asserts that "the attitudes and outlook fostered by the Church have been maladaptive as far as the pursuit of economic goals is concerned ... and particularly so in relation to enterprise" (Hawkes, 1981, 59). The influence of the Church will be manifest through its effects upon the psychological and social characteristics of individuals, and the general consensus in the literature suggests that it will tend to inhibit initiative, enterprise and risk taking. However, while the thesis advanced by Hawkes appears reasonable, if perhaps requiring some qualification, the problem is one of verification: it is extremely difficult to isolate the infuence of Catholicism per se upon the exercise of entrepreneurship in Ireland and to control for the effects of other social, cultural and economic factors.

The educational emphasis in Ireland, as in many ex-colonial countries, has been upon classical, legal and arts-orientated studies reflecting a culture with a leaning towards literature and theatre, rather than towards technology or manual dexterity. It has predominantly prepared children for employment in the Civil Service, the professions, semi-state bodies and large firms and has done little to encourage the idea that they might work for themselves. Hence, it is not surprising that the entrepreneurs interviewed by Fogarty (1973) were very critical of the educational system for several reasons: it does not produce people with a capacity for independent actions, as apart from the role of a functionary under direction; too few have obtained the dual qualification of academic knowledge and practical skills; and too few are aware of world standards of achievement. The concept that an entrepreneurial career can be consistent with social responsibility as well as providing a high income has not been transmitted and neither has a true understanding of the nature and social significance of profit (Fogarty, 1973, 134). This situation has been changing somewhat during the past decade with more attention being devoted to technical education at second and third level. Finally, it is necessary to stress that it is unclear as to how important the direct influence of education is in the subsequent decision to start a business; while education may have developed many of the abilities later harnessed in entrepreneurship, they may initially have been moulded to an employee role and situation (Gibb, Ritchie and Eversley 1981, 25). While the indirect influence of education in the development of skills, attitudes and values may be considerable, the decision to start a new firm usually arises largely as a consequence of the work and occupational experience during the post-education period of early adulthood.

Industrial Policy in Ireland: The Scope of State Intervention

There has been a long history of State intervention in the manufacturing sector in most developed countries, including Ireland, but the need for intervention and the general approach adopted is seldom seriously debated. A related and perhaps even more fundamental problem is that a succession of policy instruments including grants, tax reliefs, advisory services and a range of public agencies have been introduced in a largely ad hoc manner over several decades often on the implicit, but untested, assumption that they are correcting a market failure and moving the Irish economy to a more efficient pattern of resource use. However, the efficiency of this piecemeal system of manufacturing policies, in terms of achieving its stated objectives at minimum cost, has never been thoroughly investigated. Yet the White Paper on Industrial Policy (1984, 4) estimates that IR£433 million was spent by Departments and agencies directly or indirectly concerned with industrial development in 1983, including IR£205 million by the IDA and IR£94 million by AnCO, the training authority. In addition, a further IR£315 million in tax revenue was forgone through various tax reliefs designed to foster industrial development so that total State expenditure on industrial policies amounted to IR£748 million in 1983. None of the recent reviews of Irish industrial policy including the Telesis Report (NESC 1982), the White Paper on Industrial Policy (1984) and the National Plan - Building on Reality 1985-1987 - has seriously questioned the need for government intervention and the possible scope for radical alternative measures such as a dramatic reduction in the level of government support for manufacturing activities. Both the Telesis Report (NESC 1982) and White Paper on Industrial Policy implicitly assume that intervention in the manufacturing sector is both necessary and desirable, and that the nature of such intervention should remain broadly similar to that of the 1960s and 1970s, although there will be a shift of emphasis away from capital grants for fixed assets towards technology acquisition and export development. Could the objectives of industrial strategy be achieved by a restructuring of policy instruments and a reduction in government expenditure? Are all government interventions in manufacturing justified on the grounds of market failure? Do small indigenous firms have unique problems which merit separate policy measures?

One of the major factors underlying the justification for industrial policy in Ireland is that a country which has made a relatively late start to industrialisation in competition with strong established industries based in more advanced countries which have built up competitive advantages, faces major barriers to entry. These barriers arise because competitive success in many modern internationally traded industries depends upon factors such as achieving a large scale of production, developing strong technological and marketing capabilities, and benefiting from the externalities created by spatial concentrations of key producer services. Indigenous firms of a latecomer to industrial development, such as Ireland, would need to undertake substantial new investment in order to develop the required competitive characteristics to international standards (Blackwell and O'Malley, 1984, 127). Such investments are risky and most Irish firms lack both the management capability and working capital to undertake them. Failure to develop a pool of indigenous manufacturing firms producing traded goods is also, in part, a function of various non-price elements of competition in which Irish firms are usually weak, namely design, quality control and delivery date reliability (O'Farrell, 1982). Therefore, it is not surprising that in the period following EEC entry, existing Irish firms have increasingly restructured out of internationally traded activities and have shown few signs of developing new technology based enterprises. I shall attempt to show that the structure of incentives has also contributed to this restructuring process by not addressing some of the key bottlenecks characteristic of small firms. The evidence suggests that in Ireland there is a large number of people willing to undertake small scale entrepreneurial activities in manufacturing but perhaps a different range of qualities and an alteration in the structure of incentives and advisory systems are required for the emergence of large scale entrepreneurship, especially in technologically based firms.

The major thrust of the Telesis Consultants report (NESC, 1982) was a recommendation to concentrate upon the development of a carefully selected number of indigenous firms producing traded goods in enterprises large enough to penetrate world markets. Non-traded businesses would not be aided except in the case of skill-intensive sub-supply activities. The Government has accepted this suggestion which is sensible since grant-aiding non-traded goods firms tied to local or regional markets may simply result in displacement of output and employment elsewhere in the region with little or no net public benefit. There is an implicit assumption in such a strategy that the development agencies can determine ex ante with greater success than the market which firms are the potential winners. The principal focus in the Telesis strategy would be upon 'complex factor cost businesses' where the key competitive cost elements are likely to be factors such as skill levels, design, applications engineering, innovation, marketing and distribution rather than in low wages or transport costs.

The White Paper on Industrial Policy (1984, 109) identified the major weaknesses in Irish industry as poor management, a low level of R and D; an inadequate financial base with little equity capital; a failure to enter export markets, especially beyond the UK; and a lack of linkages with foreign industry. It accepts the broad direction of the Telesis recommendation for greater selectivity in the use of incentives and, in order to address what are regarded to be the major weaknesses inhibiting the development of Irish firms, the Government plans to introduce new or improved incentives for technology acquisition; market research; market entry; development and distribution; and export finance insurance. Grants of up to 50 per cent of the cost of acquiring technology from abroad will be available from the IDA. The market entry and development scheme will help offset costs such as travel expenses, promotion and overseas warehousing.

The White Paper does not question the basic framework of government intervention but adopts an incrementalist approach with modifications of existing policy to take account of the Telesis Report and the IDA Strategic Plan. Ruane (1984, 36) argues that the White Paper only covers in detail those policies which are the direct responsibility of the Minister of Industry, Trade, Commerce and Tourism. Hence, a critical evaluation of policies concerned with training (AnCO), industrial rescues (An Foir Teoranta), the Industrial Credit Company and fiscal incentives is not undertaken. Furthermore, policies which are not specifically industrial but have an important impact upon manufacturers (e.g. labour legislation, pay related social insurance (PRSI), energy pricing, and so on) are discussed briefly but no policy changes are proposed. This results in a situation where the issue of factor bias in the industrial incentives and the possibility of restructuring incentives towards employment are not discussed because, as Ruane (1984, 43) asserts, rates of pay related social insurance (PRSI) are not controlled by the Minister of Industry, Trade, Commerce and Tourism.

Neither the White Paper on Industrial Policy nor the plan, Building on Reality, has outlined an overall industrial budget which would enable the allocation of resources to reflect the new strategic shift of manufacturing policy away from grants for fixed assets to other types of aid to be monitored and evaluated. The projected changes in the pattern of State aid to industry amount to a framework for resource allocation which is loose, flexible and lacking in rigour (NESC 1985, 38). The Department of Industry, Trade, Commerce and Tourism has failed to take control of industrial policy; has not developed performance criteria by which to assess the various State agencies; and has not converted the general industrial strategy into an operational decision-making framework sufficient to the task of realising objectives. The failure of government departments to take responsibility for industrial policy making in the past resulted in a situation whereby policy formulation was executed by the agencies. Also, the White Paper has not explicitly identified and addressed a number of the key bottlenecks in the formation and growth of small firms and has not made the elimination of barriers associated with small size a basic principle of industrial strategy.

Biases against the Small Firm Sector: the case for Intervention

Introduction

Two types of intervention in favour of small firms may be identified - restoration of neutrality and active discrimination (Kennedy et al. 1983, 212). Restoration of neutrality involves intervening in order to remove biases against small firms which are not justified by the operation of free market forces. These may arise from various market imperfections, and legal or administrative factors. In practice, it may be difficult to determine whether the difficulties faced by a small firm arise from discrimination or diseconomies of scale

(Kennedy et al. 1983, 212). Although small firms suffer economic handicaps, intervention to remove such handicaps is only justified if differential benefits can be expected to accrue to society from such intervention. The problem is that the range of intangibles is such that evaluating the likely social benefits ex ante is likely to be difficult and imprecise, if not impossible.

Major biases against the small firm

First, employers's Pay Related Social Insurance (PRSI) payments, which have been further increased in the 1985 Budget, discriminate against small firms because they are more labour intensive. Furthermore, it must be paid whether the firm is profitable or not. Although the employment elasticity of a payroll tax cut may be rather low, there is a convincing case for reducing employers' PRSI contributions for small firms relative to large ones because of their greater labour intensity.

Second, the costs of external finance are generally higher for small firms than for large ones. Many Irish banks and the Industrial Credit Company will charge up to 3 percentage points or more extra to small firms and the additional criteria of adequate collateral and a proven 'track record' further discriminate against the small firm entrepreneur. There is no evidence that the net costs of lending to small firms as a group, even allowing for a marginally greater closure risk for non grant aided plants and higher administrative costs, is as much as the interest rate differential indicates. Banks are also more reluctant to lease plant and machinery to small firms because of the administrative costs involved and some interview respondents alleged that the banks try to persuade small businesses to purchase land and buildings to use as collateral, although it may undermine cash flow in the early stages. In the first year or two of operation many firms may make a loss (real or accounting) or only a very small profit. The smaller the firm the larger is the proportionate increase in capital base required to respond to a rise in demand; but the inability of the firm to fund internally obliges it to seek external finance at the point when its growth potential is highest but its ability to attract outside finance is lowest (Binks and Coyne 1983,

47). This brief review and our survey evidence has highlighted two major disadvantages for the small firm in raising external finance: (i) a capital market distortion, namely the higher interest rates paid on loans and (ii) the banks' insistence upon high levels of security so that a lack of collateral or the absence of a track record may prevent small businesses from being able to borrow and get themselves into a position to compete. The high cost and limited availability of capital may force the small firm to adopt sub-optimal policies. For example, because it has to purchase in smaller quantities, it may be unable to take advantage of discounts; it may have to cut advertising and promotional expenses in order to conserve scarce working capital. Hence, the limited availability and high cost of capital combine to form one of the most important causes of business failure among small firms. One policy measure which directly addresses the problem of access to capital for small manufacturers is a form of loan guarantee scheme. The strategy outlined in the White Paper (1984) implies that loan guarantees will only be available, as at present, under the Enterprise Development Programme and not for projects assisted under the much larger Small Industry programme, so for the vast majority of small manufacturers, this capital market distortion will not be corrected.

Capital market distortions: the effect of the fiscal system

Apart from institutional bias against small firms resulting from the behaviour of financial agencies, there are also capital market biases arising from the Irish fiscal system. Neary and Ruane (1982) showed that the real inflation adjusted post tax return to an individual on a 35 per cent marginal tax rate in 1980 was +6.8 per cent on an owner occupied house, -3.6 per cent on long term government security, -8.5 per cent on a building society account and -14.4 per cent on Irish equity. These differences reflect not only the effects of the fiscal system but also variations in the pre-tax rates of return, which were especially low for equities. Although return on equity is not a perfect indicator of profitability in Irish manufacturing, there is evidence from a sample of indigenous small manufacturing companies to show that profit margins (net profits before tax

relative to sales) have decreased from 6 per cent
in 1978 to 3 per cent in 1982 (NESC, 1984, 57).
Furthermore, bank borrowing by manufacturing
industry increased by 6 per cent per annum in real
terms between 1972 and 1982, while the volume of
production increased at an annual rate of only 3.5
per cent, thereby resulting in a much higher risk
profile. Interest payments rose as a percentage of
net profit before interest and tax from 23 per cent
in 1978 to 59 per cent in 1982. Promoting equity on
average accounts for only 19 per cent of finance in
a typical IDA Enterprise Development Programme
project. Since the IDA guarantees 20 per cent of
the borrowing, provides 1 per cent in equity and
supplies 27 per cent of the funding by means of a
grant, the total State exposure is 48 per cent and
the proportion of equity to debt is too low for
firms producing high technology products.

Since new firms characteristically experience
negative cash flows during their first three to
five years, high levels of debt financing (the
normal pattern in small Irish firms) with the need
to service regular interest payments, is not an
appropriate initial financial structure. Why is
there a general lack of equity investment in
indigenous manufacturing enterprises? First, there
is the poor profitability performance of Irish
manufacturing. Second, the combination of low
manufacturing profitability and the tax biases
favouring investments in Government gilts, property
and insurance linked unit trusts creates risk/
reward ratios which are highly unfavourable to
manufacturing investment. Third, as demonstrated by
an interview survey, only one-third of founders
indicated a positive willingness to allow outside
participation through the medium of share capital
(O'Farrell 1985).

The very low level of profitability in
indigenous manufacturing implies a high degree of
commercial risk which is compounded by the small
size of most companies, the limited scope of the
Irish market and the consequent imperative to
export in order to grow. This is exceptionally
difficult to achieve given the high level of
debt/equity ratios and the excessive working
capital requirements to establish a presence in
foreign markets, thereby further underlining the
need to increase the levels of equity participation
in manufacturing in order to provide a stronger
base for expansion. To strengthen the equity base
for which the financial institutions will probably

require some participation - may necessitate tax reform since the high debt/equity ratios are, in part, a function of the tax system. It is important to emphasise that the problem in Ireland is not a lack of finance but rather a shortage of two types of funding in indigenous firms, i.e. equity and long term debt.

There are two ways in which to remove the capital market imperfection which discriminates against investment in traded manufacturing firms: (i) providing reliefs for investment in traded businesses or (ii) eliminating reliefs from currently favoured areas. The Irish Government opted for the first of these alternatives in the 1984 Budget and Finance Bill by introducing a scheme to grant tax relief to individuals who provide long term risk capital for manufacturing firms.

Public procurement policy

The growth of government spending carries a threat to small firms because there is a tendency for centralised purchasing departments to place contracts with large suppliers who are able to meet bulk requirements. Public procurement policy, therefore, frequently implicitly discriminates against the small firm sector. In a study covering seven countries, Bannock (1980, 35) reported that in all but one of the countries, the share of small firms in public purchasing was lower than their share of output. The Industrial Policy White Paper (1984, 76) seeks to 'encourage' public procurement from small firms rather than to ensure that they obtain a fair share of contracts by law. However, setting targets for the share of public expenditure to be directed towards small firms will incur additional costs and, therefore, such a measure would only be justified if differential benefits can be expected to accrue to society (e.g. lower cost, or higher quality goods) from such an intervention. A more rigorous application of the instruments of competition policy, which is weak in Ireland, would also help small firms in obtaining a fair share of public contracts.

Income tax

The structure of Irish personal income tax poses considerable problems for any government seeking to diffuse entrepreneurship more widely throughout the community. The basic problem arises because higher rates are triggered at relatively low levels of taxable income: rates of 48 per cent after IR£9,000 of taxable income for a married man and 60 per cent after IR£14,600 are penal by most standards. An average waged or salaried income earner would find it exceedingly difficult if not virtually impossible given the combination in Ireland of low income levels, the direct tax burden, and the cost of living (including indirect taxation) to accumulate sufficient capital to launch a small business, while simultaneously, maintaining a reasonable standard of living.

Fiscal allowances and relative factor costs

At present, there are free depreciation allowances for machinery including that portion of the investment paid for by the IDA. The same provision does not apply to industrial buildings which are grant-aided. The case for providing depreciation allowances on machinery and equipment funded by the state should be questioned and the alternative of providing capital allowances on the basis of the net cost to the promoter, after taking account of any grants received, should be implemented.

Under Irish legislation, firms are entitled to all of the tax allowances associated with capital purchases for export production if they can avail themselves of them, even though they are not liable for any tax on the associated corporate profits (Ruane and John 1984, 37). This creates an incentive for firms to enter leasing agreements, as manufacturing enterprises can benefit through the tax provisions without incurring any costs through taxation, while banks benefit by using depreciation and interest deductibility allowances to defer tax liabilities. The IDA, however, imposes a limit of 35 per cent on the amount of grant-aided plant and machinery which may be leased. The effect of the corporation profits tax rate of 10 per cent on all manufacturing profits (both from exports and domestic sales) creates an incentive for leasing even before tax-exhaustion occurs because the allowances transferred to a banking institution can be offset against the higher tax rate. In general, the benefits of tax-based leasing are concentrated almost exclusively in the large multinational branches, while small indigenous firms have generally not benefited from tax-based lending.

Since 1971 successive governments of all political persuasions have considerably increased the cost to manufacturers of employing labour while reducing the cost of capital. Ruane and John's (1984) analysis of the cost of capital to Irish manufacturing industry incorporates the effects of the interaction between fiscal policies (e.g. through the corporate tax system) and financial policies (e.g. through investment grants) on the cost of capital. They demonstrate that since the introduction of free depreciation in 1971, tax saving from interest-deductibility and depreciation allowances combined has actually had a greater effect than the grant system in reducing the cost of plant and machinery (Ruane and John 1984, 40-41). Defining the effective (i.e. post-intervention) costs of labour (market cost plus employers' social insurance contributions), Ruane and John (1984, 44) show that government intervention steadily raised the cost of labour while the cost of capital was reduced so that the labour-capital ratio in 1982 was almost four times the 1958 level. Given some substitutibility between capital and labour in manufacturing production, such an increase in relative factor costs may be expected to lead to substitution in favour of more capital-intensive techniques of production. Even if the degree of substitutibility between capital and labour in production is low, there is a loss in efficiency from a policy which taxes labour (a factor in excess supply) and subsidises capital (a relatively scarce factor). Furthermore, the present system is biased towards fixed assets capital which therefore discriminates against firms with a high ratio of working to fixed assets capital (e.g. heavy R and D or marketing expenses); and shortage of working capital is one of the major bottlenecks to small firm expansion. In addition, one implication of the importance of fiscal allowances in reducing the cost of capital is that it discriminates indirectly against small firms since larger ones are in a better position to organise leasing arrangements and Section 84 loans. Given the clear evidence that successive governments, with employment creation as the main goal of industrial policy, have concentrated primarily upon subsidising capital rather than labour, it is remarkable that the White Paper does not address this key issue of capital bias and the possibility of restructuring incentives towards employment.

Capital grants are valuable to the firm at start-up by not only helping to remove the capital barrier to entry but also because they represent an immediate improvement in the liquidity position of the enterprise. Hence, at the time of foundation, capital grants are generally more attractive to most founders than soft loans or accelerated depreciation. In general, it is highly desirable to tailor the various incentives and awards to qualifying traded goods enterprises in order to address the key bottleneck factors preventing specific businesses from becoming internationally competitive. The system should be flexible so that a firm which, for example, purchases second-hand machinery, may be permitted to opt for a soft loan over a period of 15 to 20 years as an alternative to a capital grant. The key principle of the incentive systems for small firms should be their discretionary nature and flexibility, so necessary in order to meet the requirements of various types of business with different impediments to overcome in order to become competitive internationally, including the need for human capital aids.

Research has demonstrated that the public sector, in general, and the Civil Service, in particular, generates relatively few new firm founders (O'Farrell 1985). Hence, a considerable reservoir of potential entrepreneurial talent exists within the state and semi-state bodies. In addition, there are many occupational groups such as clerical workers and semi-skilled and unskilled manual workers which analysis (O'Farrell 1985) has shown are heavily under-represented among manufacturing entrepreneurs. The question is how to diffuse entrepreneurship more widely throughout the population, how to stimulate more people to leave pensionable and, in the public sector, tenured jobs. Research evidence (see O'Farrell 1985) suggests that the range of policy changes proposed in the White Paper of Industrial Policy will not be sufficient to attract significant numbers to leave public employment with its associated net benefits; and potential clerical, semi-skilled and unskilled manual entrepreneurs face a major entry barrier in their shortage of capital and lack of easy access to lending institutions. A policy initiative which directly addresses this problem would be to pay all new founders of traded business a salary of, say, IR£10,000 during the first year of production. The annual cost of such a scheme would be less than IR£2 million and it will not only encourage

Ireland

movement from employee to employer status but will
also greatly help cash flow during a most difficult
period thereby reducing .the probability of early
closure.

Conclusion

It appears that since EEC entry Irish firms have
not been restructuring towards skill intensive high
value added traded activities; on the contrary they
have been increasingly losing out in the domestic
and UK markets in traded business segments. They
have tended to concentrate more in sheltered
activities - the processing of local primary
resources (mainly food) and technically
unsophisticated small scale products. First,
although there has been a high birth rate of new
firms, the sample survey evidence which classified
the enterprises according to product descriptions
and the spatial structure of their markets showed
that 41 per cent of businesses were producing
highly traded outputs; 21 per cent are partly
traded and non-traded; and 38 are manufacturing
overwhelmingly non-traded goods. Second, relatively
few small indigenous firms meet the skilled sub-
supply requirements of the overseas subsidiaries
located in Ireland. Much of the growth that has
occurred in sub-supply industries has been in the
lower skill areas, such as general welding, plastic
mouldings, simple metal fabrication or packaging;
indeed packaging represented over one-third of
domestic purchases by the New Industry non-food
sectors in 1976 (O'Farrell and O'Loughlin 1981).
Third, employment growth among the stock of small
and youthful ISPs has been based to a significant
extent upon domestic demand and few firms have
entered export markets - especially outside the UK
- which is necessary if they are going to expand
substantially given the small size of the Irish
market. Fourth, for many formerly protected
indigenous firms, survival under free trade
conditions meant that they had to increase capital
investment per worker in order to raise
productivity. This capital deepening was often
associated with job losses but may have ensured
survival. It is clear from the evidence on new firm
formation rates referred to earlier in this paper
that the expression of certain forms of
entrepreneurship is as buoyant in Ireland as in
many other developed countries - although the

widespread availability of grants at start-up has clearly boosted Irish new firm formation rates. The deficiencies are apparent in the scale and type of manufacturing entrepreneurship: there are relatively few large new firms manufacturing traded goods with a high skill and technological intensity and export potential. Technologically based entrepreneurship may be subject to strong external economies as in the Silicon Valley or around Cambridge University. This external economy argument may even have some validity at a national level with Ireland's remoteness contributing to a lack of contact with the demonstration effects of other forms of entrepreneurship abroad.

This also raises the possibility that the long history of emigration - and the evidence of successful Irish entrepreneurship in the USA - may have depleted the indigenous reservoir of potential entrepreneurs. It is also uncertain as to how transferable entrepreneurial skills are between different types of activity; is it a general set of attitudes and expertise which can find expression in a wide range of manufacturing or service functions or does it tend to be specific to particular activities? Research evidence on this question is insufficient for the purposes of policy prescription.

Although it is far from clear how entrepreneurial activity will respond to changes in the parameters of public policy, the scope for policy intervention is widened if individuals are viewed as changeable throughout the course of their career with factors such as education, family background, attitudes, occupational choice and career history being potential influences in the decision to found a business. If there is to be a substantial change in the number of entrepreneurs coming forward to found and develop businesses in Ireland, cultivation of the seed-bed of enterprise must begin in the home, schools, third level institutions and in society generally through the churches, political parties and community organisations. Changes in the home environment and parental attitudes will only come about through a gradual shift in public opinion; government, therefore, has a role to play in influencing attitudes to entrepreneurship, by emphasising its social and economic desirability and in creating the appropriate social, educational and economic climate for enterprise to express itself. Many of the socio-cultural constraints cannot be removed in the short term; attitudes will respond only slowly to changes in the value systems communicated by the State, Church and educational system. Furthermore, the Irish evidence suggests that the design of an appropriate package of policy instruments and incentives is a necessary but not sufficient condition for their successful take-up. The way in which policy instruments are delivered to the small business is fundamental to the successful take-up of policy.

Notes

1. The definition of a new manufacturing firm employed in this study is founded upon the concept of the firm as one which has no obvious parent in any existing business enterprise (see Mason 1983). Independence has been defined in legal terms, recognising, however, that many independent firms may be functionally dependent. The data on new manufacturing firms is derived from the annual employment survey of the Industrial Development Authority (IDA), which operates a lower threshold size of three for inclusion in the Census.

References

Bannock G. (1980) The Promotion of Small Business: a Seven Country Study (Vol. 1) Shell UK, London

Binks M. and J. Coyne (1983) The Birth of Enterprise, Hobart Paper 98, Institute of Economic Affairs, London

Blackwell J., G. Danaher and E. O'Malley (1983) An Analysis of Job Losses in Irish Manufacturing Industry, National Economic and Social Council, Report No. 67, Dublin

Blackwell J. and E. O'Malley (1984) 'The Impact of EEC Membership on Irish Industry' in Drudy P.J. and D. McAleese (eds) Ireland and the European Community, Irish Studies Series, Vol. 3, Cambridge University Press, Cambridge, pp. 107-144

Cross M. (1981) New Firm Formation and Regional Development, Gower, Farnborough

Fogarty M.P. (1973) Irish Entrepreneurs speak for Themselves, Economic and Social Research Institute, Broadsheet No. 8, Dublin

Gibb A., J. Ritchie and J. Eversley (1981) The Shell entrepreneurs. Part 1:

Entrepreneurialism as a social process: towards a framework for analysis and understanding. Durham University, Business School

Gibb A. and J. Ritchie (1982) 'Understanding the Process of Starting a Small Business', European Small Business Journal, 1, 26-45

Gould A. and D.E. Keeble (1984) 'New Firms and Rural Industrialization in East Anglia', Regional Studies, 18, 3, pp. 189-220

Gudgin G. and G. Fothergill (1984) 'Geographical Variation in the Rate of Formation of New Manufacturing Firms', Regional Studies, 18, 3, pp. 203-206

Hawkes M.S. (1981) Graduate Entrepreneurship in Ireland with particular reference to MBA Graduates, unpublished MBA thesis, University College, Dublin

Hawkes M.S. (1982) Graduate Entrepreneurship in Ireland: the Case of MBA Graduates Working Paper, The Enterprise Centre, Faculty of Commerce, University College Dublin

Kennedy K.A., J. Bergin, T. Cellen and P. McNutt (1983) Small scale manufacturing industry in Ireland, Economic and Social Research Institute, Dublin (first draft)

Lloyd P.E. and C.M. Mason (1984) 'Spatial Variations in New Firm Formation in the United Kingdom: Comparative Evidence from Merseyside, Greater Manchester and South Hampshire', Regional Studies, 18, 3, pp. 207-220

Mason C.M. (1983) 'Some Definitional Difficulties in New Firms Research', Area, 15, 1, 53-60

Murray J.A. (1981) 'In Search of Entrepreneurship', Journal of Irish Business and Administrative Research, 3, pp. 41-55.

National Economic and Social Council (1982) A Review of Industrial Policy, Report No. 64, Dublin

National Economic and Social Council (1984) The Role of the Financial System in Financing the Traded Sectors, Report No. 76, Dublin

National Economic and Social Council (1985) Economic and Social Policy Assessment, Report No. 79, Dublin

Neary J.P. and F.P. Ruane (1982) 'Inflation and Growth', in McAleese D. and W.J.L. Ryan (eds) Inflation in the Irish Economy: a Contemporary Perspective, Helicon Press, Dublin

O'Farrell P.N. (1982) 'Industrial Linkages in the New Industry Sector: a Behavioural Analysis',

Journal of Irish Business and Administrative Research, 4, 1, pp. 3-21

O'Farrell P.N. (1984) 'Small Manufacturing Firms in Ireland: Employment Performance and Implications', International Small Business Journal, 2, 2, pp. 48-61

O'Farrell P.N. (1985) Entrepreneurship and New Firm Formation, IMI, Dublin

O'Farrell P.N. and B. O'Loughlin (1981) 'New Industry Input Linkages in Ireland: an Econometric Analysis', Environment and Planning A, 13, pp. 285-308

O'Farrell P.N. and R. Crouchley (1984) 'An Industrial and Spatial Analysis of New Firm Formation in Ireland', Regional Studies, 18, 3, pp. 221-236

O'Malley E. (1983) The Need for Selective and Active Industrial Policies, Paper presented to the Sixth Annual Economic Policy Conference of the Dublin Economic Workshop

Ruane F.P. (1984) 'The White Paper on Industrial Policy', The Irish Banking Review, September, pp. 35-45

Ruane F.P. and A.A. John (1984) 'Government Intervention and the Cost of Capital to Irish Manufacturing Industry', Economic and Social Review, 16, 1, pp. 31-50

White Paper (1984) Industrial Policy (Pl. 2491), The Stationery Office, Dublin

Chapter nine

SMALL FIRMS AND INDUSTRIAL DISTRICTS:
THE EXPERIENCE OF ITALY

Sebastiano Brusco

A Typology Of Small Firms

The significance of small firms in Italy's
industrial structure increased steadily and
consistently during both the two recent intercensal
decades, from 1961 to 1971 and from 1971 to 1981. I
do not feel it is important here to examine the
rate of this growth, which obviously could be done
by region or by industry. What, instead, may be
more useful is an examination of the changes in
quality that have come about in small firms. I feel
that the best way to do this is to refer to certain
models proposed by Brusco and Sabel in 1981 that,
in my opinion, still hold today their capacity of
interpretation.

Brusco and Sabel single out three models of
small firms:
- the traditional artisan;
- the dependent sub-contractor;
- the small firm in the industrial district.
These models will be described by reference to just
a few variables: market, tools, skill, acquisition
of skill and relations between firms.
The following three paragraphs set forth these
models, summarizing the results of Brusco and Sabel
with a few modifications of slight importance.

The Traditional Artisan

The traditional artisan is well known in those
areas and sectors where a national market is not
yet formed. Consider, in the years immediately
following the Second World War in Italy, the
tailors who were making made-to-measure suits

before the big garment firms had started to evolve;
consider the many ice-cream makers before the
large, national ice-cream manufacturers had started
up. Or, even today, consider the blacksmiths who
make fences and gates designed for single
buildings.

The market of the traditional artisan is,
therefore, fundamentally a local market which is
there not because it is highly specialized - like,
for example, certain tailors or ice-cream
manufacturers in Italy in 1985 - but because there
is backwardness in the country and in the sector.

The tools used by the traditional artisan are,
in general, simple and multipurpose. These tools
can be used to produce many different things but
not for those pieces that require close tolerances.
The skill of the artisan lies here: in being able
to cope with complex situations, working with few
tools, often with unsuitable material. The artisan
acquires his skill little by little through years
of apprenticeship to an established artisan with
very little formal schooling.

The relations between these firms are
described by a model well known in literature, that
of imperfect competition. The relationship between
customers and artisans is based, above all, on
trust and on reciprocal knowledge, and only
secondarily on price.

The Dependent Sub-contractor

The dependent sub-contractor is the figure around
which, in the early 1970s, all the controversies
about decentralization centred in Italy.

At that time, for many reasons, but primarily
because in large firms trade unions were a lot
stronger than in small ones, the large and medium
firms decentralized some stages of production to
other, smaller firms. The stages of production
which were decentralized were not always the same:
in some cases, the simplest, in others the most
harmful, in still others the most sophisticated.

The dependent sub-contractor consequently
produced - and in many sectors and regions still
produces - parts and components for larger firms
that sell on the national and the international
markets. The dependent sub-contractor, therefore,
although indirectly, works for the national and
international market. His own direct market,

however, is the large firms which place orders for his product.

The tools and machinery available to the dependent sub-contractor are not all of the same kind, as are those of the traditional artisan. In some cases, low wages and long working hours enable the dependent sub-contractor to stay on the market with backward machinery. More often, however - and this was certainly the case in Emilia in the early 1970s - the machinery used is identical to that in large firms which perform the same operations. Indeed, in many cases the machinery was the same as that used previously in the larger firm in that some medium-sized firms lent or sold their own machinery to their own workmen who continued as self-employed doing the same job as they had done as employees.

There is often a high level of skill in these firms. This depends on the fact that mostly short series are produced and, therefore, the machines must often be re-equipped for the new product. But this professional quality is strongly polarized: alongside a minority that carries out difficult and varied tasks there is a majority of lower-grade workers who perform routine tasks after the machinery has been equipped to do a given job by the more expert workers.

Very often the more skilled workers have acquired their expertise in the larger firms from which they come. There they were foremen, skilled workmen with particular responsibilities. They are frequently skilled workers who had good technical training at secondary school.

The relations between firms are very characteristic, at least in the purest form of the model: there is fierce competition among sub-contractors specialized in the same stage of production. It is truly cut-throat competition. Between sub-contractors and sub-contracting firms, on the other hand, there is a typical monopsonistic situation: the larger firms are in a position to squeeze the profits of smaller firms, forcing them to pay lower wages, to evade social security payments, to work longer hours.

The Small Firm In The Industrial District

The third model is that of the small firm in the industrial district. It coincides with what Sabel, in his recent book (1982), calls the flexible specialization model. It is the model that today predominates in many parts of Emilia, Veneto, Tuscany, the Marche. In these regions, this third model is often claimed to be an evolution of the second model.

Reference to Marshall's industrial district (Marshall 1919, 1920) is important both because it connects this structure to certain important data and because it places the accent on the fact that, in this case, what is relevant is no longer the characteristics of one single small firm, but the characteristics of the industrial structure of which the small firm is a part.

The market of these firms is always national or international. Often it is a direct market in the sense that many firms, although they are small - as a point of reference, with fewer than 20 employees - have direct relations with the markets of the finished product. It can be seen that these are small only in name; in practice, they subcontract many stages of production to other firms so that the labour-force they mobilize is ten times as great as the labour-force they have on their wages-book. In other cases these firms reach the national market indirectly through the work they carry out for parent-firms, whether large or small.

The relations between these firms are completely different from those in the previous model. A market is developed for every stage of production; there is a market of weaving, of turning, of carpentry, of dress-making. These markets are strongly competitive; sub-contractors are free to switch clients, and clients are free to switch sub-contractors. The sub-contracting firms, therefore, can no longer squeeze the profits - and the wages - of the sub-contractor. Among firms that carry out different jobs, instead, there is a great readiness to collaborate. We shall see the implications of this shortly.

This climate of competition has important effects on the type of machinery used. There is a strong incentive to invest in order to be able to offer, with more productive machinery, lower prices; and there is the scope for investment because profits are no longer squeezed by parent-firms, that is, by the firms that have direct relations with the market of the finished product and that produce on their own account. Moreover, in the industrial district there is a gradual diffusion of machines that could be called 'off-standard', those able to level a steel surface of 4 x 2 metres perfectly, or those able to carve wood according to a very complex pattern, or those able to work at extremely close tolerances. The district, that is, entrusts to a few firms the task of meeting demand on all sides for unusual, specialized and exacting jobs.

Skill in these firms, too, is strongly polarized. Some carry out simple tasks and in the course of their work they do not learn much. Others are highly specialized and their skills continually increase in their relations to other firms.

There is in these firms in the most skilled workers a particular ability that is linked with the way in which the industrial district works. It is the ability to meet and solve specific problems often in a very original way that signifies in more than one case a real capacity to innovate. To clarify this point, one must reflect on how, in different contexts, planning of new products is carried out. In large firms, planning is done in very competent technical offices; the project is defined in detail; executive plans produced by various offices are, lastly, passed on to production. In the industrial district, the parent-firm normally has a rather vague idea of what it wants. Its technical offices, which often coincide with the manager, define the new product along general lines - more in terms of requirements than in specific technical solutions. The definitive plan is perfected in talks between management and the most skilled workers, and especially between management and sub-contractors, in a common task that has no other hierarchy than that of professional quality and competence. This collaboration nearly always manages to minimize production costs, for example, through the adaptation of standard components already existing on the market. Sometimes, however, this collaboration gives place to small innovations or even important innovations that open new market prospects.

Perhaps it is worth quoting two examples. The first is of an artisan from Modena who produces pumps for weed-killer spraying. A liquid-crystal capacity gauge, which was designed by an electrical sub-supplier, found an autonomous market and is now regularly exported to Germany. The second is the story of a maintenance worker from Reggio Emilia who had inserted a small innovation into the perforated card mechanism that controls the

movement of knitting frames and who realized, after
some time, that this device of his could be used to
ring church bells automatically. Today that device
works regularly in many parishes in Northern Italy.

Some Indicators To Discriminate Between The Three Models

The three models described above, as is clear, are
stylized models not infected by all the
contradictions to be found in real situations.
There are situations, however, that may be much
more complex and in which the second and third
models may co-exist, or even all three models
together.

It must be said that, even though no specific
reference has been made to these models, much has
been said in Italy about the fact that the enormous
spread of decentralization gave place to the second
or to the third models. Today, on the whole, this
discussion is a lot less heated because the idea
has been accepted that small firms may be
qualitatively different from one another, and that
there is no endogenous force within the economic
system that drives the second model towards the
third, or, even less so, the first towards the
second. Furthermore, students of this topic have
elaborated some parameters that are easy to collect
- even if they are not collected by the Central
Statistical Office - which enable us to distinguish
these types of artisan firms. Perhaps it is useful
here to give an account of this experience. The
first type of artisan firm is easily identifiable
from the market for which it works. Working for a
local market is nearly always characteristic of the
traditional artisan. On the other hand, working
directly or indirectly for the national or
international market characterizes the second and
third types. An analysis of the clients of small
firms takes on, therefore, a decisive importance.
Very few exceptions escape this indicator: one
could be the ice-cream maker who makes a very
refined product that is not comparable with that of
the big national producers, and who finds a niche
not within a backward market but one dominated by
large firms; or like the local baker who also
defends himself from the competition of large firms
with the high quality of his product. It is to be
noted that, on close examination, these exceptions
always involve goods which are not transportable.

Italy

Although the tailors of Savile Row work as artisans, it can hardly be said that theirs is a local market.

The indicators which are easily collected and which enable us to distinguish the second from the third model are of a very different nature.

The first is represented by the percentage of small firms that have a direct relation with the market of the finished product. The higher this percentage, that is, the greater the ratio between parent-firms and sub-contractors, the closer will the industrial texture under examination be to the third model. Earlier research on the clothing industry during the second half of the 1970s (Brusco 1982) discovered, for example, that in Modena, small firms producing on their own account represented about 50% of the true artisans, whereas in Ferrara the figure was not more than 8 per cent. This, obviously, synthesizes two situations which, according to all the experts, were completely different.

The second indicator is that of the percentage of sub-contractors who have a large number of clients. When, during one year, a sub-contractor works for a large number of clients, this means that the market for spare parts and components is a competitive one; that it is not possible for subcontracting firms to squeeze the sub-contractor's profits; and that, lastly, the sub-contractor produces in short series and, therefore, tends to have a high technical standard and a good professional quality. Recent research carried out by various people shows the effectiveness of this indicator. For example, Bagnasco and Trigilia (1985) found that among the metal-mechanic sub-contractors of Bassano, only 30 per cent had more than 20 clients a year. The figure found for Modena and Reggio Emilia by Favaretto (1984) is 60 per cent. All other available indicators confirm the diagnosis that derives from this figure.

To conclude, there is a last symptom which is highly diagnostic and which enables us to distinguish the second from the third model. It is the presence, in an area that produces a certain commodity, of firms that produce the machinery necessary for the production of that commodity. A very clear example of this enriching of the industrial texture is to be found in Sassuolo where, following the growth of a large number of firms that produced ceramic tiles for floors and walls, a significant number of metal-mechanic firms producing machinery for the working of clay developed. These are almost always firms with fewer than 50 workers, which have revolutionized conveying and firing methods of materials inside the tiles factories, drastically reducing costs. These firms, by exploiting the professional quality of maintenance workers, have gradually developed a capacity for autonomous planning and they are now beginning to gain markets for themselves at home and abroad (Russo 1983). Similar things have happened elsewhere - for example, in Sardinia where the industrial district of cork, in the province of Sassari, is beginning, although slowly, to innovate machinery for the production of bottle corks and the recovery of working waste.

Obviously, the indicators possible, apart from the four I have quoted, are innumerable. A whole family of indicators is concerned with identifying labour market parameters: working conditions, autonomous workers' profits and so on. Still others can be found from the quality of machinery used.

But parameters concerning the labour market are, for an independent researcher, very difficult to collect; if it is easy to observe working conditions, it is not so to obtain information on wages, especially when these wages are high, paid in such a way as to avoid social security payments. Lastly, it is almost impossible to obtain any data on the level of profits of autonomous workers.

The same goes for finding out about machinery used. A recent research experience (Brusco 1985) shows that when machinery is not radically backward, its assessment must be made only after a very careful, competent analysis of the product. In short, the point is that multipurpose machinery, as long as it has close tolerances, is the best for working short series, even if such machines are not suitable for long ones. In other words, it would be nonsense to judge the machinery that produces a Ferrari or a Maserati as having a low productivity simply because it is different from that used by Fiat.

Summing up, therefore, in order adequately to assess the machinery used by a small firm, the mixture of products that the machinery produces must be known. So too must be the different combinations of short and long series worked during a year; whether a short series, as often happens, is put into production periodically, with time intervals; and whether, lastly, the firm has the use of special equipment, to be mounted on multipurpose machines to produce longer series. This analysis, of course, is not simple to conduct.

To conclude, the importance given to the three indicators defined at the beginning is justified by the fact that they are easily collected and effective. Any other data on technology, on the labour market or on the product market will always be useful, but it is very likely that, in general, these will be qualitative data.

Small Firms And Economy Of Scale

In the previous discussion it was maintained that industrial structures composed of small firms can be very efficient and capable not only of using but indeed of producing innovations. It was also specified, although only incidentally, that by the term "small firms" we refer to firms with fewer than 50 employees, and more often fewer than 20.

Up to what point do these conclusions contrast with the usually widespread opinion that large firm size is a necessary condition for the enjoyment of economies of scale and, therefore, for economical and efficient production? Up to what point can the estimates carried out by leading industrial economists like Bain (1956) and Pratten (1971) be accepted in contrast with what has been maintained? The problem may also be presented in other terms. One might ask, that is, how much of what we have maintained is in opposition to many current texts, according to which the small size of a firm is a powerful indicator of bad technology.

The fact is that, both in large-scale economy estimates à la Bain or à la Pratten, and in the use of the small-scale as a symptom of low technical level, two fundamental assumptions are implicit.

The first assumption is that a product of a long or very long series is being considered. The cars that Bain refers to are probably produced in at least a million units.

Instead, the small firms considered here typically produce in short series. Maserati does not produce more than 8,000 cars a year or more than 2,000 of the same model; women's garments manufactured by small firms are produced in not more than 5,000 copies per model; the machine tools of Emilian firms are often produced in just a single model for a given client, like the automatic packaging machines in Bologna; the cloth of Prato is very often produced in limited quantities and

its exclusive use is granted to a single, leading
tailor. In this type of production, the advantages
of large-scale production quickly disappear. On the
other hand, the advantages of flexibility, of being
able to make special plans or designs on demand, of
being able to move about within the market, are
much greater.

It could be objected, here, that we are
talking about small segments of the market: the
interstices that Penrose (1959) talks about. But,
on careful investigation, it would seem that whole
sectors have converted to short series. At least
within the markets of capitalist countries, high
quality accompanied by the price that derives from
good technology suitable for small series often
comes off best against low quality, even though
accompanied by prices that derive from a production
technique of the Taylorite type.

But in those estimates of the minimum
efficient size and in those identifications of the
'small' with the 'backward', there is another
important assumption. It is assumed that firms
around which discussion centres have a level of
vertical integration similar to that, we might say,
of representative firms existing in the 1950s and
1960s.

Both the dependent contractor and the small
firm in industrial districts, on the contrary, have
a much lower level of vertical integration. In
practice, one type of firm corresponds to every
stage of production. There are firms that only
supply, or weave, or plan the product, or cook
mortadellas, or assemble a machine tool, or carve
the legs of a fake Louis XV chair, or cut the
uppers of women's shoes. So it is with reference to
the single phase of production that the minimum
size for efficiency must be estimated. And, in
fact, if this is the reference, these firms nearly
always reach the minimum size for efficiency. If a
worker can operate three looms, we can be sure that
a textile artisan firm will have these three looms.
In this case, the minimum size for efficiency,
measured in terms of labour force, is that of one
worker. And a software house, giving a service to
third parties, may be completely efficient with
fewer than ten workers. In other words, the
situation is that described by Marx when he refers
to the production of clocks in the nineteenth
century. Those who remember the long list of trades
and firms that Marx mentions in the fourth section
of Das Kapital first book will have a clear idea of

what is meant.

Of course, one may wonder what the costs of this radical fragmentation of the productive apparatus are. A reply to this question is given elsewhere (Brusco 1975). Here, it is sufficient to say that fragmentation is possible only because many small firms that complement one another are grouped together in a relatively restricted area. It is the already quoted notion of an industrial district proposed by Marshall, where interrelations between firms, competition and collaboration, availability of services, the differentiated presence of suppliers, and the appeal to final purchasers, are elements essential to efficiency.

It is the same consideration, the fact of being a 'system' rather than a 'single firm', that defines the degree of sophistication of these industrial structures and that makes it difficult, as will be seen, to reproduce these experiences on the basis of incentives or measures of industrial policy.

Regional Variations In The Characteristics Of Small Firms In Italy

What is the regional distribution in Italy of the three models? The data placed at the disposal of students by the Central Institute of Statistics do not, in fact, give any indications. The only phenomenon that emerges from the 1981 Industrial Census data is that the number of employees in firms with fewer than 20 workers increased compared with 1971 in almost all regions and almost all provinces in Italy.

In contrast, however, there are now available a large number of studies based on non-official findings which do identify the areas in which there are systems of firms with the features previously outlined. Some of these studies, like those of the Unioncamere (1982, 1983) and those of Garofoli (1981, 1983) try to construct a map of these areas, localizing them over the whole country. Although the procedure cannot be exact, it may be that where no industrial district has been found the small firms still possess the features described in the first model, that of the traditional artisan who operates within the local market.

On this basis - although with a high degree of uncertainty common to residual determinations of this type - it is possible to maintain that the subdivision of the country proposed by Bagnasco in 1977 is still quite valid. In the South, in fact,· small firms that serve the local market predominate, even if it is to be noted that, especially in Puglia and Campania, it is possible to identify some areas that are similar to the second and third models explained previously. In older industrialized areas of the North, many studies show that big factories are often surrounded by a large number of dependent sub-contractors. But even here, industrial districts of recent formation are quite frequent. Among these, one of the most interesting cases is represented by a group of small electronic and data processing firms operating in the area between Turin and Ivrea (Bianco and Luciano 1982). But of course it is in the 'Third Italy' that industrial districts are most diffused: in Veneto, Emilia, Tuscany, Umbria, and the Marche. Some are old, others are of more recent formation. Some are more developed and capable of innovations, others are more backward, with low wages, without steady relations with foreign markets, and exposed to the competition of the newly industrialized countries.

A Tentative Explanation Of The Industrial District Formation

How can the irregular distribution of industrial districts within the national territory be explained? Why is it that in Southern Italy industrial districts are so infrequent compared to other parts of the country, although considerable incentives of various kinds in favour of small firms have been available?

An important contribution to the analysis of this problem has been made by Bagnasco and Pini (1981). Among other things they stress two main points. First of all it may be noted that the 'Third Italy' areas correspond to the diffusion of métayage (share-cropping) agricultural areas. The coincidence is not surprising. In spite of the fact that some recent studies (Forni 1985) show that the métayer often played a role which was little different from that of a wage-worker, it is clear that, mostly, it was the family living on the farm who took all fundamental business decisions regarding its management. Therefore, in some way the spreading of métayage favoured the growth of managerial capacities, the capacity of relations

with supplier and purchaser markets, the capacity
of calculating the convenience of investment, the
capacity of book-keeping, and, in some cases, of
keeping the pay-rolls. Obviously, these are the
same capacities which, a few years later, would be
needed for the management of a small industrial
firm.

It should be noted that, contrary to what has
been maintained by Paci (1982), the relationship
between the métayage condition and the artisan-
entrepreneur condition is not based on personal
experience. In fact, as shown by Forni (1985) the
proportion of entrepreneurs having had previous
métayage experience is not particularly high.
Indeed, the relationship between métayage and
entrepreneurial capacities is more complex and
passes through a slow sedimentation of managerial
competence within the whole social texture.

Secondly, Bagnasco illustrates the basic role
of towns in the development of industrial
districts. The town is important as a place of
trade, of commercial and financial organization, as
a place of markets. It is no mere coincidence,
perhaps, that a considerable proportion of first-
generation entrepreneurs - those setting up their
own businesses in the post-war period, when the
active population rate engaged in agriculture was
still 45 per cent - came out of the ranks of
stall-keepers. It is not possible here to go deeper
into this question, as it would need a detailed
analysis of the social texture and of the
competences spread in the 'Italy of the Towns'. But
it is certain that, for example, in Modena, the
building which until 1861 housed the Austrian
Embassy bears witness to the great richness of
relations, interactions and acquaintances which may
have played a part, later on, in determining the
direction and path of development.

Bagnasco's observations, however, do not seem
entirely sufficient to explain the territorial
differences hinted at in the preceding paragraph.
It is necessary in addition to refer to at least
two other elements which are very important, not
only because they explain what happened in the
past, but also because they indicate some prospects
for future operation.

First of all it should be observed that the
historical origins of industrial districts often
stem from the previous existence of one or more
large firms which - sometimes a long time ago -
were working in the field where small and artisan

firms are now operating. There are many examples of this, which are often clear and unambiguous. At Castelgoffredo, in the province of Mantova, the stocking industry was begun by one factory, NOEMI, which was established there in the 1920s; already at the end of the last century, Vigevano, in the province of Pavia, housed the large footwear factory of the Bocca brothers; in Reggio Emilia and Modena the 'Officine Reggiane' and 'Fiat Trattori' have played a decisive part in stimulating the growth of the agricultural machine sector and so on. Many districts of newer formation, too, directly derive from the establishment of a branch plant by a large firm having its head office in another region. Indeed, as happened in the Serra de' Conti territory of the Marche (Bronzini and Grassini 1981), often the firm of extraprovincial origin closes down a few years after its establishment and is replaced by a local firm uniting the dismissed workers in a co-operative firm. From this first company, then, all the other firms of the actual district derive.

The logic of this pattern of evolution is very clear. It is the large or average firm which, with its daily work, manages to introduce the necessary technical and professional competence into a peasant social texture with few market connections. The workers learn to manage the productive process, the employees learn the connections to suppliers and to the market of the product. Then, under certain conditions, workers and employers little by little tend to change into independent workers doing on their own the work they have learnt in factories. What these conditions are has already been hinted at several points: that the market asks for customized goods, that the large firms tend to decentralize, and that the productive process can easily be divided into phases (Brusco 1982).

Finally, the importance of the school system should be remembered. From the very beginning of this century technical schools - spread all over the areas with many small autonomous firms - have been furnishing the workers with the fundamental theoretical elements of their trades. Until less than ten years ago (Capecchi 1983), people with a diploma of the Aldini-Valeriani School of Bologna represented the backbone of the Bolognese metal-mechanical industry.

As may easily be verified, there is a single red thread uniting the four factors that have been mentioned: the métayage, the role of the town, the large firms, and schools. Essentially it is a question of courses along which - in different ways - the local communities have accumulated managerial, technical and commercial competence and capacity. And it is a distinctive feature of the industrial district that this knowledge is not characteristic of one particular group within the community, but that it is spread to all social strata. Considering the fact that in Emilia-Romagna, where the active population is now approximately 1.5 million workers, there are 150,000 artisans, one cannot but notice that, essentially, everybody in Emilia has a direct experience of what a firm means, of what it means to apply to a business consultant, to resolve a technical problem, to meet with certain market difficulties, to deal with banks, to accept association with a friend to start a new activity. Certainly, this is a knowledge of a not very sophisticated level, but it is a knowledge settled deep within the social texture, which, little by little, feeds and incites the growth of new firms. And, notice, it is the same diffused competence which lies beneath the innovation model that Sabel (1982) elaborated very precisely and which has been shown here with reference to the industrial districts: because it is only a collaboration between thousands of workers and technicians which can explain how a not very clear need may be transformed into a minimizing of costs or into a new product by means of workmeetings and friendly discussions.

If all this is true, if actually the fundamental factor of growth is diffused competence, a further observation is necessary. One cannot but notice, in fact, the very limited relevance of the availability of capital - or, even more directly - of savings in the evolution of these areas. This is not the place to go further into the question, which would take us too far, but it should be observed that, fundamentally, the capital invested in these areas does not represent the alternative to a commodity which one has renounced in order to improve one's future conditions. It is rather an alternative to rest; it is the transformation of the income earned by working a number of hours per year above the average. A model describing this economy should not base its data on the level of employment and consumption and hence deduce the saving. As crucial variables, instead, it should take the number of

persons that every family is capable of employing
in the family-firm, and the number of working-hours
of each person during the day; as data it should
take consumption and hence deduce the level of
investment. The crucial starting-point, the
condition which permits the mobilization of the
work of the old and the young, and which is an
incentive to longer working-hours, is know-how. The
know-how which - alone - is capable of transforming
rest into work, and work into capital.

Local Government And Industrial Districts

What role has been played by municipal government
in the development of industrial districts in
Italy? The answer to this question has important
implications, especially with reference to
industrial policy. The basic data to take into
consideration are probably two. The first datum is
that industrial districts are just as frequent in
Emilia and Tuscany - where the local authorities
are mainly left-wing, controlled by the Italian
Communist Party - as in Veneto, where almost all
local authorities are controlled by the Christian
Democrats. Secondly, it is necessary to point out
that, as may be observed from many data, the
industrial districts of Emilia are probably the
most developed of all, where the rate of
development has been highest. However, this primacy
should be taken into consideration while
remembering that, in many cases, the development in
Veneto has also been enormous and striking.

It might be maintained, as Bagnasco and
Trigilia have done (1985), that in practice, no
matter what their political ideology may be, the
local authorities involved have, above all, sought
to create the conditions of consensus around the
new industrial structure which has been asserting
itself from the post-war period until today.

Actually, apart from the usefulness of a
mainly sociological and politicological literature
as the one quoted, perhaps the vicissitudes of
these years may be read in a more articulate way.
Even a superficial observation, in fact, will show
that generally the red local authorities have been
the most efficient ones. The pollution deriving
from new industries has been held at a tolerable
level in spite of the lack of effective national
legislation. And the comparison between Sassuolo,
where the ceramic tile factories could have

degraded the whole environment substantially, and Vicenza, where only very recently has pollution from the leather industries been brought under control, is certainly in favour of the Emilian Authorities.

Abundant quantity of high-quality public services have been made available for the family. Today the availability of places in day-nurseries and kindergartens is at a European level. Obviously, this has favoured the rate of participation.

Urban development has been programmed. Wide and orderly streets - which do not expand as oil spots around the towns - characterize the artisan villages, where the work-sheds of the small firms can be found together with the homes of their owners. Land speculation is under control, preventing the owners of land from putting obstacles in the way of investment by the firms.

However, one cannot believe that these have been the decisive incentives for a development of this type of productive structure. The development of the industrial districts in Veneto or in the Marche - where the Christian-Democratic authorities have certainly been less efficient - is a significant proof, by now, of the fact that this way of organizing the production process on a territorial basis is strictly connected with basic forces, engrafted into the whole social texture, as those described in the preceding paragraph. These are the forces which, in certain particular conditions - as referred to above - have given rise to the growth of the districts. Probably the more alert local authorities in Emilia have accelerated development. But the main references for an understanding and explanation of what has happened are not the experts of industrial policy, programming incentives for underdeveloped areas, but Hirschman and Braudel.

References

Bagnasco A. (1977) Tre Italie - la problematica territoriale dello sviluppo italiano, Il Mulino, Bologna

Bagnasco A. and R. Pini (1975) Sviluppo economico e trasformazioni sociopolitiche dei sistemi territoriali a economia diffusa, Quaderni Fondazione Feltrinelli, No. 14

Bagnasco A. and C. Trigilia (eds.) (1985) Società e

politica nelle aree di priccola impresa: il caso di Bassano, Arsenale, Venezia

Bain J.S. (1956) Barriers to new competition, Cambridge University Press, Cambridge

Bianco M.L. and L. Adriano (1982) La sindrome di Archimede, Il Mulino, Bologna

Bronzini F. and C. Grassini (1981) 'Alcuni effetti dello sviluppo industriale in un'area arretrata dell'entroterra marchigiano', in Economia Marche, No. 9

Brusco S. (1975) 'Organizzazione del lavoro e decentramento produttivo nel settore metalmeccanico', in Sindacato e piccola impresa (a cura della FLM di Bergamo), De Donato, Bari

Brusco S (1982) 'The Emilian model: productive decentralization and social integration', Cambridge Journal of Economics, 6

Brusco S. (1985) 'Il livello technologico degli artigiani metalmeccanici di Modena', Mimeo

Brusco S. and C. Sabel (1981) 'Artisan production and economic growth', in Wilkinson, Frank (ed.), The dynamics of labour market segmentation, Academic Press, London

Capecchi V. (1983) 'Diplomati e mercato del lavoro', in Capecchi, V. (ed.), Prima e dopo il diploma: percorsi maschili e femminili, Il Mulino, Bologna

Favaretto I. (1984) 'Subfornitura. Dove scopri che a Modena non si fa bene soltanto il prosciutto', Argomenti, No. 13-14

Forni M. (1985) Storie familiari e storie di proprietà, Mimeo, Bologna

Garofoli G. (1981) 'Lo sviluppo delle aree periferiche nell'economia italiana degli anni settanta', L'industria, No. 3

Garofoli G. (1983) Industrializziazione diffusa in Lombardia, Franco Angeli, Milano

Marshall A. (1919) Industry and trade

Marshall A. (1920) Principle of Economics, 8th edition

Paci M. (1982) La struttura sociale italiana, Il Mulino, Bologna

Penrose E.T. (1959) The theory of the growth of the firm, Basil Blackwell, Oxford

Pratten, C.F. (1971) Economies of scale in manufacturing industry, Cambridge University Press, Cambridge

Russo M. (1983) Technical change and the industrial district, Studi e ricerche dell'Istituto Economico, Modena, No. 14

Italy

Sabel C. (1982) Work and politics - the division of
    labour in industry, Cambridge University
    Press, Cambridge
Unioncamere (1982) Rapporto 1982 sullo stato delle
    economie locali, Vol. 1, Franco Angeli, Milano
Unioncamere-censis (1983) Rapporto 1983 sullo stato
    delle economie locali, Vol. 1, Franco Angeli,
    Milano

Chapter ten

URBAN DYNAMICS AND THE NEW FIRM;
THE POSITION OF AMSTERDAM IN THE NORTHERN RIMCITY

Mark de Jong
Jan Lambooy

Cities As Incubators

In the literature, cities are usually seen as
incubators for new economic activities. In their
well-known study on the economy of New York, Hoover
and Vernon (1959) already indicated a concentration
of innovations in parts of Manhattan. A focal point
in their current of thought is the importance of
'external economies' to small firms and for
developing new activities. Because of the many
uncertainties these enterprises have to deal with,
they settle in areas where "sudden needs could be
easily met from sources outside the plant".
    Herewith, this study also formed the basis for
the original incubator hypothesis, which states
that new firms, because of agglomeration effects,
start in the centres of big cities and leave their
starting location (mainly because of expansion and
- therefore - a lack of space) after a gestation
period. This current of thought predominantly
concerns certain parts of the manufacturing sector,
where information (for example on dynamic markets)
played an important role, as is the case in the
publishing or clothing (garments) industries (cf.
Steed 1976).
    Research in the 1970s indicated that the
incubator hypothesis could not be satisfactorily
validated, new economic activities in general no
longer being concentrated in inner cities. Both
techno-economic changes and structural spatial
transformations play their parts in this respect.
In the first place, the shift from manufacturing-
dominated toward service-based economies has many
implications for the role of small firms within
economic life and consequently for the spatial
pattern of firm formation. Moreover, due to

technological developments, major parts of manufacturing industry - especially in the 'maturity' phase of the product life cycle, which is reached much earlier than in the past - do not need urban economies. Furthermore, external economies may be found in the much wider area of the urbanized territory and therefore many tertiary industries and new (manufacturing) activities, which do need these economies, may have a wider choice of locations than the (inner) city itself (Lambooy 1976, Gudgin 1978, Fagg 1980).

Consequently, firm formation cannot be studied independently from technological developments and structural spatial dynamics, in particular with regard to the evolution of cities toward urban zones. Research on the relationship between new firms and their environment has to deal with questions regarding the spatial scale, the time span chosen, and the technology or branch of industry involved. We will deal with these three factors first, before highlighting some empirical evidence from the Northern Rimcity of the Netherlands.

The spatial scale at which the analysis is carried out is of great importance, because with the help of this scale, the contents of the production structure and the production environment are shaped. The notion 'production environment' may be seen as a further specification of the notion 'environment', which is used in the market theory. In market theory, attention is paid especially to the market relations of a firm, and sometimes also to the formal political relations. In our opinion, 'environment' should also include at least the physical infrastructural artefacts and the non-formal political (institutional) relations. Thus the notion 'production environment' would include three types of relations of a firm, viz.:

1. the market relations (labour, raw materials, sales, capital, real estate), in so far as these lie within the field to be studied;
2. the institutional political relations (relationships with government, labour unions, action groups; the attitude vis-à-vis business; image elements); and
3. the infrastructural environment (or, as Francois Perroux has put it: the 'espace technique').

The spatial scale of the analysis, as we choose it, then determines which firms and which environments will be studied. The basic idea here is that the various elements are functionally interrelated; regional economic analysis therefore cannot take place without considering these regional 'profiles'. The urban environment could then be regarded as including first the cities themselves; second the spatial scale of the city region (in a functional sense); or third an urban zone (e.g. the Northern Rimcity). We will use the notion 'urban production environment' in the broad sense, as a city region (or as several interwoven city regions), which, by entrepreneurs and by 'commuters', is considered to be the dominant reference area for their locational choice.

The element of time also plays an important role, in two different ways. It cannot be denied that innovations, openings and bankruptcies of firms, fluctuate with time. Generally, a relationship is supposed to exist with the 'long wave', in the sense that in certain periods the prospects for firm formation are more favourable than in others (Van Duijn 1983, Freeman 1984). Furthermore, the 'age' of a product, of a production process, or of an enterprise, is considered to be relevant. In the "Dynamic Market Theory" of H.W. de Jong, therefore, much attention is paid to the concept of the 'product life cycle' (De Jong 1981).

Technological developments in the economy as a whole, and the development of industrial sectors, are connected with these concepts. Firm formation is related to technological opportunities, and therefore differs with industrial sectors (Rothwell and Zegveld 1982). From a dynamic point of view, the notion of the 'industrial sector' actually is not satisfactory as a 'hard' mechanism for classification. New activities, such as the information technology sector, bio-technology, and parts of the business services sector, therefore are very difficult to study in a purely statistical manner (De Jong and Lambooy 1985, Lambooy and Tates 1983).

Urban Dynamics In The Northern Rimcity

We have already stressed the importance of the urban zone as the relevant scale for analysing economic phenomena, such as the formation of new firms. Without too much elaboration on this point, we would like to mention a few important aspects of the urban dynamics of the Northern Rimcity. This urban zone has some special characteristics, because of the unusual clustering of cities and city regions in the Western part of the Netherlands, which is also known as the 'Randstad Holland' (Rimcity - cf. Hall 1977).

Whereas the name suggests a single continuous zone, functionally speaking this is not valid. We should at least distinguish between a southern wing (consisting of the Rotterdam harbour area and The Hague) and a northern wing. The Northern Rimcity is a functionally integrated labour market, with two million inhabitants, stretching from the steelplant complex of Hoogovens and the provincial capital of Haarlem in the West, to the city of Amersfoort in the East. Amsterdam is situated in the heart of this area, with the largest concentration of employment, predominantly 'white collar' jobs (financial sector, business services, (international) trade and headquarters, producer services, and education). Residential areas, as well as manufacturing industry and the wholesale trade, have gradually and deliberately been spread over the whole of the Northern Rimcity. Physical planning has (also) played an important role in forcing economic activities out of the monumental inner city of Amsterdam, out of considerations for preserving the inner city. Therefore, unlike many other cities, Amsterdam does not have a strong Central Business District (CBD), but major office developments are increasingly located near the Beltway, at relatively short distances from the inner city. Together, these (sub-)centres constitute by far the largest (non-governmental) office market in the Netherlands.

New Firms In The Northern Rimcity

Two recent studies of the Institute of Economic Geography at the University of Amsterdam provide information on our basic question, namely the relationship between urban dynamics and new firms. The first concerned a study of the spatial dynamics of small and medium sized manufacturing firms in the Northern Rimcity (De Jong 1984); the second one focused especially on the 'information technology sector' in Amsterdam (De Jong and Lambooy 1985). In both cases, we specifically looked at the importance of urban environments to new (technologically advanced) business and employment. The first question examined, was: Are urban environments important for the rise of new enterprises? Some years ago, the Nederlandse Middenstands Bank (Dutch Tradespeople's Bank -NMB), in its Annual Report, published a map of the Netherlands, which provided an overview of the areas with more (or less) openings of new firms, when compared with the whole of the Netherlands. From this map it could be concluded that the 'halfway zone' (the provinces bordering on the Rimcity) showed an over-representation, whereas the peripheral regions showed an under-representation of firm formation; the regions containing the big cities were well below average in this respect.

These data were valuable, in particular as an incentive for further research, since a number of questions still remained to be answered. For instance, one might ask which pattern would appear if we were to differentiate for industrial sectors. Furthermore, it remains to be seen to what extent the picture drawn is determined by service industries (since these activities have followed a shift of the population to the suburbs in the 'halfway zone'), the more so because we know that many mutations are being realized by retail establishments. Also, the spatial division used does not provide information about the controversy between urban and rural areas in this respect, whereas from the literature it appears - in most Western countries anyway - that the growth of industrial employment in rural areas in the past decade has started to surpass the developments in urban areas (Fothergill and Gudgin 1982, Jackson et al. 1981, Keeble et al. 1983). And lastly, firm size could not be taken into account, let alone the type of business opening.

When we tried to map the establishment data for a selected number of manufacturing industries[3] (in total about 16,000 establishments), the NMB-picture became somewhat differentiated. Firstly, it appeared that the 'high-tech' business groups (office machines, electro-technical and instruments industry) were especially located in the Rimcity and in the big cities. This has been confirmed by recent research by Bouman et al. (1985) for a comparable selection of high-technology industries in the Netherlands. Also, these results are in line with the situation in the 'high-tech' sector in the United States, which also is concentrated in urban agglomerations. A 1982 survey for the US Congress indicated that "most high technology companies prefer an urban environment to a rural environment"

(Premus 1982, 16, also Malecki 1984).
Secondly, we found that the Rimcity as a whole
contained the highest percentage of (surviving)
young firms, with the halfway zone in a good second
place, and followed at some distance by the
periphery (Table 1). Within the Rimcity, most of
the newly established firms were located in the big
cities, but their share is declining. Relatively
speaking, the suburban communities (especially
'urbanized rural municipalities') within the
Rimcity and the 'halfway zone' are an increasingly
important location for new firms. Therefore,
incubation (on the general level of the sectors
researched) is no longer confined to within the
boundaries of the big cities, but should be
considered in relation to the urbanization of large
parts of the Netherlands. Taking into account the
rather small differences shown in Table 1, we
should stress this last statement and the general
irrelevance of a centre/periphery concept for the
Dutch case.

Table 1. Share of Enterprises established after
1975 (selected manufacturing industries)
per Municipality as a percentage of total
enterprises existing in the Rimcity, the
'Halfway zone' and the Periphery in 1982.

	Rimcity no. in %	Halfway no. in %	Periphery no. in %	Total* no. in %
Rural municipalities	201 43.0	197 35.2	239 31.0	640 35.5
Urbanized rural municipalities	868 41.9	899 41.3	487 35.5	2,277 40.3
Small cities	209 42.1	239 35.9	231 36.0	686 37.8
Medium-sized cities	414 36.6	252 38.0	278 35.5	954 36.8
Big cities	1,119 37.6	374 36.9	189 38.5	1,689 37.6
Total	2,811 39.4	1,961 38.6	1,424 35.1	6,246 38.2

* Some 50 firms could not be classified
Source: De Jong 1984, 25.

When we take a closer look at the location
pattern within the Northern wing of the Rimcity,
the position of Amsterdam is a good example of the
gradual 'suburbanization of new activity'. Of the
young enterprises, about one third are located in
Amsterdam itself, and in total 50 per cent are in
the three large cities. However, it is clear that
the suburban fringes of the study area are gaining

new firms, whereas the still considerable dominance of the cities is diminishing.

Interestingly enough, most firms are not located within the city centre or on designated industrial estates. Only in the machinery industry are 45 per cent of the small firms to be found in industrial areas, against on average a mere 21 per cent of all small firms. The city centres contain 17 per cent of all small enterprises, whereas more than half the total (36 and 18 per cent respectively) are located in both older and post-war residential areas. New firms are even more heavily represented in residential neighbourhoods (66 per cent), implying that there is probably some mobility of firms from one area to another.

Therefore, we have mapped the locational dynamics of over 2,100 enterprises in the northern wing of the Rimcity at a more detailed level. We found that half of the businesses had started after 1970 and that about one third had moved at least once since that time. This means that only a minority of the existing firms has been located at a fixed place for a longer period of time.

All of these individual location decisions could, in principle, have a considerable impact on the spatial structure of the area. However, no large shifts have taken place; the location pattern has indeed remained rather stable (cf. Cross 1981, 236). Three quarters of the migrant firms remained within the same municipality. Of the migrant firms, no less than 38 per cent went to another location in the same kind of environment; that is, within residential areas, or within the city centre, and so on. Only industrial areas attracted many firms, in particular growing areas.

Based on a subsequent questionnaire among nearly 400 firms, it could be concluded that this rather stable locational pattern should be seen as a consequence of the spatially limited view of small entrepreneurs where their choice of location is concerned. We will elaborate on this point in the context of the firm formation process, in the next section.

The study of new economic activities, also from a spatial point of view, implies an emphasis on the qualitative aspects of processes of change. This is because it is all about 'new', and not so much about 'more'. If we were to draw conclusions with regard to locational dynamism, based only upon the figures about the number of newly-established firms in comparison to the existing number of enterprises, we should be confronted with a number of problems connected with the quantitative nature of these conclusions. Such statistical considerations therefore have to be interpreted with caution. Cities, contrary to suburbs, have an extensive number of older, stagnating firms; the dynamic group of firms may therefore be blurred in statistical figures. We then see many new firms - in absolute terms - in the cities, but, because of the large population of existing firms, the relative figures appear to be lower than those in the smaller municipalities.

Therefore, we certainly cannot limit ourselves to quantitative material only; we also have to take into consideration the nature of the new activities concerned. The developments in the computer sector in Amsterdam, for instance, show remarkable results (De Jong and Lambooy 1985). From the beginning this sector has been heavily concentrated in Amsterdam and, although a certain measure of dispersal did take place, the share of the Amsterdam region appears to be growing again over the last couple of years. At the moment, according to our study, the city region offers employment in this sector to about 10,000 people (about 3 per cent of the total labour force), spread over about 300 firms. The exact size of this sector is hard to establish, because of the fact that, for the time being, the industry has not been defined in a uniform way, and because of the enormous dynamism with regard to establishment and closures of firms.

In the Amsterdam city region, about 100 computer sector firms are established yearly, the greater part of which disappears again within a (very) short time. The fact that we are dealing with a very young branch of industry, is indicated by the very small number of enterprises (21 firms) that started in Amsterdam and its environment before 1970, and were still operating in the area in 1984. The largest growth has taken place after 1980: almost two thirds of the number of firms has started since then.

So we are dealing with a young, technically advanced sector, which is yet (again?) developing in an urban environment. This is the more surprising because, when asked, the enterprises concerned in general appear to see only few specific benefits connected with locating in Amsterdam, when compared to other places. Therefore, the reason why they are located in Amsterdam and its environment may be understood only in relation to the genesis of the firms concerned.

With some simplification, two types of enterprises may be distinguished. Firstly, we can discern the establishments of large (American) computer firms, that have often been active in the regions since World War II, as regional headquarters or as wholesalers in office equipment (e.g. IBM, NRC). Secondly, many computer service bureaus have started in Amsterdam. By interviewing entrepreneurs in this sector, we were able to get a picture of the factors behind this spatial concentration.

Spatial Dimensions Of Firm Formation

In the two studies mentioned, we have paid attention to the process of firm formation, both through a telephone questionnaire among 100 new entrepreneurs in the northern wing of the Rimcity, and through interviews with about 20 small entrepreneurs in the computer industry in the Amsterdam agglomeration. Partly based on this research, we would like to propose an evolutionary interpretation of firm formation and of some spatial dimensions in that process. We will refer to new firms only if one or more independent entrepreneurs play a central part in this process, excluding those ventures that are initiated by existing firms, or other capital suppliers. We therefore may assume that there will be no new firm without there also being a new entrepreneur. This does not mean that the causality also works the other way around; there are many more entrepreneurs than there are new firms. What do we mean by this?

Shapero has suggested that it looks as if "the world is divided into categories of people; those who act as if they have free will and all the rest" (1984a, 8-9). Indeed, many people are 'enterprising' before, or without ever, becoming an entrepreneur. This also means that it is difficult to decide whether, and if so at what moment, a new firm is being established, because the "start-up is a continuous process rather than a discrete event" (Birley 1984). The incubation activities appear in varied ways. Sometimes they merely consist of experimenting in a technical sense (as with typical inventors), but sometimes they also include a market orientation, by working for somebody else, for instance as a consultant. Also, many entrepreneurs are involved in the 'informal economy', often without ever starting a formal business.

This pre-establishment or 'incubation phase' (Falk 1982: 'embryonic stage') has a few particular characteristics in common. Sectorally, entrepreneurs generally are venturing in a direction in which they already have acquired a certain knowledge, skills, and experience. Sometimes this has been acquired in formal education, but more often this is not the case and 'learning by doing' in (former) employment is more usual. In our research, four out of five new entrepreneurs already had working experience in a similar firm.

The incubation phase also is of interest from a geographical point of view, in that these activities nearly always take place at home. This implies that potential entrepreneurial efforts are taking place everywhere where people live: that is to say, in residential areas. At least in the Amsterdam case, selective outmigration of middle class residents has caused a diminished concentration of 'potential entrepreneurs' within the city limits. In fact, most new firms start at home. As we have seen before, two thirds of the new firms in the Northern wing of the Rimcity started in residential areas and not in city centres or on industrial estates. The tendency for suburban and residential locations to become more important as a first location for small firms in their first years of existence has also been noted earlier.

From an economic development perspective, it is of crucial importance whether this process of 'trial and error' leads to the establishment of a real firm, which provides at least a full-time job for the entrepreneur himself. Whether or not a new firm gets established depends on a series of factors. First of all, the matching of supply and demand is at stake here. Rapidly growing markets provide special incubation opportunities for entrepreneurs who possess the relevant skills. The computer service industry is a good example. Many founders of new firms in this sector have formerly been employed in the automation departments of banks, insurance companies, large foreign companies, computer firms, or universities, all of which are strongly concentrated in Amsterdam. Thus, both with regard to the (initial) market, and with regard to technical know-how, the pre-conditions for successful business ventures were present.

Moreover, the (perceived) opportunities of the

entrepreneur in relation to his or her present position ('displacement' factor) is of relevance. Unemployment or an insecure job situation can be push factors, although in the Netherlands this is not as important as is sometimes conceived. More important is the relatively weak career opportunity for today's generation of younger executives in large firms, because of demographic factors and because of a stagnation in growth in many large companies. Even so, it also depends on the amount of risk involved, which is related to the scarcity of one's skills in the labour market. In particular in the computer service industry, many respondents told us that they hoped that their venture would be successful. They were not really concerned about their future, however, because they could always return to a well-paid job, the moment they would like to do so. In other words, the risk of starting a business is limited both in the case of lack in demand of someone's skills and in the opposite case when the labour market prospects are extremely good.

Finally, institutional factors play a role in determining whether or not people will persist in establishing their own business firm. In a very direct sense, firm formation is stimulated by measures such as business technology centers, small entrepreneurs courses, and spin-off facilitating instruments. Even more important, also from a geographical point of view, are indirect effects of a supportive institutional climate, including the fiscal and business climate, and publicity about small firms.

We would like to stress some geographical dimensions of the firm formation process as described above. Firstly, although most new firms 'incubate' at home, after a certain period of operation an entrepreneur may decide to become established and to choose - more deliberately than before - a business address. From a spatial point of view, this really is a more crucial moment for the entrepreneur, because the location decision then is more influenced by external factors, such as the industrial or office space available, market factors, and the institutional climate. We can see this happen, because most migrations in fact result in a shift from residential neighbourhoods to industrial areas, while older firms tend to choose more formal business sites. Whereas 17 per cent of the new firms were located in separate industrial or office areas, 60 per cent of old firms are situated in these locations. The questionnaire showed that 25 per cent of the new entrepreneurs did not have any locational preference at all and that the others were largely satisfied with their existing locations. Furthermore, (spatial) bottlenecks only became an issue after one or two years of existence; a typical answer stated that "we are too young to decide on these issues".

A related topic is illustrated in Fig. 1. When we asked small business owners in general where they would preferably be located, their replies revealed a discrepancy with the existing location pattern. At the same time, it underlines the proposition that most entrepreneurs who are located in residential neighbourhoods do not do so because of a deliberate preference or decision. Given the net outmigration of firms from the inner cities, it is remarkable that the core areas still exert considerable attraction to small and medium sized firms. The 'no preference' category is predominantly filled with new entrepreneurs. These results are similar to the findings of Gudgin (1978, 105-106), who concluded that "the founders of new firms will rarely make active location decisions. Instead, new firms are located within the entrepreneur's home area. Also, the industry in which the firm operates will normally be that one

Fig. 1.   The location of SME's in comparison with entrepreneurial preferences of neighbourhood types.

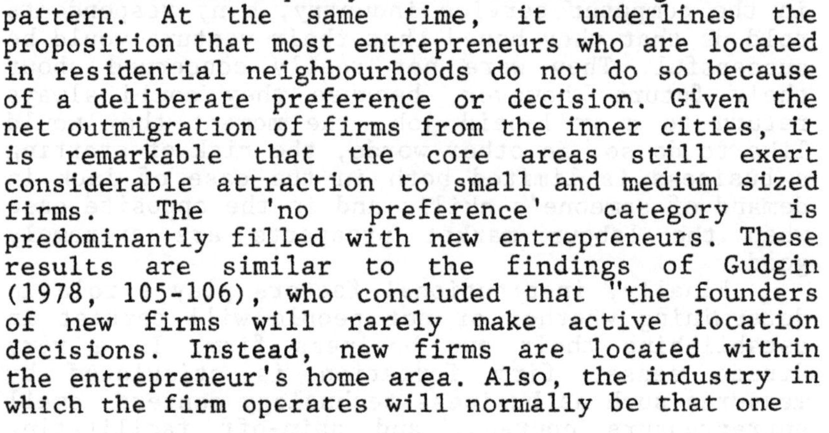

inner city	46 / 71 (+25)
old residential neighbourhoods	12 / 87 (-75)
new residential neighbourhoods	10 / 48 (-38)
industrial sites	89 / 98 (+9)
near certain facility[1]	-/16 (-)
miscellaneous	16/18 (+2)
no preference	-/61 (-)

--- = existing location
—— = preferred location
[1] For example, a highway, port, shopping centre

Source: De Jong (1984, 88).

214

in which the entrepreneur previously worked. The decision which is made is whether or not to go into business; the location and form of production are to a large extent predetermined".

Secondly, by placing the entrepreneur in the key position of a new business venture, we also assume the importance of the background and skills of the entrepreneur. Jacobs (1970, 55) observed the important role of experience for entrepreneurs and for skilled labour alike: "New work arises upon existing work". This assertion also has important geographical consequences by way of the gradual developments taking place in and between urban areas. We may now turn our attention toward an evolutionary interpretation of the locational patterns described.

Toward An Evolutionary Interpretation Of Urban Dynamics

The theory of 'Evolutionary Economics' is based especially on the ideas of Cyert, March and Simon with regard to the decision-making process of and within organizations. In short, Nelson and Winter (1982) argue that, because of the nature of such decision-making, structural changes come about only at an extremely leisurely pace. The direction of the development has largely been determined by the previous situation. But although routines and skills "are a persistent feature of the organism and determine its possible behaviour", they also stress that "actual behaviour is determined by the environment" (Nelson and Winter 1982, 14-15). Thus, changes often have an unpredictable dimension, due to stochastic developments, which could, of course, also be explained by creative (i.e. unpredictable, innovative) actions. Therefore, this theory may be considered to be an extension of and an elaboration on the theory of Schumpeter.

From a spatial point of view, this theory leads to the hypothesis of the cumulative unfolding of an already existing economic situation (Harris 1954, Myrdal 1957) on the one hand; and - spatially - to a "sidelong increase" (Lambooy 1984, Lambooy and Huizinga 1976) on the other hand. In the long term, urban economic development is a result of the diversified and finely branched production structure of certain urban areas. Earlier writers (e.g. Lampard 1966, Thompson 1965) have of course also developed this idea: indeed, it is present in the writings of Adam Smith and Von Thünen.

If urban economic development can indeed largely be characterized by evolutionary patterns of change, we might ask what exactly will grow, and how this growth will affect urban economies? However, we will take the position that it will only be possible to define the nature of future development, and, moreover, that it is even undesirable - from a policy perspective - to be too specific in this respect.

Future Developments And Policy Implications

It is crucial that we establish the fact that uncertainty exists about the question, which sectors and which enterprises will grow in the future, because this also implies that our view at the location of new economic activites is clouded. Given a number of basic technologies that are strongly developing at the moment (e.g. information technology, telecommunications, bio-technology), we can at the most form some ideas on possible promising fields of application. From experiences gained, it appears that precisely by application in other parts of the economy, the more important employment and output growth may be realized. Roobeek (1984, 139-140) has developed such a conceptual 'technology web' for bio-technology, and Freeman, Clark and Soete (1982) have described the working of 'new technology systems'.

Precisely because of the complex way in which new technologies influence the economy (and certainly the service sector), it is hard to predict which new firms will be successful. The chance that the same firms that have been growing in the most recent past will also provide employment in the future is uncertain. This has again recently been confirmed by the problems confronting many so-called 'excellent enterprises', only a few years after they had been held up as examples to their colleagues by Peters and Waterman (cf. Business Week of 5 November 1984).

Although a great many new enterprises are currently being established, and although many new initiatives are being taken, not all of these will, of course, be successful. Many new founded firms usually disappear again within a period of a few years, or remain at about the same level of employment after the start. Only a minority will expand (in the study of the Rimcity, it appears that only about one third of the surviving firms did show a growth of employment) and at most a few per cent of new firms show considerable employment growth. This means that really expanding enterprises are very rare indeed, while it should also be noted that most of these are not - or are only to a limited degree - technically advanced. Gregerman (1984) states in this respect that many municipalities are wrong in focusing their attention exclusively on 'high-tech' industry, and that their goal should be to create healthy jobs in general (that is to say: they should be oriented toward 'high growth' industry). From a geographical viewpoint, the situation is even more complex. Evidence is accumulating that different urban economies show different growth opportunities (Pascal and Gurwitz 1983, Noyelle and Stanback 1984). Although in general certain service industries seem to possess the largest growth potentials, it then depends on the assets of a particular urban or regional economy as to which new firms will have the greatest growth opportunities. Instead of competing to generate the same kind of so-called 'high-tech' firms, a more adapted strategy might then be more opportune.

Because of the uncertain future and the risks involved, those regions where the most new initiatives are established do possess an advantage. Solely because of their size, urban areas therefore are in a better position than their rural counterparts. But besides the number of initiatives, their quality is also important: in a diversified economy there is a greater chance that those initiatives will be developed that will prove to be successful in filling the opportunities provided by market 'niches' as yet unknown.

Therefore, the size and variation of local demand on the one hand, and of the labour market on the other hand (know-how, potential entrepreneurship), are of crucial importance in the rise of new economic activities. Although neither of these factors can easily be changed in the short term, this may well be possible in the long run, as may be shown, for example, by the rise of new growth centres in the South of the United States. Furthermore, it is certainly possible to carry out policies oriented toward improving the conditions for creativity and dynamism at the start of a firm, and toward expansion afterwards. In this respect, we should think of the improvement of the 'production environment', for example by way of facilities for spin-off and mobility of labour, investment in the physical and institutional infrastructure, and by improving the 'quality of life' and the business climate (cf. Keeble 1985, 33). Especially with regard to the infrastructural characteristics of the production environment, impetus may be generated from co-operative projects between government and industry.

This appears to be the case, for example, in the Teleport project which has been initiated in Amsterdam by a group of private developers. In a now co-operative effort of both public and private sectors, a new subcentre will be developed around a satellite earth station (or 'Teleport'). Besides being an improvement to the telecommunications infrastructure, this project also has a distinct positive influence on the image of activity business and on overall investment in Amsterdam. Although it is not quite clear how such mechanisms work, we found in the information technology study that the 'image' of a particular locality is very important in the decisions that entrepreneurs have to make. Some (parts of) municipalities are considered to be attractive locations ("That's the place to be"), whereas for others the opposite holds true. We may conclude that (local) government policies can play a major part in this respect.

Concluding Remarks

Research on new firm formation shows that traditional incubation theory is far too simplistic in that it takes into account only a few factors, whereas the relationship between firm formation and urban dynamics is much more complicated. The two basic questions are, whether or not urban areas possess advantages with regard to the local potential for entrepreneurship (supply) and regarding the demand for new products or services. In answering these questions, we cannot limit ourselves to factors such as external economies, because these have a different impact for different economic activities. Since large urban regions have increasingly become centres of information exchange and decision-making, they tend to generate related activities. The information technology sector is presumably the clearest example of an innovative industry, which is dependent on both know-how and demand concentrated in cities and city regions. But also more generally, the transfer mechanism for innovations is largely defined by the relation and information networks. Although these networks do have a spatial bias, they are not necessarily tied to the (inner) city itself. Firstly, firms operating interregionally or internationally often have a much wider action radius, where transfer of innovations or the exchange of technological information is concerned. Secondly, the spatial scales on which these networks operate, differ and change gradually.

In a Dutch context, it is very difficult to describe the radius of these information and relation networks, since - in the words of Pred - "almost the whole physical area of the Netherlands lies within a 100-mile radius, or the 'urban field', of the Randstad metropolitan complex, and can therefore benefit from its external economies to some extent" (Pred 1977, 194). However, research in other countries - for instance in the US - does suggest that there is an urban/rural difference, at least with regard to the important category of high technology firms, which may be particularly concentrated in urban environments.

The most attractive city regions for technically advanced enterprises appear to be those characterized by a diversified economic structure, a major labour market, a scientific infrastructure, and good (international) transportation links (see e.g. De Jong 1983). This means that certain large city regions, such as Boston, New York, San Francisco (Silicon Valley) and Los Angeles, are particularly favoured for high-technology development, since the existing economic structure has been extended in an advanced direction. Malecki (1984) has recently drawn attention to this growth effect, which "tends to reinforce the agglomeration economies already present in these areas, and which cumulatively adds to their attraction for future high-tech enterprises".

In addition, however, there is evidence that "agglomeration economies may operate at a lower size threshold" (Malecki 1984, 267), so that new urban areas may also participate in the growth of technologically-innovative industries. We may point to Austin, Dallas, Denver and Phoenix, in the so-called 'Sun Belt' of the US. However, in this case it must be stressed that the urban areas concerned have been able to develop only after a long period of slow evolution (De Jong and Terhorst 1983). These American developments also give rise to the possibility that new locational (innovative) clusters are now evolving, but are doing so only after a long period of time, and mainly in addition to, rather than instead of, the existing urban agglomerations. Such developments may also be found in France (specifically in the South - the Côte d'Azur, Toulouse - and in the Alpes - Grenoble; cf. Aydalot 1984).

It is not clear yet whether also in the Netherlands - be it at a totally different level of scale than in the examples mentioned above - new locational clusters might develop. There are some signs of clusters of new firm formations near the Technical Universities of Twente and Eindhoven, and indeed manufacturing industry in general can benefit from external economies in the whole of the Netherlands, as Pred rightly observed. But as we have seen, new firms in 'high-tech' branches and certainly those in advanced tertiary activities are more concentrated in the urbanized western part of the country.

It may therefore be argued that particular economic functions are tied to urban regions. Since new entrepreneurs build on existing activities, the spatial pattern of new firms is to a large extent a reflection of the preceding situation. The concentration of human capital in urban regions provides a major reason for the clustering of advanced new firms either within or near cities (or within the "Daily Urban System"). Whether or not this potential of human capital will lead to successful firm formation, depends above all on two factors, namely whether this 'supply' matches 'niches' in the market, and the general conditions in the 'production environment'.

So far, we have discussed the importance of the urban environment to new firm formation in certain sectors of the economy. But often the opposite causality is stressed, in the sense that new firms are considered to be vitally important to (urban) economic development. Shapero (1984b, 19) has clearly described this interaction, as follows: "To attain the desired characteristics of diversity, innovativeness, and resilience that have been identified with a dynamic economy implies a multiplicity of companies and, by inference, the kind of industrial ecology or environment that facilitates the formation of new companies in answer to opportunities or problems". This statement should not be interpreted too narrowly. Storey (1982) has rightly warned against overestimation of the role of new firms in solving problems in the short term. In the long run,

however, the vitality of cities and urban regions
will be preserved and improved precisely through
new business ventures.

Note

1. Data for the 1983 situation in printing, metal,
   office machines, electro-technical and
   instruments industries.

References

Aydalot, Ph. (1984) 'Reversal of spatial trends in
    French industry since 1974' in Lambooy, J.G.
    (ed.), New spatial dynamics and economic
    crisis, IRPA-Yearbook 1984, Finnpublishers,
    Tampere, pp.41-62
Birley, S. (1984) Finding the new firm,
    Proceedings of the 44th Academy of Management
    Conference, Boston
Bouman, H., T. Thuis and B. Verhoef (1985) High
    tech in Nederland, Doctoral thesis, GIRUU/VU,
    Utrecht
Cross, M. (1981) New firm formation and regional
    development, Gower, Farnborough
Duijn, J.J. van (1983) The long wave in economic
    life, Allen and Unwin, London
Fagg, J.J. (1980) 'A re-examination of the
    incubator hypothesis: a case study of Greater
    Leicester', Urban Studies, pp. 35-44
Falk, N. (1982) 'Premises and the development of
    small firms' in Watkins, D., J. Stanworth and
    A. Westrip (eds.)' Stimulating small firms.
    Gower, Aldershot, pp. 127-163
Fothergill, S. and G. Gudgin (1982) Unequal
    growth; urban and regional employment change
    in the UK, Heinemann, London
Freeman, Chr. (ed.) (1984) Long waves in the world
    economy, Frances Pinter, London
Freeman, Chr., J. Clark and L. Soete (1982)
    Unemployment and technical innovation; a study
    of long waves and economic development Frances
    Pinter, London
Gregerman, A.S. (1984) 'Competitive advantage;
    framing a strategy to support high-growth
    firms', in Commentary of the National Council
    for Urban Economic Development, Washington
    D.C., pp.18-23
Gudgin, G. (1978) Industrial location processes

and regional employment growth, Saxon House, Farnborough

Hall, P. (1977) The world cities (2nd ed.), Weidenfeld and Nicholson Ltd, London

Harris, C.D. (1954) 'The market as a factor in the location of industry in the United States' Annals of the Association of American Geographers, pp.315-348

Hoover, E.M. and R. Vernon (1959) Anatomy of a metropolis, New York

Jackson, G., G.Masnick, R. Bolton, S. Bartlett and J. Pitkin (1981) Regional diversity. Growth in the US 1960-1990. Auburn House, Boston

Jacobs, J. (1970) The economy of cities, Vintage Books, New York (original edition 1969)

Jong, H.W. de (1981) Dynamische markttheorie Stenfert Kroese, Leiden

Jong, M.W. de (1983) 'Regionale kondities voor nieuwe hoogwaardige bedrijvigheid; industriële vernieuwing in Greater Boston', Economisch Statistische Berichten, 16-11, pp.1059-1063.

Jong, M.W. de (1984) Ruimtelijke dynamiek van het midden- en kleinbedrijf; het lokatiepatroon van kleine industriële ondernemingen in de Noordvleugel van de Randstad, Institute of Economic Geography, Amsterdam

Jong, M.W. de and J.G. Lambooy (1985) De informatica-sector centraal; perspectieven voor de Amsterdamse binnenstad, Institute of Economic Geography, Amsterdam

Jong, M.W. de and P. Terhorst (1983) Innovaties en ruimtelijke concentratie; de opkomst van de 'Sunbelt' in de Verenigde Staten, Institute of Human Geography, Publication nr.9, Amsterdam

Keeble, D. (1985) 'The changing spatial structure of economic activity and metropolitan decline in the UK', in Ewers H.J. (ed.), The Future of the Metropolis, De Gruyter, Berlin

Keeble, D., P.L. Owens and Chr. Thompson (1983) 'The urban-rural manufacturing shift in the European Community', Urban Studies, 20, pp. 405-413

Lambooy, J.G. (1976) 'Verstedelijkingsnota en agglomeratievoordelen', Economisch Statistische Berichten, 31-3. pp. 318-322

Lambooy, J.G. (1984) 'The regional ecology of technical change' in Lambooy J.G. (ed.), New spatial dynamics and economic crisis. IRPA-Yearbook 1984, Finnpublishers, Tampere, pp.63-76

Lambooy, J.G. and J.H. Huizinga (1976) 'Twintig jaar 'Het Westen des lands en Overig Nederland'; de ontwikkeling van het 'Nieuwe Westen'', in Intermediair, 13, 12

Lambooy, J.G. and N. Tates (1983) De zakelijke dienstverlening in Amsterdam, Institute of Economic Geography, Amsterdam

Lampard, E.E. (1966) 'Urbanization and social change' in Handlin, O. and J. Burchard, The historian and the city, Cambridge, Mass.

Malecki, E.J. (1984) 'High technology and local economic development', Journal of the American Planners Association, summer 1984, pp.262-269

Myrdal, G. (1957) Economic theory and underdeveloped regions, London

Nelson, R.R. and S.G. Winter (1982) An evolutionary theory of economic change Cambridge, Mass.

Noyelle, Th.J. and T.M. Stanback (1984) The economic transformation of American cities Rowman and Allanheld, Totowa

Pascal, A. and A. Gurwitz (1983) Picking winners; industrial strategies for local economic development, Rand Publication Series, Santa Monica

Pred, A.R. (1977) City systems in advanced economies, London

Premus, R. (1982) Location of high-technology firms and regional economic development, Joint Economic Committee US-Congress, Washington

Roobeek, A. (1984) De relatie tussen technologie en ekonomische ontwikkeling; een literatuur-analyse, Dept. of Economics, University of Amsterdam, Amsterdam

Rothwell, R. and W. Zegveld (1982) Innovation and the small and medium sized firm, Frances Pinter, London

Shapero, A. (1984a) Why entrepreneurship?, Mimeo, The Ohio State University

Shapero, A. (1984b) 'Entrepreneurship in economic development', in Farr, C.A., (ed.), Shaping the local economy. International City Management Association, Washington D.C., pp.12-24

Steed , G.D.F. (1976) 'Centrality and locational change: printing, publishing, and clothing in Montreal and Toronto', Economic Geography, 52-3, pp. 193-205

Storey, D.J. (1982) Entrepreneurship and the new firm, Croom Helm, London

Thompson, W.R. (1965) A preface to urban economics, Baltimore

Chapter eleven

THE REGIONAL IMPACT OF PUBLIC POLICY TOWARDS SMALL
FIRMS IN THE UNITED KINGDOM

Colin Mason
Richard Harrison

Introduction

Since the publication in 1971 of the report of the
Committee of Inquiry on Small Firms, better known
as the Bolton Report (HMSO 1971), successive
governments in the United Kingdom have introduced a
wide variety of measures designed to promote new
firm formation and small firm growth (Beesley and
Wilson 1982). Both the Conservative Government of
the day and the subsequent Labour administration
acted upon a number of the Committee's
recommendations in order to remove sources of
unintended discrimination against small firms and
to create a climate favourable to their growth. The
momentum increased towards the end of the Labour
administration with the appointment of a special
study under Lord Lever, a senior Minister in the
Government, to investigate the problems of small
firms and to recommend and initiate remedial
action. This led to the incorporation of a number
of fiscal measures to assist small firms in the
budgets of 1977 and 1978. In addition, the Labour
Government appointed a committee, under the
chairmanship of Sir Harold Wilson to inquire into
the role of the financial institutions and the
provision of funds for industry and trade; its
interim report on the financing of smaller firms
was published in 1979 (HMSO 1979) and a number of
its recommendations have subsequently been acted
upon.
The election in 1979 of a Conservative
Government pledged to create a thriving private
enterprise economy in which the entrepreneur would
play a key role - described by Riddell (1983, 165)
as an attempt to construct a society which is "a
cross between nineteenth century Birmingham and

224

contemporary Hong Kong, located in Esher" - has turned the steady stream of measures to assist the small firm sector into a torrent. Indeed, one of the Government's claims during the general election campaign of 1983 was that it had introduced 108 such measures since coming into office four years earlier, many of them intended to positively discriminate in favour of the small firm sector. However, since its re-election for a second term in office the Conservative Government has concentrated its efforts on 'repacking' and publicising the plethora of small firms schemes available to take account of the criticism that there is only limited awareness amongst the small business sector of the assistance that is on offer (for example, as shown in a survey by the Economists Advisory Group 1983) while the sheer number of different measures is confusing to the target clientele (Dickson 1984). To this end, the Government is proposing to condense and simplify the 64 schemes under the remit of the Department of Trade and Industry into four groups covering investment, innovation, export and advice in an attempt to create a more 'user friendly service' (Dawkins 1985).

The measures introduced since 1979 by the Conservative Government· address four main constraints on small business activity. First, the availability of finance for new and small firms, consistently identified as one the most important limitations on their growth, has been tackled by the Loan Guarantee Scheme, while the fiscal incentives embodied in the Business Start-up Scheme, subsequently extended and renamed the Business Expansion Scheme, have made it more attractive for individuals to invest in new and established small businesses. In addition, the Enterprise Allowance Scheme was introduced to provide a payment in lieu of unemployment benefit to encourage more unemployed individuals to consider setting up their own business. Second, the provision of inexpensive or free business information and advice has been enhanced by an expansion of the activities of the Small Firm Service (e.g. the introduction of additional services such as the Small Firms Technical Enquiry Service) and through the creation of local enterprise agencies whose establishment has been encouraged by the availability of tax relief on the contributions in cash and kind (e.g. seconded staff) from companies which support them. Third, legislative and administrative burdens on small firms have also been reduced by exempting them from certain obligations under various pieces of legislation (e.g. dismissal procedures under employment legislation and the provision of detailed financial information with the Registrar of Companies). According to recent reports the Government is currently exploring, by means of a high level inter-departmental committee, ways of further deregulating the small business sector as the most likely (perceived) way of generating a significant number of jobs (Hamilton Fazey 1985). This process has now cumulated in the publication of a Government White Paper on deregulation (HMSO 1985), which proposes the establishment of a central task force to scrutinize the impact of new and existing regulations on business. Finally, the 100% Industrial Buildings Allowance on capital expenditure by property developers has increased the supply of small industrial premises.

The evaluation of the impact of this expanding volume of assistance to the small firms sector has featured in two recently compiled research agendas as an important area which warrants detailed analysis by academics and policy-makers (Frank, Miall and Rees 1984; Mason and Harrison 1985). In fact, there are already a substantial number of studies, conducted both within and outside Government, which have attempted to evaluate the operation of a number of the measures recently introduced to assist the small firm sector. Prominent examples include reviews of the Small Firms Counselling Service (Howdle 1979, 1982, Research Associates Ltd 1981), the Small Business Loan Guarantee Scheme (Department of Industry, 1982a, Robson Rhodes 1983a, 1983b, 1984a, 1984b), the Small Workshops Scheme (Department of Industry 1982b), the Small Engineering Firms Investment Scheme (Research Associates Ltd 1984), the pilot version of the Enterprise Allowance Scheme (Department of Employment 1984) and the New Enterprise Programme (Morris and Watkins 1982; Dyson 1982; Johnson and Thomas 1983a, 1983b).

In many cases these studies have merely attempted to measure the direct outcome of the particular scheme under consideration. However, more sophisticated evaluations have also attempted to estimate their net benefits in order to provide a more detailed and realistic assessment of the effectiveness of the policy. This has involved deriving estimates of the displacement effect on unaided businesses by those businesses in receipt of assistance. It has also involved attempts to measure deadweight - the extent to which assistance has been made available to businesses or individuals to do what they would have done in any case - and its converse, additionality - the number of individuals starting their own business or existing firms expanding which would not have been able to do so in the absence of assistance. Indirect benefits, in the form of the additional economic activity which is created by the input demands of assisted businesses, have also been taken into account. Despite these efforts, however, it would be fair to say that the definitional and methodological problems involved in the assessment of such issues have yet to be adequately overcome.

One significant issue which has either been omitted or given only cursory attention in evaluations of national small firms policy is its spatial outcome. This is important because it has increasingly been argued that the capacity for small business development varies across the UK space-economy. The case has been put most forcefully by Storey (1982a), who has constructed an index of regional entrepreneurship based on measures of the plant-size structure, industry mix, occupational structure, educational attainment, wealth and market size of each region - all important factors that are associated with entrepreneurship. This index highlights the South East as the most favourable region for small business activity, followed some way behind by the South West and East Anglia. At the other extreme, the North, Wales, Northern Ireland and Yorkshire-Humberside emerge as the regions with the poorest potential for entrepreneurial activity. New firm formation rates derived from VAT registration statistics (Ganguly 1984, Whittington 1984), the Department of Trade and Industry's Record of Openings and Closures (Pounce 1981, Johnson 1983) and independently-constructed establishment databanks (Gould and Keeble 1984) each confirm the existence of spatial variations in business start-ups that are broadly in line with variations in regional entrepreneurial potential.

The implication of these differences among regions in both entrepreneurial potential and performance is that although the assistance to small firms is available on a national basis, take-up rates are likely to vary substantially among regions. Specifically, it seems probable that take-up rates will be highest in the South

227

East, South West and East Anglia, which are economically prosperous areas with already well-developed small firms sectors, and lowest in the depressed regions of northern Britain where small business activity is poorly developed. At a time when the small firm sector is regarded as the primary vehicle for economic recovery, the existence of such variations in take-up rates will serve to widen, rather than reduce, existing regional disparities in economic well-being in the United Kingdom. Our purpose in the remainder of this paper is therefore to examine the regional take-up rates of measures introduced since 1979 to assist the small firms sector in the UK to assess the extent to which this anticipated variation is in evidence.

Spatial Outcomes Of Small Firms Measures: Four Case Studies

In the introduction we identified four main groups of measures to support and develop the small firms sector in the UK (financial assistance, information and advice, deregulation and the provision of premises). However, in view of the large number of specific schemes that have been introduced in recent years to assist the small firms sector in the UK, our examination of the regional outcome of this policy must inevitably be selective. For the purposes of this paper we have been able to obtain from the relevant Government departments regionally-disaggregated data on the take-up of assistance under the Loan Guarantee Scheme (LGS), the Business Expansion Scheme (BES), the Small Engineering Firms Investment Scheme (SEFIS) and the Enterprise Allowance Scheme (EAS). The study is therefore restricted to an examination of regional variations in the take-up of schemes of financial support for the small business sector and does not consider regional differences in the usage of small firms advisory services and business training facilities which are equally significant elements in the overall 'package' of support for small firms. Nor do we examine the regional impact (if any) of deregulation and the provision of small industrial premises. However, the four schemes examined here are particularly important for three reasons. First, the existence of the 'finance gap' - the general unavailability of adequate financing for small firms - has been identified in the past as a constraint on the development of the sector in the UK. Second, these four measures have been given a particularly high profile by the Government and are the subject of considerable debate within the small firms community and in the financial press. Third, these schemes have been responsible for channelling a considerable amount of finance from both the public and private sectors into the UK small firms sector. We estimate that some £1.0 to £1.5 bn has been invested in small firms over the last three years as a result of these four measures (including the full value of investments made under SEFIS and the BES, but not adjusting for deadweight and non-additionality).

For each scheme in turn we briefly outline its objectives, development and national impact and then proceed to examine in more detail the regional distribution of its recipients. Because the available data are compiled only as absolute values - giving the numbers of firms assisted and the volume of expenditure in each region - it has been necessary for the purposes of regional comparison to derive for each scheme an indication of the relative take-up in each region. This is achieved by relating the actual take-up in each region, expressed as a proportion of the UK total, to an 'expected' share based on the best approximation of the regional distribution of each scheme's target clientele.

The Small Firm Loan Guarantee Scheme

The promotion of the small firm sector in the United Kingdom has always been linked with their finance. Over the last 50 years a number of official reports (Macmillan 1931; Radcliffe 1960; Bolton 1971; and Wilson 1979) have identified a gap in the market for funds for small businesses. Primarily, concern was expressed about the absence or low take-up of equity finance for small businesses. However, partly in the light of the experience of the Small Business Administration in the United States, the concept of a Loan Guarantee Scheme was raised in the Wilson Report (HMSO 1979) on the financing of small businesses as a potentially cost-effective means of increasing bank lending to small firms with viable projects but lacking proven track records or sufficient personal security. The scheme was also viewed as being a second-best alternative to improving the source of equity capital finance available to small firms.

The Loan Guarantee Scheme (LGS) was introduced for an experimental three year period in England, Scotland and Wales in June 1981 following negotiations and discussions with the banks prior to the 1981 Budget. However, the operation of the scheme by the Northern Ireland clearing banks only commenced on 1 April 1982, ten months after its introduction in the rest of the United Kingdom. According to evidence given by the banks to the Northern Ireland Assembly (Northern Ireland Assembly 1984) there were two reasons for this delay. First, the LGS was offered to the Northern Ireland banks a considerable time after it had been offered to the banks in Great Britain. Second, when the Scheme was finally offered to the banks in Northern Ireland it was on different terms to those offered to the other banks and they had to spend some nine months negotiating with the Government in order to get terms which were reasonably similar to those available elsewhere. Because of this, as will become clear below, the take-up of the LGS in Northern Ireland was very low in the first year.

The original LGS was introduced as a selective measure, available under section 8 of the 1972 Industry Act (now replaced by the 1982 Industrial Development Act). Although specific guidelines for the Scheme were not set out by the Department of Trade and Industry, and there were no formal criteria for eligibility, the purpose of the Scheme has since been defined as the provision of finance to new or existing small businesses in any sector which appear to be soundly based and to have a fair chance of success but which cannot raise funds from a conventional source. Government guarantees under LGS are not intended to replace existing security or provide additional support for lendings which may be at risk. They are only for new or additional lendings which are considered by the bank to be unacceptable because of high gearing and the lack of adequate security.

Under the original experimental scheme the Government undertook to guarantee 80 per cent of medium to long-term loans (2 to 7 years) up to a maximum of £75,000. For this they levied a premium of 3 per cent per annum on the guaranteed portion of the loan, in addition to the interest charged by the lender, to cover anticipated losses due to the failure of businesses participating in the Scheme. It was intended that the LGS should be self-financing, with premium income covering any claims

made due to business failures. Between 1 June 1981
and 31 May 1984 the Department issued 15,253 loan
guarantees in respect of £501.3 million of bank
lending: this represents about 4 per cent of total
bank lending to small businesses (Robson Rhodes
1984a, 38). Just over half of the guarantees issued
went to new businesses, and around 43 per cent went
to manufacturing businesses. The average loan value
of £32,900 was less than half the maximum permitted
under the scheme and, as one would expect, was
higher in manufacturing businesses, which accounted
for 49 per cent of total bank lending under the
scheme, than in retailing and the service sector.

Two of the most important criteria for
evaluating the overall national impact of the LGS
are, first, the additionality of the bank lending
which is guaranteed, and, second, the viability of
the business supported under the scheme. Both of
these have been subject to comment by consultants
appointed to review the operation of LGS (Robson
Rhodes 1984a). Despite the Government's intentions
it appears that only about half the loans made have
been genuinely additional - that is, where in the
absence of the scheme borrowers would not have been
able to raise finance from elsewhere on any terms.
This compounds the problem caused by the extreme
financial precariousness of many of the firms
benefiting under the scheme, which is reflected in
high failure rates. By the time the consultants
prepared their report up to one in three of
guarantees issued had been drawn on and the failure
rate for the first cohort of loan guarantees has
now risen to 40 per cent.

Because of this the Government extended the
scheme for a further six months in June 1984 under
revised terms. Under this amended scheme only 70
per cent of a LGS loan would be guaranteed by the
Department and the borrower would have to pay an
annual premium of 5 per cent (3.5 per cent above
bank interest rates) compared with 3 per cent (2.4
per cent above bank rates) under the old scheme.
From December 1984 a further £50m has been made
available to extend the scheme for another 12
months. However, in addition to paying a higher
premium, applicants with personal assets (including
their own homes) who were unwilling to provide
security for a commercial loan would not be
eligible under the scheme. Furthermore, reflecting
the recommendations of the Robson Rhodes (1984a)
report, all potential borrowers will in future face
much stricter vetting and monitoring of their

financial progress to reduce the number of failures under the scheme.

The regional distribution of loan guarantees under the LGS is shown in Table 1. As one would expect, the South East/East Anglia region dominates, with 38 per cent of guarantees issued and 41.7 per cent of loans by value. While this position has changed little since the scheme's inception, there has been a progressive fall in the proportion of loans issued in the North West, East and West Midlands, and Wales, and a recent rise in the share accounted for by Scotland, Yorkshire and Humberside and Northern Ireland. In their 1983 report on the LGS, Robson Rhodes (1983b) suggested that there was a significant North-South division in the pattern of lending under the scheme, with the peripheral regions of the United Kingdom losing out to the South East. Similarly, Storey (1982b) and Whittington (1984) have suggested that the regional distribution of scheme loans in 1981 closely followed that expected on the basis of Storey's index of regional entrepreneurship, and have concluded that this demonstrated a marked regional bias in the take-up of small firms incentives.

From the most recent evidence available, however, there does not appear to be any clear cut regional division: the location quotients in Table 1 indicate that regions with more than their 'fair share' of scheme loan guarantees (in descending order) were the North West, Northern, South East and Yorkshire and Humberside regions. Take-up in the Midlands (East and West) and South West was only slightly lower than expected on the basis of their share of the national stock of businesses registered for VAT purposes in 1983. Scotland and Wales, however, obtained less than their 'fair share' of loans, while the very low take-up in Northern Ireland is, at least in part, a function of the administrative delay in introducing the scheme which we referred to above.

Turning to failure rates under the scheme, it is clear from unpublished DTI data which relates notified claims to the month of loan sanction that national failure rates for the earlier cohorts have risen to very high levels. By 13 November 1984, 44 per cent of guarantees issued in the period June to September 1981 had been called upon, and over one-third of all guarantees issued up to June 1982 had been claimed against. This may reflect the fact that there was a great deal of uncertainty about

Table 1: Loan Guarantee Scheme (original version): regional distribution of guarantees issued and loans guaranteed.

Region	Guarantees Issued No	%	Value of Loans £m	%	Average Loan £000	Location Quotient* No	Value
South East & East Anglia	5,790	38.0	209.2	41.7	36.1	1.04	1.14
South West	1,364	8.9	42.6	8.5	31.2	0.95	0.91
West Midlands	1,327	8.7	42.3	8.4	31.9	1.00	0.97
East Midlands	964	6.3	32.2	6.4	33.4	0.93	0.95
Yorkshire & Humberside	1,213	8.0	34.7	6.9	28.6	1.02	0.88
North West	2,004	13.1	61.8	12.3	30.8	1.36	1.28
Northern	649	4.3	19.8	3.9	30.5	1.06	0.96
Wales	700	4.6	21.1	4.2	30.1	0.85	0.78
Scotland	1,076	7.1	31.3	6.2	29.1	0.95	0.83
Northern Ireland	166	1.1	6.5	1.3	39.2	0.32	0.38
United Kingdom	15,253	100.0	501.5	100.0	32.9	-	-

* Location Quotient =

Regional share of number of loans (or value of loans)
Regional Share of UK stock of VAT registered businesses
Source: Department of Trade and Industry

the operation of the scheme in its early stages; as the banks' knowledge and experience of what is in many ways venture capital (high risk) rather than conventional bank lending has grown so has their ability to weed out marginal applicants at the outset. The Robson Rhodes (1984a, 141) report does suggest that there has been an improvement in the average life of loans, and hence in failure rates, in more recent cohorts and they tentatively conclude that failure rates on current loans may not reach the heights reached on earlier loans quite so quickly. The consultants also note that failure rates are highest in the second six months of a loan's life.

Regional failure rates for the original LGS up to 13 November 1984 are shown in Table 2. Although there have been some variations over time, the ranking of regions by failure rates now appears to be well established. Failure rates in the North West (which has the highest take-up of loans) and Wales (with the lowest take-up rate apart from Northern Ireland) have consistently been higher

United Kingdom

Table 2: Regional Failure Rates Under the Loan
Guarantee Scheme (original version) up to
13 November 1984

Region	LGS failure rate by date of loan (%)*				Average stop rate (%)**
	1.6.81/ 31.3.82	1.4.82/ 31.3.83	1.4.83/ 31.3.84	1.6.81/ 31.3.84	
South East & East Anglia	38.8	27.0	9.3	21.9	10.7
South West	35.3	26.8	6.6	21.2	8.3
West Midlands	33.9	27.3	9.2	22.1	9.4
East Midlands	38.1	27.0	7.5	22.1	8.9
Yorkshire & Humberside	35.7	19.1	9.5	17.9	9.3
North West	41.3	32.0	11.7	26.5	10.4
North	34.0	30.1	10.6	21.5	8.9
Wales	38.4	35.4	10.5	28.9	7.4
Scotland	37.9	22.6	9.5	18.4	8.2
N. Ireland	50.0	22.2	7.8	14.3	4.8
UK	37.8	27.4	9.3	22.1	

* Number of claims made up to 13 November 1984 as a % of
number of loans sanctioned during the period.
** Average stop rate 1981-1983 as a % of annual regional stock
of VAT registered businesses (Ganguly, 1984).
Source: Department of Trade and Industry

than in other regions, while Scotland, Yorkshire
and Humberside and, to a much lesser extent, the
East and West Midlands, have experienced the lowest
failure rates. Although included in the analysis,
the figures for Northern Ireland must be treated
with great caution for two reasons. First, for
reasons discussed above the bulk of Northern
Ireland loans are concentrated in later cohorts
which will lead to a downward bias in overall
failure rates. Second, the actual number of loans
in Northern Ireland in many of the early cohorts is
so small that the failure rates may be subject to
large random fluctuations. For example, one
additional failure in Northern Ireland of a
guarantee issued in the period 1 June 1981 to 31
March 1982 would increase the failure rate by 10
percentage points. When compared with failure rates
calculated from VAT registration data between 1981
and 1983 (Ganguly 1984) it appears that these
regional LGS failure rates largely follow the same
pattern (Table 2). There are, however, two major

exceptions. In Wales the LGS failure rate (rank 1) is much higher than would be expected from the overall failure rates for VAT registered businesses, which is the second lowest in the United Kingdom. In Yorkshire and Humberside, on the other hand, the very low LGS failure rate does not reflect the relatively high overall failure rate.

The Business Expansion Scheme

The Business Expansion Scheme (BES) was introduced in 1983 as successor to the more restricted Business Start-up Scheme which was established two years earlier. It is aimed at overcoming the problems encountered by new and established small businesses in attracting venture capital on account of their lack of a track record and consequent higher risk. The objective of the scheme is to increase the flow of equity capital into small firms by offering substantial tax breaks to investors. Under the BES, private individuals can claim tax relief at their top rate on investments in new equity of unquoted UK companies up to a maximum investment of £40,000 per year. Such investments can be made both directly in companies by individual taxpayers and also indirectly through specialist BES investment funds which can both provide expertise in choosing and managing investments and, by investing in a portfolio of small companies, spread the risk of failure and loss of the invested capital. Most of the leading financial institutions in the UK have established such funds, but in addition some regional specialist funds have been set up to invest in small companies in a particular geographical area. For example, the Mercia Venture Capital Fund is restricting its operations to the Midlands, while the Solent Business Fund is intended to be limited to South Hampshire.

The Inland Revenue scrutinizes the investments to ensure that they are within the rules of the scheme. In brief, the investor must be a UK resident and must not be 'closely connected' with the company in order to qualify for tax relief. Broadly, this means that an individual must not (together with any associate) own more than 30 per cent of the company, taking into account the BES investment, and is neither an employee, partner nor a paid director in the company. The relief is granted for investments in new, genuinely additional and full-risk ordinary share capital and the investor must retain his shares for at least five years. Trades which do not qualify under the scheme include: dealing in land, shares or commodities; leasing and letting assets on hire; banking, insurance and other financial services; and, since the 1984 Finance Act, farming. Qualifying companies must carry on their trade wholly or mainly in the UK. Property companies were also excluded from the BES in the 1985 Finance Act, which also extended eligibility for the first time to R&D companies.

An Inland Revenue analysis of the operation of the BES during 1983-84 (Inland Revenue 1984) estimated that investments under the scheme have amounted to about £80m (see The Treasury, 1984 for a summary). To put this figure in perspective, the Industrial and Commercial Finance Corporation (ICFC), the UK's major provider of medium and long term loan and equity finance for owner-managed small businesses, invested less than £30m during the preceeding year (Dickson 1983). Taking into account the tax relief which has been granted to investors (an average of 50 per cent), the overall 'cost' of the scheme to the Exchequer in 1983-84 is likely to have been in the order of £40m. The Inland Revenue statistics exclude at least 100 companies which raised money directly, for which information is not yet available. Details are available on 312 companies which raised a total of £73m under the scheme. Two-thirds of them were start-up (i.e. less than five years old), attracting 57 per cent of the total investment funds. 'Genuine' start-ups - companies under a year old - comprised 46 per cent of the total and received £30m in investments, a 41 per cent share. The median investment made in a company was around £100,000; however, the typical investment by a specialist BES fund was £160,000 whereas the median value of direct investments (typically involving more than one investor) in any firm was £40,000.

The majority of those companies which had raised investment under the scheme were small. In terms of turnover, 42 per cent had either not yet traded or had only nominal amounts of turnover, while 18 per cent of the companies that were trading had an annual turnover of less than £100,000. However, a further 30 per cent had turnover in excess of £1m. Measured by the size of their workforce, 62 per cent had less than 25 employees and just 6 per cent had over 100 employees. There was considerable diversity in the

trades of the companies invested in: 41 per cent
were in the manufacturing sector, accounting for 35
per cent of the total investment under the scheme;
27 per cent of companies were in services;
attracting 18 per cent of the investment capital;
and 17 per cent were in wholesale and retail
distribution, with a 12 per cent share of the total
investments.

The regional distribution of companies raising
investment finance under the BES scheme, where
their locations are known to the Inland Revenue (a
total of 262 companies), and the amount of
investment finance raised by companies in each
region is presented in Table 3. It is clear from
this information that in absolute terms the South
East region has been the major beneficiary with 42
per cent of the companies raising investments and
36 per cent of the total investment. East Anglia
attracted a further 24 per cent of the total amount
of investment under the scheme although it
contained only 5 per cent of the companies invested
in. The South West contained the second largest
share of companies, with 10 per cent of the total,
followed by Scotland (9 per cent) and the East and
West Midlands (both 8 per cent). In contrast,
peripheral regions with the exception of Scotland
contain only a small proportion of the companies
which have raised finance under the BES, the lowest
shares being in the Northern Region (1.5 per cent)
and Northern Ireland (0.4 per cent). Moreover,
except for Wales and Yorkshire-Humberside, the
average amount of investment finance raised by
companies in the peripheral regions has been below
the national average. Consequently the proportion
of total investment going to these regions has been
even smaller. BES investments in start-up companies
was concentrated to an even greater extent in the
South East, with 43 per cent of such investments by
company and 47 per cent by value, although the
overall regional ranking was similar to that for
all BES companies.

Assessing the extent to which this uneven
regional outcome of the BES is genuine rather than
simply a reflection of the underlying regional
shares in economic activity is somewhat
problematical: it is impossible to calculate rates
of take-up under the scheme because the size of the
potential clientele cannot be identified, in part
because the scheme lacks clear parameters which
could identify the number of eligible companies
(e.g. in terms of their maximum size or industries)

United Kingdom

Table 3: The Business Expansion Scheme: regional
distribution of assisted companies and
invested capital

Region	Companies No.	%	amount £m	%	average invest. £000	location quotient* companies	finance
South East	109	41.6	23.3	36.3	213.8	1.28	1.11
East Anglia	12	4.6	15.2	23.7	1266.7	1.15	5.93
South West	26	9.9	3.9	6.1	150.0	1.05	0.65
West Midlands	22	8.4	5.2	8.1	236.4	0.97	0.93
East Midlands	22	8.4	3.2	5.0	145.5	1.24	0.74
Yorkshire-Humberside	15	5.7	3.6	5.6	240.0	0.72	0.71
North West	18	6.9	3.0	4.7	166.7	0.72	0.49
North	4	1.5	0.2	0.3	50.0	0.37	0.07
Wales	10	3.8	3.3	5.1	330.0	0.70	0.94
Scotland	23	8.8	3.2	5.0	139.1	1.17	0.67
N. Ireland	1	0.4	0.1	0.2	100.0	0.12	0.06
unallocated	(50)	–	(8.8)	–	–	–	–
UK	312		73.0		234.0		

* Location Quotient =

$$\frac{\text{regional share of BES companies or amount of investment}}{\text{regional share of UK stock of VAT-registered businesses}}$$

Source: Inland Revenue (1984) Table 7

but also because newly formed as well as
established businesses qualify. So, in the absence
of any more suitable alternative measure, data on
each region's share of the total stock of VAT-
registered businesses in 1983 is used (Ganguly
1984) to provide the 'expected' regional shares
against which the actual regional distribution of
BES investment can be assessed. This comparison, in
the form of a location quotient (Table 3),
highlights three southern regions - the South East,
East Midlands and the East Anglia - plus Scotland
as containing disproportionately large relative
shares of companies raising investment finance
under BES, although only East Anglia and to a
lesser extent the South East had more than their
'fair share' of the total amount of investment
under the scheme. At the other extreme, the
regional allocation of BES investments is
significantly under-represented in Northern Ireland
and the Northern Region and also, but to a lesser
extent, in Yorkshire-Humberside and the North West.
It would seem plausible to suggest that one of the

more significant factors which has contributed to this uneven distribution of investments is the spatial concentration of the banking and finance sectors in the South East Region and, to a lesser extent, in Scotland.

Small Engineering Firms Investment Scheme

The Small Engineering Firms Investment Scheme (SEFIS) was established following the 1982 Budget to assist small firms in the engineering industry to undertake investment in certain types of advanced capital equipment, notably numerically controlled and computer numerically controlled machine tools, but also non-robotic welding machinery, physio-chemical machine tools, metal working machine tools incorporating lasers or plasma, and metrology equipment. The underlying objective was to strengthen the innovative capacity of small engineering firms by helping them to introduce new products and production techniques, and to secure improvements in their productivity and reliability. The scheme, which operated on a selective basis, offered a capital grant of one-third of the cost of one project up to a maximum project cost of £200,000. Companies operating in Division 3 of the 1980 Standard Industrial Classification (Metal Goods, Engineering and Vehicle Industries) and employing not more than 200 full-time staff were eligible to apply under the scheme. Moreover, the scheme was unusual in having an implicit regional bias in the sense that companies receiving a SEFIS grant and located in an Assisted Area could also qualify for Regional Development and European Community grants. In these cases the SEFIS grant was determined as one-third of the cost of the project net of Regional Development Grant (RDG). In Special Development Areas, where the RDG was 22 per cent (until the recent revisions to regional policy) the total subsidy available came to 48 per cent; in Northern Ireland, where the automatic capital grant was then available at 30 per cent, the total subsidy available under SEFIS was equivalent to 53 per cent of project costs.

The Government allocated £30m to the scheme (although it was initially intended to have a £20m limit) but its popularity was such that this amount was used up in less than two months. A second version of the scheme - SEFIS II - was therefore

introduced in the 1983 Budget with an allocation of
£100m. It was open to all small firms instead of
being restricted to Division 3 of the SIC as
previously, the maximum firm size was raised to 500
employees and all businesses, including
subsidiaries of foreign firms, were eligible.
However, the level of demand was much lower than
for SEFIS I and the available funding had not been
fully allocated by its closing date in September
1984, a situation which has been widely ascribed to
the depressed condition of the UK engineering
industry. Many companies simply did not have
sufficient orders to justify the extra financial
commitment involved in a major high technology
re-equipment programme.

An evaluation of the original scheme by
Research Associates Ltd (1984) on behalf of the
Department of Trade and Industry concluded that
SEFIS I had clearly met its original objective of
stimulating investment by small engineering firms
in advanced capital equipment. Moreover, the scheme
has had a favourable aggregate impact on the firms
that benefited, with the creation of 1,279 new jobs
and the saving of 1,520 jobs, an increase in annual
output of £77m and in profits of £5m. However, only
about 66 per cent of SEFIS I recipients made
genuinely 'additional' investments in new
machinery; the remainder would have made
investments even in the absence of the grant,
although in some cases by purchasing smaller or
less sophisticated machines. When fully discounted
for this additionality element, SEFIS I was
estimated to have created 512 new jobs and saved
172 existing jobs amongst recipient firms and
increased their annual output by £31m and their
annual profits by £2m. But because 75 per cent of
SEFIS recipients were sub-contract engineering
firms serving what is a finite market, it is highly
probable that their extra business and jobs have
been gained at the expense of competitors, thus
resulting in a substantial displacement effect.
Favourable indirect impacts of SEFIS I include
'imitation effects' whereby other small engineering
firms have been encouraged to invest in advanced
machinery in order to remain competitive, and
'knock on' effects on the customers of SEFIS firms
in the form of faster delivery, improved quality
and price reductions which might be expected to
enhance their competitiveness. In addition, UK
manufacturers supplied 59 per cent of the machines
purchased under SEFIS I, providing a welcome boost

to the machine tool industry.

The regional distribution of firms in receipt of SEFIS I grants shows a marked concentration in the South East Region which contained 36 per cent of the total, but because the average size of grant in the region was below the national figure, its share of total funding was somewhat lower at 32 per cent. The West Midlands, in second place, contained 18 per cent of SEFIS recipients and received a similar proportion of total funding (Table 4). Of course, as in the case of the other schemes discussed in this paper, the regional shares of recipients and funding under the SEFIS scheme are not particularly meaningful on their own and require to be related to the proportion of potential SEFIS applicants in each region in order to derive an indication of spatial variations in take-up rates. However, because of the way in which the data in the Annual Census of Production is disaggregated by size of firm, the only measure available refers to the regional distribution of manufacturing units with less than 100 employees and operating in Division 3 of the 1980 Standard Industrial Classification. Although, as noted above, SEFIS I was open to firms with up to 200 employees, 93% of recipients had less than 100 employees (Research Associates Ltd, 1984), hence the use of this measure as an indicator of 'expected' regional shares should not be misleading.

Comparing the regional shares of SEFIS recipients and funds with the distribution of engineering firms with less than 100 employees in the form of a location quotient (Table 4) highlights Northern Ireland and the South West as regions with 'excessive' shares under SEFIS, although the position of Northern Ireland is likely to have been exaggerated by the large number of 'missing values' in the Annual Census of Production tables to preserve the confidentiality of individual companies. The South East Region also has more than its 'fair share' of SEFIS recipients. At the other extreme, Wales, the North West, Yorkshire-Humberside and, to a lesser extent, Scotland are under-represented in terms of both their proportions of SEFIS recipients and shares of SEFIS funds. The West Midlands, which the scheme was implicitly designed to help the most (as the core of the UK engineering industry) obtained more or less its 'fair share' of SEFIS grants, a less favourable outcome than might have been anticipated.

241

United Kingdom

Table 4: Regional Distribution of Companies Receiving Grants Under the Small Engineering Firms Investment Scheme (SEFIS) (payments made in the period 1st July 1982 to 30th September 1984).

Region	No of firms	Assistance £000	Average grant (£)	Location quotients* no of firms	amount
South East/ East Anglia	374	6754.5	18,060	1.13	1.02
South West	114	2363.6	20,733	1.82	1.88
East Midlands	67	1456.3	21,736	0.90	0.97
West Midlands	193	3882.5	20,117	0.97	0.98
North West	94	2036.0	21,659	0.78	0.84
Yorksh.-Humber.	75	1668.4	22,245	0.73	0.82
North	40	907.1	22,678	0.97	1.10
Wales	26	465.6	17,908	0.68	0.68
Scotland	47	1004.6	21,374	0.83	0.89
North. Ireland	20	428.9	21,445	2.11	2.22
United Kingdom	1050	20,967.5	19,970		

* Location quotient is calculated as the regional share of firms receiving SEFIS grant/amount of grant, divided by regional share of manufacturing units with less than 100 employees and operating in Division 3 of the 1980 Standard Industrial Classification (1983 Annual Census of Production, PA 1003).
Source: British Business (various issues)

The Enterprise Allowance Scheme

The objective of the Enterprise Allowance Scheme (EAS) is to encourage unemployed people to set up in business for themselves or to become self-employed. It is widely believed that one of the biggest disincentives faced by unemployed people wanting to set up their own business is the loss of a guaranteed income from unemployment or supplementary benefit as soon as they start trading whereas the receipts in the early stages of a new business are likely to be uncertain, low and fluctuating. Under the scheme a flat rate, taxable allowance of £40 per week for 52 weeks is paid to people qualifying under the scheme in order to supplement their business receipts while it is becoming established. In effect, therefore the EAS provides participants with an independent source of working capital. In addition, information and guidance is provided to all who join the scheme by the Department of Trade and Industry's Small Firms Service.

Entry into the scheme is strictly controlled by the Manpower Services Commission. Only people unemployed or under a formal redundancy notice for at least 13 weeks can apply, and if jobless they must be in receipt of unemployment or supplementary benefit. In addition, the applicant must be willing to work full-time in the business, have at least £1000 to invest in it (or a bank loan or overdraft for that amount), and be over 18 and under pensionable age. The business itself must be new, independent and employing less than 20 people in its first three months.

The EAS began on a pilot basis in February 1982 in five areas - Medway, North East Lancashire, Coventry, North Ayrshire and Wrexham/Shotton - and started as a national scheme in August 1st 1983. Initially, the budget allocated to the national scheme was sufficient for 600 people to join per week. Hoewever, the demand for places has considerably exceeded the supply and in order to reduce the long waiting lists the Government in mid-1984 increased the funding to allow 1000 entrants per week. In November 1984 the Government announced a further increase of £325m to the budget, allowing the weekly intake to be raised to 1250 entrants, with effect from the next fiscal year. From August 1st 1983 - when the scheme started on a national basis - until the end of November 1984 nearly 60,000 people had received, or were currently in receipt of, an Enterprise Allowance.

Under the pilot scheme a total of 3,331 people set up in business. A study based on a 20 per cent sample of participants in the pilot areas noted that 90 per cent were male and over 35 per cent of those in receipt of an allowance were under 35 years of age. One-quarter of participants had been unemployed for over 12 months and, not surprisingly, the biggest single reason given for joining the scheme was the failure to find a job, although this accounted for under one-third of the total number of participants. Three-quarters of the businesses established were in the service sector - notably construction (especially repairs), retailing, and garage repairs, all activities where barriers to entry (skill and capital) are low - whereas only 13 per cent of businesses were in manufacturing, despite the fact that over 40 per cent of participants were previously employed in this sector. The job creation generated under the scheme was estimated at 50 additional employees per 100 businesses after nine months, but as 75 per cent of businesses had no employees it is clear that a relatively small number of firms have generated a substantial proportion of the extra jobs (Department of Employment 1984).

In addition, the survey estimated that the deadweight in the pilot scheme was around 50 per cent; in other words, for every 100 businesses formed under the scheme only around 50 did so only because the EAS was available. Moreover, deadweight businesses were on average larger in employment terms than non-deadweight ones. However, a follow-up survey of EAS participants after they had left the scheme concluded that the allowance had made a significant contribution to the survival of both types of firm during the vulnerable first year of trading. Indeed, 80 per cent of businesses were still in existence six months after leaving the scheme. Overall, the pilot version of the scheme is estimated in its first year to have involved a net cost to the Exchequer of £2,690 per person taken off the unemployment count. Moreover, under EAS there is no additional public expenditure after twelve months but if a firm continues to trade after this period there are continuing Exchequer savings from lower unemployment and higher taxation receipts, thereby reducing significantly the longer term net costs, perhaps to £650 per person removed from the unemployment register over two years (Department of Employment 1984).

Take-up rates under the pilot scheme displayed considerable variations between the areas, with North East Lancashire having the highest levels of participation when weighted by unemployment while lowest rates were in Coventry and Medway (Mason and Harrison 1985). The national scheme has also experienced differential take-up rates at the regional scale (Table 5), although the pattern is more complex than a simple distinction between northern and southern regions. Indeed, it is the North West which has the highest unemployment-weighted take-up rate when measured both in terms of the cumulative number of EAS participants and number of participants at November 1984, followed by the South West and Wales, another 'peripheral' region. The Midlands (both East and West) and the Southern area (East Anglia and the South East Standard Regions, excluding Greater London) also

United Kingdom

Table 5: Enterprise Allowance Scheme: regional take-up rates.

region	no of EAS particip. (cumul. total*)	cumulative particip. rate per 1000 unemployed**	no of EAS particip. November 1984	particip. rate/1000 unemployed***
London	5545	15.4	3744	9.9
Southern	9067	22.1	5983	13.6
South West	4740	27.1	3148	15.9
Midlands	10446	20.7	6757	14.7
North West	11484	27.9	7667	17.9
Yorkshire-Humberside	5454	20.3	3624	12.7
Northern	3301	15.3	2144	9.4
Wales	3821	24.3	2505	14.6
Scotland	4748	15.1	3152	9.7
N. Ireland	1900	16.4	1403	11.9
UK	60506	20.4	40127	13.0

*   1 August 1983 to 30 November 1984
**   excluding school-leavers, unemployment at June 1984
*** excluding school-leavers, unemployment at November 1984
Source: Manpower Services Commission; NI Dept. of Economic
        Development

had take-up rates above the national average. However, lowest take-up rates are typically found in certain peripheral regions, namely the North, Scotland, and Northern Ireland, but also in Greater London.

One possible explanation for the lack of a clear-cut distinction in the take-up rate of the EAS between the southern regions and the remainder of the country is that participation under the scheme is allocated according to regional quotas which reflect differences in 'need'. Hence the total number of places available has been divided amongst the regions on the basis of the numbers of long-term unemployed, although subsequently this has been modified to take account of the differing level of demand in each region (MSC, pers. comm.). It may therefore be that the take-up rate in southern regions is constrained by the quota of places available on the scheme, which in turn might be reflected in longer waiting lists of EAS applicants than in peripheral regions. Indeed, this feature has been confirmed by the Financial Times (8th May 1984) in a report on the early operation of the national scheme, although data are not available for a detailed evaluation of the extent and persistence of such variations.

Discussion

We have been able to demonstrate on the basis of an examination of four nationally-available schemes to assist the small firm sector that take-up rates are not uniform across a regional system. Moreover, although not the central concern of the paper, it is possible that additionality and displacement will also differ between regions. Evidence on this point is extremely sparse even at a national scale, but the examination of SEFIS recipients by Research Associates Ltd (1984) does suggest that under this scheme the additionality element was greater in the northern and midland regions than in the south. The proportion of firms obtaining additional business as a result of installing advanced machinery with the aid of a SEFIS grant was also found to be higher in peripheral regions than in the south, which might in turn imply a similar regional variation in displacement effects. However, this study was based on a small sample size, consequently such conclusions derived from regional sub-samples must inevitably be highly tenuous.

The pattern of regional variations in take-up rates that has been identified here does not reflect the clear-cut south-north dichotomy that is suggested by Storey's (1982a) index of regional entrepreneurship. Indeed, only the BES has a regional distribution that approximates to this anticipated pattern, but even in this scheme Scotland has a greater proportion of BES-funded companies than is 'expected' on the basis of its share of the total stock of UK business activity. Certainly, it is a consistent feature of all the schemes examined in this study that the South East and East Anglia have more recipients and a greater share of the funds than is 'expected' on the basis of their proportion of eligible applicants in each scheme, while the South West contains more than its 'fair share' of EAS and SEFIS participants. In addition, three peripheral regions, namely Wales, Yorkshire-Humberside and Scotland, have fairly consistently displayed low take-up rates under the schemes examined here. However, there are some other peripheral regions with take-up rates under particular schemes that are greater than 'expected' on the basis of their share of potential recipients, notably in the case of the LGS, although there is no peripheral region that has consistently received more than its 'fair share' under each of the schemes examined. Indeed, some peripheral regions have experienced widely contrasting performances under different schemes. For example, Northern Ireland - the region with the largest relative shares of SEFIS recipients and funding - also has the lowest relative share of any region under both the LGS and the BES. Similarly, the North West has the highest take-up rate under both the LGS and EAS but has considerably less than its 'fair share' of SEFIS grants and BES investments, while the North has more than its 'fair share' of loan guarantees and SEFIS grants but fewer than 'expected' EAS participants and BES investments.

Regional differences in entrepreneurial potential plus the associated differences in regional economic environments, notably the size and growth prospects of different regional markets, can help to interpret the broad contrast in take-up rates between the southern regions of the South East, East Anglia and the South West on the one hand and the remainder of the country on the other. However, the variability between regions, especially peripherally-located ones, in take-up rates under different schemes is to be explained by other factors.

Considering technical issues first of all, it is obvious that our conclusions are derived from the calculation of location quotients which are in turn determined by the data that are used to measure the 'expected' regional share under each scheme. As stressed on a number of occasions in this paper, because of both the eligibility criteria that apply to each scheme and the lack of suitably disaggregated data on the UK small business population it has been necessary to use very approximate measures of the eligible target population in each region. Different measures will therefore produce different 'expected' values. However, as experimentation with alternative measures results in relatively few changes in regional rankings based on location quotients, this factor can be dismissed as being of only minor significance.

More plausible is the suggestion that the awareness amongst small firm proprietors of government schemes of assistance, which is generally low throughout the UK (Economists

Advisory Group, 1983; Research Associates Ltd, 1984), may be greater in some regions than in others. This will occur if specific schemes are vigorously promoted only in certain areas, either by Government agencies or by interested private sector organizations such as the banks in the case of the LGS, venture capital firms in the case of BES, and machine tool suppliers in the case of SEFIS. For example, according to the survey of SEFIS recipients more owner-managers (29 per cent) became aware of the scheme through machine tool suppliers than from any other source (Research Associates Ltd, 1984). Such a channel of information seems likely to hold great potential for spatial bias. The survey of SEFIS recipients also noted that industry trade associations in the South West and West Midlands had been particularly active in promoting the scheme to their member companies.

It may also be the case that in some regions the use of certain schemes is 'crowded out' by the activities of other organizations. For example, the more active involvement of Scottish banks in lending to small businesses than their English counterparts may have served to lessen the number of applications under the LGS in Scotland (Hood, 1984). The under-representation of both Scotland and Wales in the LGS and BES may also be related to the operation of the Scottish and Welsh Development Agencies which have made available alternative sources of loan and equity finance, often on very favourable conditions. Similarly, the low take-up rate of the LGS in Northern Ireland is likely to reflect not only the administrative delay in introducing the scheme, as noted earlier, but also the alternative availability of finance through the region's small firms agency, the Local Enterprise Development Unit (Hart 1984), which does not carry with it the cost penalty inherent in the LGS.

It is important that researchers in the fields of industrial geography and regional economics should examine in more detail these and other possible interpretations of regional variations in take-up rates under various schemes to assist the small firm sector. Specifically, how important are differences in the awareness, promotion and delivery of particular measures in producing variations in take-up rates? The extent to which the take-up rate is simply a reflection of the underlying dynamism (or lack of it) amongst the regional stock of small businesses similarly requires to be appraised. However, research which seeks to evaluate the spatial outcome of schemes to assist the small firm sector must move beyond a concern simply with take-up rates to consider such issues as additionality, displacement and failure rates which may, in fact, be of greater significance in determining the overall impact of such measures on the regional system.

Conclusion

Industry aid schemes which have been introduced in an attempt to enhance UK economic efficiency and competitiveness by making assistance available on a national basis have typically operated in a way which is counter to policies whose objective is to reduce regional economic disparities by encouraging industrial regeneration in depressed areas. For example, Cameron (1979) has noted that the Industrial Strategy of the Labour Government (1974-79), with its emphasis on encouraging key rapid-growth economic sectors, favoured the South East. The take-up rates of various innovation schemes similarly show a strong bias towards the South East (DTI, 1983). The consultancies licensed by the Department of Trade and Industry to provide advice to firms on micro-electronics applications under the MAPCON scheme are also heavily concentrated in the South East (Goddard, 1983). Small firms policy in the UK represents a further element in the strategic objectives of achieving 'a profitable, competitive and adaptive productive sector' (Frank et al, 1984). Support for this sector in the UK, as in other Western economies, is justified by the contribution that small businesses are believed to make to competition, innovation and job creation. The generally higher take-up of assistance by new and small businesses in southern regions of the UK is therefore yet another example of a lack of co-ordination between policies with the objective of promoting national economic growth and those attempting to reduce regional economic disparities.

Whether this situation is to be condoned or condemned will ultimately depend on personal value judgements concerning the relative weighting of regional economic problems vis-a-vis the national economic malaise. However, if the case is accepted for maintaining a regional policy under the particular economic conditions facing the UK economy, then some method of reconciling the apparently incompatible objectives of schemes to encourage greater industrial efficiency with those aiming to promote regional economic development is required. Indeed, this is all the more pressing in view of the recent Regional Policy review (HMSO 1983) which has reduced the size of the regional aid budget and therefore increased the relative amount of spending on industry aid schemes. Assisted areas are doubly disadvantaged by this change, firstly as a result of the reduction in the spending on direct regional assistance, and secondly, as shown in this paper, by their generally low take-up under industry aid schemes which prevents these areas from obtaining their 'fair share' of such expenditure.

An acceptable compromise might involve the creation of nationally-available industry-aid schemes in which the level of assistance varies according to regional 'need'. The EAS already incorporates this feature in the sense that the regional distribution of unemployment has been taken into account in determining the regional allocation of places available under the scheme. However, as we have shown, the regional variations in take-up rates fail to accurately match those of unemployment. An even more radical approach might therefore be required which restricts the availability of certain schemes only to depressed regions.

Support for such an approach is based primarily on a concern for regional equity. However, it can also be justified on economic and political grounds and thereby meet the present Government's concern to minimize its financial commitment to small firm policy while maximizing its effectiveness. This can be illustrated with reference to the LGS. As noted in our discussion of this scheme, the higher than expected failure rate amongst participating small businesses has meant that it has run at a substantial cost to the Exchequer instead of being self-financing as originally envisaged. The Government has attempted to reduce the public expenditure cost of the LGS by raising the premium that is charged and reducing the proportion of the loan that is guaranteed. Critics have claimed that by watering down the scheme in this way its effectiveness has been reduced; certainly, since the amended version of the LGS was introduced in June 1984 monthly applications have been running at half the previous rate. The view has also been expressed that this change signals the Government's declining commitment to supporting the small firm sector. Yet the objective of reducing the cost of the LGS could equally have been satisfied by restricting its operation to peripheral regions where its effectiveness would have been maintained. Indeed, given the lower average owner-occupancy levels, lower average house prices and lower average personal savings in peripheral regions which combine to make it more difficult for potential new firm founders to raise capital (Storey, 1982a; Lloyd and Mason, 1984) the need for such a scheme is likely to be particularly great, hence its overall effectiveness may even be enhanced by restricting its operation to peripheral areas. Certainly, the limited evidence available on the operation of SEFIS suggests that measure may have been more cost-effective in peripheral areas on account of the greater level of additionality and also because the grant stimulated a higher proportion of firms in such areas to invest in CNC machinery <u>for the first time</u> than in southern regions (Research Associates Ltd, 1984).

The general introduction of regionally-differentiated levels of assistance for small firms is likely to lead to a reduction in the efficiency of such schemes in promoting a thriving small firm sector nationally. However, as we have tentatively suggested, the incorporation of a regional dimension into such policies will not only strengthen the indigeneous sector in peripheral regions but will also reduce the total costs while enhancing overall cost-effectiveness. However, trade-offs involved in the introduction of a regional dimension to nationally-available schemes of assistance for small businesses are poorly understood and imprecisely elaborated. In view of this, it would seem reasonable to suggest that, alongside the conventional concerns about additionality and displacement, the Government should include in its terms of reference for future evaluations of the effectiveness of small firms measures a specific requirement that the impact in different regions is examined as a first step towards minimizing the inconsistencies and conflicts between national economic objectives and regional economic development.

United Kingdom

Acknowledgements

We gratefully acknowledge the assistance of officials in the Department of Trade and Industry, Inland Revenue, Manpower Services Commission and Northern Ireland Department of Economic Development who provided the data on which this paper is based. However, they are in no way associated with the interpretation of this data which is entirely our responsibility.

Appendix: Standard Regions of the United Kingdom

References

Beesley, M. and Wilson, P. (1982) 'Government aid to the small firm since Bolton' in J. Stanworth, A. Westrip, D. Watkins and J. Lewis (eds.), Perspectives on a Decade of Small Business Research, Gower, Aldershot, pp. 181-199

United Kingdom

Cameron, G.C. (1979) 'The national industrial
    strategy and regional policy' in D. Maclennan
    and J.B. Parr (eds.), Regional Policy: Past
    Experience and New Directions, Martin
    Robertson, Oxford, pp. 297-322
Dawkins, W. (1985) 'Small business aid shake-up',
    Financial Times, 13th March
Department of Employment (1984) 'Evaluation of the
    pilot Enterprise Allowance Scheme', Employment
    Gazette, 92, pp. 374-377
Department of Industry (1982a) Interim Assessment
    of the Small Business Loan Guarantee Scheme,
    London
Department of Industry (1982b) Small Workshops
    Scheme: Survey of The Effects of the 100%
    Industrial Building Allowance, London
Department of Trade and Industry (1983) Regional
    Industrial Policy: Some Economic Issues,
    London
Dickson, T. (1983) 'New investment scheme can boost
    unquoted companies', Financial Times, 20th
    September
Dickson, T. (1984) 'UK Government policy',
    Financial Times Survey: Small Businesses, 12th
    June
Dyson, J. (1982) 'The position of the New
    Enterprise Programmes in the process of
    start-up: an approach to matching founding
    programmes to different categories of business
    founder' in T. Webb, T. Quince and D. Watkins
    (eds.), Small Business Research, Gower,
    Aldershot, pp. 99-116
Economists Advisory Group (1983) The Small Firm
    Survivors, Shell UK Limited, London
Frank, C.E.J., Miall, R.H.C. and Rees, R.D. (1984)
    'Issues in small firms research of relevance
    to policy-making', Regional Studies, 18, pp.
    257-266
Ganguly, P. (1984) 'Business starts and stops:
    regional analysis by turnover size and sector
    1980-83', British Business, 2nd November, pp.
    350-353
Goddard, J.B. (1983) 'Industrial innovation and
    regional economic development in Great
    Britain', in F.E.I. Hamilton and G.J.R. Linge
    (eds.), Spatial Analysis, Industry and the
    Industrial Environment. Vol. 3: Regional
    Economies and Industrial Systems, Wiley,
    Chichester, pp. 255-277
Gould, A. and Keeble, D. (1984) 'New firms and
    rural industrialization in East Anglia',

Regional Studies, 18, 3, pp. 189-201

HMSO (1971) Report of the Committee of Inquiry on Small Firms (Chairman: J.E. Bolton), London, cmnd. 4811

HMSO (1979) The Financing of Small Firms: Interim Report of the Committee to Review the Functioning of the Financial Institutions (Chairman: Sir H. Wilson), London, cmnd. 7503

HMSO (1983) Regional Industrial Development, London, cmnd. 9111

HMSO (1985) Lifting the Burden, London

Hamilton Fazey, I. (1985) 'Dilemma on small business deregulation', *Financial Times*, 22nd February

Hart, M. (1984) 'Local agencies and small firm promotion: the case of Northern Ireland, 1971-1983', in B.M. Barr and N.M. Waters (eds.), Regional Diversification and Structural Change, Tantalus Research Ltd, Vancouver, pp. 276-295

Hood, N. (1984) 'The small firm sector', in N. Hood and S. Young (eds.), Industry, Policy and the Scottish Economy, Edinburgh University Press, Edinburgh, pp. 57-72

Howdle, J. (1979) An Evaluation of the Small Firms Counselling Service in the South West Region, Department of Industry, Bristol

Howdle, J. (1982) 'An evaluation of the small firms counselling service in the South West Region', in T. Webb, T. Quince and D. Watkins (eds.) Small Business Research, Gower, Aldershot, pp. 177-191

Inland Revenue (1984) Business expansion scheme: results for 1983-84, mimeo

Johnson, P.S. (1983) 'New manufacturing firms in the UK regions', Scottish Journal of Political Economy, 30, pp. 75-79

Johnson, P. and Thomas, B. (1983a) 'Training means (small) business: an economic evaluation of the New Enterprise Programme', *Employment Gazette*, 91, pp. 17-20

Johnson, P. and Thomas, B. (1983b) 'Entrepreneurial training and high fliers', paper presented to the National Small Firms Research Conference, University of Durham

Lloyd, P.E. and Mason, C.M. (1984) 'Spatial variations in new firm formation in the United Kingdom: comparative evidence from Merseyside, Greater Manchester and South Hampshire', Regional Studies, 18, 3, pp. 207-220

United Kingdom

Mason, C.M. and Harrison, R.T. (1985) 'The geography of small firms in the United Kingdom: towards a research agenda', Progress in Human Geography, 9, pp. 1-37

Morris, J. and Watkins, D. (1982) 'UK government support for entrepreneurship training and development', in T. Webb, T. Quince and D. Watkins (eds.), Small Business Research, Gower, Aldershot, pp. 85-98

Northern Ireland Assembly (1984) Economic Strategy: volume III, NIA 151-III, HMSO, Belfast

Pounce, R.J. (1981) Industrial Movement in the UK 1966-1975, HMSO, London

Research Associates Ltd (1981) The Value of the Counselling Activity of the Small Firms Service, Department of Industry, London

Research Associates Ltd in consortium with Inbucon Management Consultants Ltd (1984) Policy Study for the Department of Industry: the Small Engineering Firms Investment Scheme I, Research Associates Ltd, Stone: Staffs

Riddell, P. (1983) The Thatcher Government, Martin Robertson, Oxford

Robson Rhodes (1983a) An Analysis of Some Early Claims Under the Small Business Loan Guarantee Scheme, Department of Industry, London

Robson Rhodes (1983b) Small Business Loan Guarantee Scheme: Commentary on a Telephone Survey of Borrowers, Department of Industry, London

Robson Rhodes (1984a) A Study of Businesses Financed Under the Small Business Loan Guarantee Scheme, Department of Trade and Industry, London

Robson Rhodes (1984b) Commentary on a Telephone Survey of Borrowers Financed Under the Small Business Loan Guarantee Scheme, Department of Trade and Industry, London

Storey, D.J. (1982a) Entrepreneurship and the New Firm, Croom Helm, London

Storey, D.J. (1982b) 'Small firms and economic recovery', Northern Economic Review, 2, February, pp. 14-20

Treasury (1984) 'The Business Expansion Scheme', Economic Progress Report, 173, pp. 5-6

Whittington, R.C. (1984) 'Regional bias in new firm formation in the UK', Regional Studies, 18, 3, pp. 253-256

Chapter twelve

THE ECONOMIC IMPORTANCE OF SMALL AND MEDIUM-SIZED
FIRMS IN THE FEDERAL REPUBLIC OF GERMANY

Frans-Josef Bade

Introduction

In recent years small and medium-sized firms have
once again become the focus of political interest.
Some of the arguments for this increased interest
have been known for a long time. The fact that in
the Federal Republic of Germany (FRG) about 95% of
all firms are small and medium-sized was documented
seventy years ago (Passow 1915). Equally well-known
is the fact that in the FRG these firms employ
three-quarters of the total employed workforce and
account for nearly two-thirds of total sales (cf.
the official publications of the last Census 1961
and 1970 by the Federal Statistical Office).
        Instead, what is new about the increasing
political interest is the atmosphere in which these
reasonably well-known results are being discussed
once again. As recently as 1976 - at the IFO-
symposium about the "economic function of small and
medium firms" (IFO 1976) - a general scepticism
about the competitiveness of small and medium-sized
firms was prevalent. Although a few authors
discounted the thesis of the general inferiority of
small firms as 'folklore and economic myth' (Petry
1969/70, 18), most studies of small or new
businesses were somewhat defensive in character.
The general idea that large size is a condition
sine qua non for economic efficiency and
performance was too predominant. This view was
supported by prominent and influential economists
such as Schumpeter (1943), Galbraith (1956) and
Lilienthal (1952). In the West German case, Bombach
(1969) also emphasized the economic advantages of
large firms and was convinced of both the necessity
and the inevitability of the economic concentration

process. Impressed by the predominance of' the corporate system of economy Galbraith (1973) even believed that the market system as the residual component of an economy dominated by large corporations could only be preserved if the state protected small firms by subsidies, production quotas and price coordination. Without such means of guaranteeing a minimum entrepreneurial income, competition and the market segment in the economy would be eliminated in the long run.

Recent and current publications have however lost much of this defensive attitude (Aiginger and Tichy 1984). Instead, they argue that structural changes in economic demand and production in the last decade have basically shifted the balance of competitive advantage from large to small enterprise (Schätz 1984). An essential contribution to the change of atmosphere in German studies is the work of Birch (1979) and others in the USA (e.g. Armington and Odle 1982). Their findings suggest that in recent years small and young firms have been the winners in the process of structural economic change. According to Birch (1979, 1983) two-thirds of job increase in the USA has taken place in firms of less than 20 employees. Large enterprises, defined as firms of more than 500 employees, have contributed only 13% to the job increase, while their share in total employment was 45%.

This chapter considers whether a similar trend, of growth of new, small firms, has also occurred in the FRG. It is therefore primarily concerned with the available empirical evidence, its results and methodology, as well as theoretical aspects. As most information is available only on a national level, regional aspects of the growth of small and new firms are perforce discussed only briefly, at the end of the chapter.

Empirical Evidence For The Growth Of Small And Medium-Sized Firms

Results and methodological aspects

The most remarkable feature of the Birch study - apart from the results - is its data base. By using Dun and Bradstreet information employment figures relating to individual firms for different years are available. Thus, in principle individual growth processes could be followed up. Moreover the data base is said to contain information about more than 5 million firms which would imply a coverage of 80% of total firms in the USA and a highly representative sample. However, as will be noted shortly, some of the data recorded and, consequently, some of the results seem to be rather questionable (Schmenner 1982, Eckart et al. 1985).

For the FRG, cohort analyses based on representative samples of this scale do not exist. There are however four longitudinal studies which have recently investigated the size-influenced growth of firms in West Germany. These are by Friedrich and Spitznagel (1981), Fritsch (1984), Steinle (1984) and Hull (1984); cf. Table 1.

Briefly summarizing their results, all authors are more or less convinced that small firms performed relatively well during the 1970s in comparison to large firms; at least the thesis of the superiority of large firms is not proven by their results.

However, each of the four studies has methodological shortcomings which raise serious doubts over their interpretation of the findings. One critical issue, for example, is the representativeness of the data sets. For example, growth prospects for the leather or clothing industries are obviously not so favourable as they are for the electrical engineering or plastic industries or even consumer and producer services. If the sectoral structure of the sample deviates from the sector structure of the whole economy, and if these deviations are not taken into account, the conclusions are necessarily biased with regard to the economy as a whole.

Information about the degree of sample bias and representativeness is only given by Friedrich and Spitznagel and by Steinle. However, the former only indicate that the responding firms developed relatively well in respect to total manufacturing industry. And in the latter study the statement about the sample's representativeness is actually incorrect: in comparison to the whole economy the firms recorded in the Hoppenstedt data base are relatively large organisations (that is why the publication of the data base is called 'Handbook of Large Firms').

Another critical issue refers to the date of questionnaire. If firms are asked for their growth in the past, the information is necessarily restricted only to surving firms. It is generally

Table 1. Studies of Size-Influenced Growth of Firms in the FRG.

Friedrich and Spitznagel (1981)	Results:	"Larger firms show a better development" (p. 11f) But also: "Thesis that large firms are growth-promoting is to be refuted" (p. 61)
	Source:	Own questionnaire
	Period:	1973 - 1977
	Cases:	844
	Sector:	Manufacturing industry
	Miscellan.:	- 'Survivor'-analysis - Representativity: bias towards firms of relatively favourable development - Only classes of growth rates, no exact growth figures
Fritsch (1984)	Results:	Small firms grow faster whereas large firms decline
	Source:	Recordings of Kreditanstalt für Wiederaufbau
	Period:	1976 - 1981
	Cases:	888 (550)
	Sector:	Mining, manufacturing and services
	Miscellan.:	- 'Survivor'-analysis - No information about representativity - Weighted average growth rates
Hull (1984)	Results:	Young firms grow more rapidly
	Source:	Own questionnaire
	Period:	1974 - 1980
	Cases:	458
	Sector:	Manufacturing industry
	Miscellan.:	- 'Survivor'-analysis - No information representativity - Analysis of individual growth rates
Steinle (1984)	Results:	Small firms more stable in declining industries, large firms grow faster in expanding industries
	Source:	Sample of Hoppenstedt-addresses
	Period:	1973 - 1980
	Sector:	Manufacturing and services
	Cases:	ca. 11 000 firms
	Miscellan.:	- Analysis includes closures - Not representative for small firms - No exact figures of growth rates

agreed that small firms close down more frequently than others. Consequently, what may be called 'survivor-bias' is likely to affect estimation of the growth of firms more strongly.

Finally another kind of bias must be mentioned which, likewise, cannot be exactly calculated. Only Hull uses individual firm growth rates. In spite of the availability of this information, the other authors used only weighted averages; thus the total employment in one cohort at the end of the analysis period is compared to employment in that cohort at the beginning. The effect of this weighted average approach is that larger firms within a cohort influence the overall cohort growth rate to a disproportionate degree. Particularly in the higher size classes with their larger size ranges it is possible that one extreme case distorts the whole picture.

Employment: an adequate indicator for growth?

In addition to methodological problems associated with these analyses, they raise the more fundamental question as to whether employment is an adequate measure of economic growth. It is understandable that in times of acute shortages of jobs employment is regarded as a major economic issue. But to measure the success of a firm exclusively by its change of employment (which means in the 1970s by the amount of job losses) ignores the most important indicators of economic performance. Labour is after all only one input factor among others, whereas the success of a firm centres on its performance in the market, i.e. its sales and production, or only its value added if its particular contribution to the overall value of its production is to be taken into account.

Certainly an increase of production can be connected with additional employment. But this relationship does not exist in each case. There are many ways of improving performance without increasing the number of jobs - more capital inputs, change of production processes or even changes of products. Given the strength of international competition and the importance of productivity growth the achievement of output growth without additional employment may even have become a necessity, as is shown in one of the cited studies.

According to Friedrich and Spitznagel the

number of jobs increased in less than one third
(29%) of all firms with a rapid growth of
production; more than half of these fast-growing
firms diminished their employment. Conversely,
there were cases where, in spite of production
decline, the number of jobs remained stable or even
increased (12% of all firms with production
decline).

Other growth indicators than employment are
only available from official statistics which do
not permit cohort analysis. Thus only comparison of
size structures for different years is possible. In
consequence, direct inference from temporal changes
of size structure of trends in the growth process
of firms is not feasible. Most probably, the firms
of one size class at the beginning of the period
are, to a large extent, not identical with those in
the same class at the end.

Essentially, there are two official sources in
the FRG which provide information about recent
changes in the size structure of firms. The first
one is the official statistics on the mining and
manufacturing industries, which provide size-
differentiated data about the number of firms,
their employment, sales and investment.

In Table 2 the shares of different firm sizes
are calculated for total manufacturing industry as
well as differentiated for the production-,
investment-, consumer- and food/beverages-
industries. As in 1976 there was a systematic
change in the scope of the statistics - handcraft
firms with more than 20 employees have been
included - a direct comparison between 1970 and
1982 shares is not possible. Instead, the figures
for 1976 and 1977 (before and after the change in
definition) are also given.

In the first period 1970 to 1976 many firms
closed down and the total number of firms therefore
decreased. The contraction in the higher size
classes was particularly marked, presumably due to
the overall employment decline shifting firms to
the lower size classes. In the following period the
contraction was less intensive and the growth
differences between the different size classes less
distinct. The shares of large firms remained quite
stable, while the share of very small firms
declined favouring firms with 100 to 199 employees
which had the smallest loss.

Trends in employment were fairly similar.
Unequivocal changes in the size structure favouring
the share of small firms can be observed only in

Germany

Table 2. Firms, Employment, Sales and Investment by
         Size Classes in the Manufacturing
         Industry.

N. of	1970	1976	1977	1980	1982
Empl.	%	%	%	%	%
20- 49	41.90	42.14	47.92	46.57	47.38
50- 99	23.23	24.06	23.28	23.72	23.38
100-199	15.84	15.69	13.71	14.23	14.31
200-499	11.96	11.52	9.63	9.85	9.47
500-999	3.90	3.68	3.10	3.18	3.12
≥1000	3.17	2.91	2.36	2.45	2.34
Total Firms	35123	31046	36856	36545	34714

N. of					
Empl.	1970	1976	1977	1980	1982
20- 49	5.57	5.82	7.66	7.34	7.56
50- 99	6.85	7.31	8.17	8.11	8.11
100-199	9.28	9.48	9.61	9.69	9.91
200-499	15.52	15.39	14.87	14.84	14.44
500-999	11.21	10.91	10.65	10.78	10.77
≥1000	51.58	51.09	49.04	49.23	49.20
Total Empl.	8396548	7199509	7346695	7462689	6978753

N. of					
Empl.	1970	1976	1977	1980	1982
20- 49	5.06	4.78	6.00	5.70	5.54
50- 99	5.99	6.05	6.74	6.43	6.32
100-199	8.29	8.13	8.29	8.52	8.42
200-499	14.55	13.96	13.37	13.36	12.78
500-999	10.58	10.44	10.48	10.28	10.35
≥1000	55.54	56.64	55.11	55.72	56.60
Total Sales in mio DM	558646	888848	949605	1184298	1259428

N. of					
Empl.	1970	1976	1977	1980	1982
20- 49	0.00	4.78	6.95	5.78	4.93
50- 99	5.25	6.08	7.30	7.25	5.47
100-199	7.14	7.99	8.26	7.97	7.57
200-499	13.60	13.49	13.14	11.97	11.70
500-999	9.80	10.29	9.96	9.86	9.92
≥1000	64.22	57.38	54.39	57.17	60.41
Total Inv. in '000DM	37518817	36236044	39086547	52713501	50381540

Source: Federal Statistical Office, own calculations

the first period. After 1976 the direction of structural change even appears to have been reversed: the shares of medium and large firms slightly increased.

As was briefly noted earlier, total sales are not entirely appropriate as an indicator of output. Sales - or gross production value - do not only contain the value which a firm produces with its own employees and capital, but also the value of intermediate goods and services. Thus, while it is true that sales measure the firm's success in the market, an even better index of actual performance, i.e. the earned income for labour and capital, is gross (or net) value added.

In respect to the influence of size on the economic performance of firms this aspect is of importance insofar as some authors suggest that the share of intermediate goods and services is higher in larger firms (e.g. Krengel 1976). Consequently, sales would overestimate the economic efficiency of larger firms. However, official statistics restricted to the mining and manufacturing industry do not in fact reveal any remarkable or unequivocal differences (cf. Table 3). Nor is the rank-order between large and small firms changed: the larger the firm, the higher is not only its sales in relation to its employment, but also its value added per employee. On average and for total production industry, the smallest firms attained only two thirds (67.5%) of the value added earned by the largest firms in 1982.

Even cautiously interpreted, however, the statistics on sales growth and the changes in the size structure of sales (Table 2) do not offer any evidence that smaller firms performed better. In both periods the largest firms with more than 1,000 employees increased their share of total sales by more than 1%-point. The shares of all other classes declined or remained stable. The picture for industry groups is more complex. In the production- and investment-goods industries large firms seem to have been more successful, whereas in the consumer-goods and food industries smaller- or medium-sized firms performed better. Interestingly, the latter industry group had a much smaller total growth of sales in both periods.

With regard to investment, changes in size structure appear similar to those for employment. In the first period to 1976 characterized by an economic recession, the decrease of employment as well as of investment chiefly affected the share of

Germany

Table 3. The Share of Intermediary Goods and
Services by Size of Firm in the Mining and
Manufacturing Industry.

| | Gross Prod. Value mrd. DM | Share of | | Gross Value Added per employee '000 DM |
		Interm. goods and services in %	Gross Value Added in %	
20- 49	70.4	63.6	36.4	48.6
50- 99	80.8	63.4	36.6	51.9
100-199	109.0	66.4	33.6	52.5
200-499	161.7	61.5	35.5	56.9
500-999	131.1	61.3	35.7	62.9
1000	755.9	65.2	34.8	72.0
Total	1,309.0	61.9	35.1	63.8

Source: Federal Statistical Office, Serie 4.3.2, 1982, Table
9; own calculations

the largest firms. In the second period of economic
recovery from 1977 to 1982, however, the share of
larger firms again reached nearly the same level as
at the beginning of the 1970s.

In short, these official statistics for the
mining and manufacturing industry do not provide
much support for the assumption that the
competitiveness of smaller firms has particularly
increased in the last decade. As far as inputs like
labour (employment) and capital (investment) are
concerned the varying directions of share changes
conform to the thesis that larger firms behave more
cyclically, i.e. react to business cycles more
rapidly and with greater intensity. In respect to
sales no particular tendency in the changes of
shares can be observed taking into account the
large deviations between groups of industries.

The second set of statistics which is
available also does not reflect the supposed
success of small firms. This is the statistics of
sales taxes which has several advantages in
comparison with the first data set. Firstly, all
sectors of the economy are included, not only
manufacturing industry, but also the large service
sector. Secondly, the size threshold adopted is
very low; each firm or person having sales of more
than 20,000 DM (nearly £5,000) must pay sales taxes
and is therefore registered. This low

inclusion threshold is especially important for the service sector since many personal and consumer-oriented services consist primarily of small firms. Thirdly, the low threshold results in large numbers of firms and persons being registered. This allows a fine sectoral differentiation without raising the problem of confidentiality. And fourthly, apart from an increase in the threshold (from 12,000 to 20,000 DM) the framework of recording did not change essentially during the period of study. A fairly lengthy temporal comparison is therefore possible.

Figures calculated from these sales tax statistics are shown in Table 4 where the tax payers are grouped into three large size classes. Three main results are worthy of note. First, the table reveals very large differences between the size structures of different industries. Although their share of total firms is rather low (less than 7%), firms with sales of more than 100 mio. DM produced nearly 90% or more of total sales in energy, mining and chemicals. On the other hand, there are many industries in which large firms account for a sales share of less than one third; examples include plastics-rubber, stone-glass, timber-printing and leather-clothing. Thus, differences in sectoral growth must have selective consequences for the size structure of the whole economy.

Secondly, with respect to changes in size structure among the total 23 industries there are only four in which firms in the large enterprise class did not perform better than the average for the industry between 1970 and 1982. In contrast, there are only two economic sectors where small firms with sales of less than 1 mio. DM increased their share of total sales. And these sectors - agriculture, and education and science - are hardly representative of the whole economy as the number of persons having to pay sales taxes because of secondary earnings is extraordinarily high in these sectors.

Thirdly, in 1970 the share of small and medium-sized firms was much higher in the service than in the production sector (74% to 53%). Although sales of services increased much faster than those of production activities between 1970 and 1982, no shift towards smaller firms can be observed at the level of the whole. One amongst several reasons for this was the particularly rapid expansion of large firms within the service sector,

Germany

Table 4. Sales by Size Classes.

	Shares 1970			Total sales in mio. DM
	0.02-1	1-100 millions DM	100- DM	
Agriculture	52.37	30.02	17.61	4310
Energy	1.68	21.67	76.65	33394
Mining	0.16	3.41	96.43	24311
Manufacturing	9.21	43.17	47.62	643078
- Chemicals	0.92	19.65	79.43	73626
- Plastics, rubber	5.60	53.94	40.46	17018
- Stone, glass	10.46	65.12	24.42	26091
- Iron making	5.18	22.93	71.90	83428
- Struct. steel, vehicles	5.97	39.76	54.26	145139
- Electrical engineering	6.31	47.78	45.91	88574
- Timber, print	18.91	60.48	20.60	54627
- Leather, clothing	11.44	72.69	15.88	49926
- Food	19.33	46.34	34.33	104649
Construction	37.44	55.02	7.54	74236
- Building	25.05	64.86	10.08	55533
- Finishing	74.23	25.77	0.00	18703
Trade	20.38	52.95	26.67	503255
- Wholesale	9.88	59.96	30.17	333613
- Retail	41.02	39.18	19.80	169642
Transport, communications	20.90	37.45	41.65	44601
- Transport	27.48	49.25	23.27	33919
- Post, railways	0.00	0.00	100.00	10682
Business-related services	39.78	43.55	16.66	40043
- Banks, insurances	41.34	45.71	12.95	4499
- Other bus.-r. services	39.59	43.28	17.13	35544
Household-related services	58.60	28.15	13.25	48077
- Education, sciences	12.53	49.90	37.56	15295
- Other house.-r. serv.	80.10	17.99	1.91	32782
Non-profit organisations	7.83	52.40	39.77	13461
Total economy	17.28	45.43	37.29	1428766
- Production	11.30	42.13	46.56	775019
- Services	24.18	49.46	26.36	649437

Sources: Own calculations of sales tax statistics

266

Germany

Table 4. Sales by Size Classes (continued).

	Shares 1982			Total sales in mio. DM
	0.02-1	1-100 millions DM	100-	
Agriculture	45.16	46.77	8.07	12211
Energy	0.61	10.67	88.73	141563
Mining	0.07	2.58	97.34	40120
Manufacturing	4.60	32.88	62.51	1447973
- Chemicals	0.22	8.56	91.22	271752
- Plastics, rubber	3.43	61.56	35.02	36647
- Stone, glass	5.74	60.88	33.38	50973
- Iron making	4.85	23.64	71.50	145478
- Struct. steel, vehicles	2.76	28.23	69.01	348067
- Electrical engineering	4.18	37.93	57.89	201422
- Timber, print	11.02	57.66	31.32	108527
- Leather, clothing	7.06	65.71	27.24	74496
- Food	9.30	37.37	53.34	210611
Construction	23.80	64.87	11.33	196186
- Building	13.84	70.35	15.81	136113
- Finishing	46.37	52.45	1.18	60073
Trade	10.59	50.00	39.41	1135567
- Wholesale	4.22	50.28	45.50	733564
- Retail	22.21	49.50	28.29	402003
Transport, communications	12.48	44.08	43.44	108072
- Transport	15.14	53.47	31.39	89093
- Post, railways	0.00	0.00	100.00	18979
Business-related services	22.39	51.44	26.17	189817
- Banks, insurances	5.16	59.83	35.01	22470
- Other bus.-r. services	24.70	50.31	24.99	167347
Household-related services	46.64	37.10	16.26	124833
- Education, sciences	16.56	47.12	36.31	44591
- Other house.-r. serv.	63.35	31.53	5.12	80242
Non-profit organisations	4.33	47.91	47.76	21870
Total economy	10.39	40.82	48.80	3418212
- Production	6.26	33.93	59.81	1825842
- Services	14.89	48.72	36.38	1580159

Source: Own calculations of sales tax statistics

especially in the retailing and wholesaling industries.

To sum up, the sales tax statistics do not confirm the hypothesis of a recent increase in the competitiveness of small firms. It is true that the monetary constant delineation of size causes some problems of interpretation. In the course of time sales figures have more or less continuously risen. Consequently, even below-average growth can lead a firm in the long run to change its size class. Due to the limitations of the data, this can be neither excluded nor can the effect exactly be calculated.

On the other hand, however, the actual shifts observed render it unlikely that the increase in the share of the largest size class is caused only by the constant margins effect. The sales tax data show that over the 1970-82 period, the number of tax payers increased in all three size classes. However, the largest increase occurred in the highest class, especially in the category of sales greater than 250 mio. DM. Furthermore, not only the number of tax payers, but the ratio of sales per tax payer, too, grew fastest (+20%) in this class - in spite of an already very high value in 1970 (1,040 mio. DM). In all other size classes, even on a more differentiated level of 14 size classes, the increase never exceeded 4%.

The data do not allow us to identify the forces underlying these processes; nonetheless, the increase in share of sales recorded by the highest class, which was the largest in respect to the number of firms as well as to average sales per firm, hardly conforms to the thesis that the economic position of large firms has weakened in the last decade.

Plants - Firms - Corporations

The results of the sales tax analyses are confirmed if corporate relationships are taken into account. Principally, the discussion about the importance of small and medium-sized firms focusses on the size of the economic decision unit. Though perhaps oversimplifying, one may say that plants are of importance only insofar as large plants imply large firms. The reverse relationship is less valid as large decision units own small plants, too. The definition of decision units is usually based on the legal status of a particular plant. By this means, however, the direct influence of large corporations is widely underestimated. In 1981, the largest 32 industrial enterprises owned more than 1,000 legally independent German subsidiaries in the manufacturing sector alone (Bade 1983). Even more surprising was their growth: from 1971 to 1981 the number of subsidiaries increased by nearly 50%.

Consequently, in the West German case legal independency does not necessarily imply economic independency. To what extent small and medium-sized German firms are connected to larger corporations by ownership rights is not possible to identify, in the absence of comprehensive information. However, instead of a bottom up procedure (of analysing all smaller firms) a top-down-approach is possible using concentration statistics. It is true that these data are limited to measuring the degree of dominance of the largest three, six etc. firms and do not afford direct information about the importance of small firms. But, the changes of concentration ratios perhaps allow some indirect conclusions.

It is somewhat surprising that virtually none of the studies investigating the success of small firms make any reference to this kind of information, provided for example by the German monopoly commission. As a selective summary, four important conclusions based on concentration analyses should be noted:

A. The share of the ten largest industrial firms in total sales of their respective line of business has risen continuously since 1954, the first year of report. By 1982 the average for all industrial groups was 44% compared to 31% in 1954.

B. Most of the industries in the manufacturing sector which have attained an above average growth in recent years and which are expected to continue expanding are highly concentrated. Consequently, a deconcentration due to future changes in the sectoral structure cannot be anticipated.

C. Concentration ratios possess two critical features.

    a. First, the share of the ten largest firms is based on legally independent units; consequently, it fails to take account of the influence firms exert on their subsidiaries. The monopoly commission therefore also analyses the consolidated business areas of the largest 100 industrial corporations. According to the commission the share of these firms in total sales of mining and manufacturing industry rose from 37% to 40% between 1978 and 1982. Even this share is probably underestimated as the sales figures for these corporations exclude internal sales within the respective corporations whereas these are included in the total sales figure for production industry as a whole.

b. Secondly, as is mentioned above, sales may overestimate the economic performance of firms. That is why the commission determines not only the sales, but also the value added of the 10 largest corporations. From 1978 to 1982 their value added rose at the same rate as that for production industry as a whole. Their share in total value added therefore remained unchanged at 19%.

The discrepancy between the increasing share of sales and the unchanged share of value added does not necessarily imply that the economic performance of the largest corporations has only increased on average. Instead, the difference may be explained by a considerable growth of their foreign activities. In recent years, large West German corporations have transferred an increasing part of their production activities to foreign countries with the consequence that the supply of intermediate goods and services from abroad has risen strongly. According to Koubek and Scheibe-Lange (1983), in the case of their analysed large firms the value added produced abroad was nearly half as much (43%) of total value added; in the case of large chemical corporations the share was as high as two thirds (68%). If foreign activities are ignored, the value added statistics for larger firms substantially underestimate their total economic performance.

D. In the light of these considerations, the following observation of the monopoly commission becomes even more important. Although foreign activities are omitted, since 1970 the (domestic) value added of the largest 10 firms (all sectors included) in the FRG has grown faster than the value added of the whole economy.

Regional Aspects

Unfortunately no regional information is available on the economic performance of small and medium-sized firms in the FRG. In view of the discussion above this is perhaps not surprising. Firstly, the data base for small firms is rather weak in general. Secondly, for the opposite segment of the economy, the very large firms, some information is provided by concentration analysis. However, in most cases large firms are regionally dispersed. Thus their regional classification is - apart from the location of certain obvious functions such as headquarter offices - rather problematic.

There is some evidence that most headquarters, especially those of the largest firms, are concentrated in the main agglomerations (Bade 1983). The picture with regard to branch plants is less clear; they can be observed in the more peripheral areas of the FRG as well as in the agglomerations. Thus the degree of external control does not appear to vary greatly according to a centre-periphery scheme. One major regional difference exists in the importance of single-plant firms, which are usually smaller than multiplant firms.

It is often supposed that single-plant firms occur more frequently in peripheral areas than in the FRG's agglomerations. But as a generalization this assumption is open to question. According to interim results of an ongoing research project (Gräber et al. 1985) the frequency of single-plant firms in less agglomerated areas is actually lower, not higher. However, if the share of employment or of investment is taken as a basis, then their importance appears to be much greater: in the peripheral areas nearly half of total employment or of total investment is accounted for by single-plant firms.

The main reason for the difference lies in the size of multi-plant firm branch plants. On average, branch plants in the major agglomerations are much larger (300 employees) than those in the less agglomerated areas (170 employees). In contrast, no clear regional differences can be observed between single-plant firms.

This result is of particular interest because some authors (e.g. Derenbach and Wittmann 1984) view small single-plant firms as being of key importance for regional policy. Essentially, their arguments are based not so much on instrumental and implementation aspects of regional policy (small and indigenous firms can be more easily addressed by regional policy makers). Rather, these authors draw a direct connection between the undoubted and surprising recent employment success of less agglomerated areas on the one hand, and the small and medium-sized structure of their plants on the other.

At present, information is not available to prove or disprove this supposed relationship. Firstly, we do not know whether the above average growth of employment is due to a larger job increase in the smaller plant classes and/or to minor job loss in the larger plants. Secondly, plants are not identical with firms and neither small plants nor firms are necessarily independent enterprises, as mentioned above. The provisional results of Gräber et al. show that many small establishments are externally-controlled branch plants. Thus on the basis of the available data we cannot exclude the possibility that the relative gains of employment in less agglomerated areas are in fact more reflections of adaptation processes in the agglomerations transmitted through the corporate location networks of multi-plant firms (decrease of employment in central plants with transfer of jobs to less central locations or, at least, no job losses in the latter plants).

Finally, even if the relative job increase is largely due to the employment behaviour of indigenous small firms, some further scepticism should be mentioned which is connected with employment as performance indicator. If, confronted with intensifying international competition many enterprises try to increase their competitiveness by externalizing non-profitable activities and by intensifying the rationalization and automation of production processes, it may be questioned whether firms which do not follow this strategy are better off because of better products and less intense competition. Rather - as the sectoral structure of industries in less agglomerated areas does not appear to be particularly favourable - is it not possible that these firms 'only' reveal somewhat conservative or defensive behaviour in trying to retain the structure and volume of activities as long as possible?

References

Aiginger, K. and G. Tichy (1984) Die Grösse der
    Kleinen, Signum Press, Vienna
Armington, C. and M. Odle (1982) 'Small Business -
    How many jobs?' The Brooking Review, 1-2, pp.

Germany

14-17
Bade, F.J. (1983) 'Large Corporations and Regional Development', Regional Studies, 17, 5, pp. 315-326
Birch, D. (1979) The Job Generation Process, M.I.T., Mass.
Birch, D. (1983) 'The Contribution of Small Enterprise to Growth and Employment', Paper for the conference on 'New Opportunities for Entrepreneurship', June 22-24, Kiel
Bombach, G. (1969) Technischer Fortschritt und Konzentration, Basel
Derenbach, R. and F.T. Wittmann (1984) 'Betriebsgrössenstruktur und Regionalwirtschaft', Informationen zur Raumentwicklung, 12, pp. 1234-1238
Eckart, W., E. v. Einem and K. Stahl (1985) 'Dynamik der Beschäftigten-entwicklung - Stand der empirischen Forschung', University of Dortmund, Department of Economic and Social Sciences, Working paper 8501
Friedrich, W. and E. Spitznagel (1981) Wachstum, Beschäftigung und Investitionstätigkeit im Verarbeitenden Gewerbe, IFO-Studien zur Industriewirtschaft, 22, München
Fritsch, M. (1984) 'Die arbeitsmarktpolitische Bedeutung kleiner und mittlerer Betriebe bzw. Unternehmen im Prozess des Strukturwandels in der Bundesrepublik Deutschland' in: Regionale Entwicklung durch Förderung kleiner und mittlerer Unternehmen (ed. by The Federal Department for Regional Planning), 06.053, Bonn, pp. 43-81
Galbraith, J.K. (1956) American Capitalism - The Concept of Countervailing Power, Boston
Galbraith, J.K. (1973) Economics and the Public Purpose, New York
Gräber, H., M. Holst, K.P. Schackmann-Fallis and H. Spehl (1985) 'Interregionale Kontrollverflechtungen im Verarbeitenden Gewerbe', 2. intermediary report, University of Trier, Department of Town and Regional Planning
Hull, C. (1984) 'Job Generation among Independent West German Manufacturing Firms 1974-1980', International Institute of Management, IIM/LMP 84-15, Berlin
Koubek, N. and I. Scheibe-Lange (1983) 'Konzentration und Internationalisierung der Grossunternehmen und Konzerne in der deutschen Wirtschaft von 1960 bis 1980', WSI-Mitteilungen, 7/1983, pp. 394-408

Lilienthal, D. (1952) <u>Big Business: A New Era</u>, New York

Monopolkommission (1984) <u>Fünftes Hauptgutachten der Monopolkommission 1982/83</u>, Bundestagsdrucksache 10/1791, Bonn

Passow, R. (1915) 'Der Anteil der grossen industriellen Unternehmungen am gewerblichen Leben der Gegenwart in Deutschland, England und den Vereinigten Staaten, <u>Zeitschrift für Sozialwissenschaften</u>, 6, pp. 491-518

Petry, H. (1969/70) 'Technischer Fortschritt, Integration, internationale Wettbewerbsfähigkeit und Unternehmensgrösse', <u>Jahrbücher für Nationalökonomie und Statistik</u>, Vol. 183, pp. 271-299

Schätz, K.-W. (1984) 'Die Bedeutung kleiner und mittlerer Unternehmen im Strukturwandel', <u>Institut für Weltwirtschaft</u>, dicussion paper 103, Kiel

Schmenner, R. (1982) <u>Making Business Location Decisions</u>, Englewood Cliffs

Schumpeter, J.A. (1943) <u>Capitalism, Socialism and Democracy</u>, London

Steinle, W.J. (1984) 'Der Beitrag kleiner und mittlerer Unternehmen zur Beschäftigungsentwicklung', <u>Mitteilungen zur Arbeitsmarkt- und Berufsforschung</u>, 2184, pp. 257-266

Chapter thirteen

RELEVANCE AND NATURE OF SMALL AND MEDIUM-SIZED
FIRMS IN SOUTHERN ITALY

Alfredo Del Monte
Adriano Giannola

Introduction

This chapter is organized into two sections. The
first presents an analysis of the growth of small
manufacturing firms in Southern Italy, describing
the peculiarities of the South both with respect to
Italy as a whole and with respect to the Northern,
Eastern, and Central (NEC) regions taken together.
The analysis is based for the most part on census
data collected by the ISTAT and is concerned with
the period 1971-81.

In the second section we will consider the
problem of obstacles to the growth of local firms
in less developed areas [1]. A first attempt will be
made at testing the hypothesis that the rate of
growth of local firms in Southern Italy was
significantly higher in the seventies than it had
been in the sixties. It will be argued not only
that there has been an improvement in this respect
but also that in some industries (e.g. Metal
products, Mechanical, electrical and instrument
engineering, Vehicles) the improvement was closely
connected to the regional industrial policy
followed at the beginning of the decade. For other
industries (e.g. Clothing, Footwear), the
improvement seems to be independent of the action
of industrial policy.

In general, it seems reasonable to conclude
that during the seventies the obstacles to growth
tended not to be as strong as they had been
previously, although this seems to be more
particularly true for the period 1970-74 than for
the rest of the decade.

The Increase In The Number Of Plants And Employees, According To Plant Size, 1971-81.

A comparison of the census data for the period 1971-81 shows a relatively high rate of growth of employment in local manufacturing industries in Southern Italy: 25.76%, as against an overall national rate of increase of only 11.63% and an increase of 25.67% for the most dynamic of the NEC regions. A characteristic feature of the development of Southern manufacturing industries during this period was the absolute decline in the number of plants, a decline that affected exclusively those firms belonging to the smallest dimensional classes (at this dimensional level, 'plant' is synonomous with 'firm'.) In contrast, in Italy as a whole and especially in the NEC regions, the smallest-sized firms experienced the greatest increase in the number of plants and employees, both in terms of their rate of growth and in terms of their relative share of the total increase which occurred during this period. For the NEC regions, the growth of plants with 1 to 9 employees accounts for 81% of the total increase in plants and more than 33% of the total increase in employment. The gains made by firms with 10 to 19 employees account for another 15% of the total increase in plants and 30% of the total increase in employment. At the national level, the trend is the same (see Table 1). Here, firms with 10 to 19 employees have a greater share of the total increase than those with 1 to 9 employees, a phenomenon which is actually determined by the peculiar performance of firms in the Southern regions.

As we have said, the trend in the South was the opposite. The declining rate of growth of plants (-8%) was entirely determined by the decline in growth experienced by firms with 1 to 9 employees. For firms of this size, the decline in the number of plants (-12%) was accompanied by a corresponding decline in the number of employees (-3%). There was an increase in the number of plants with 10 to 19 employees (see again Table 1), but in spite of this increase, the growth in employment experienced by the firms belonging to this dimensional class accounts for only 24% of the total growth in employment in the South. At the national level, they account for 50% of the total increase and in the NEC regions, for 30% of it. For the two dimensional classes taken together, we find

Southern Italy

Table 1. Percentage change in the number of plants and employees by firm size in manufacturing industry (1971-81).

Size	Southern Italy Plants	Employees	%E	North, East, Centre Plants	Employees	%E	Italy Plants	Employees	%E
1 - 9	-12.23	-3.10	-4.58	32.23	35.79	33.35	15.10	6.12	10.74
10 - 19	86.79	82.36	23.84	67.72	66.57	30.32	62.37	77.47	51.39
20 - 49	40.57	37.66	15.65	30.73	26.98	16.83	19.52	17.33	19.57
50 - 99	16.01	14.83	4.67	14.01	14.11	6.78	4.82	4.82	4.44
100-199	3.35	-10.43	-4.06	-4.17	-10.38	-5.81	-9.39	-18.16	-21.54
200-499	83.47	70.44	18.94	75.89	51.44	15.72	53.02	33.78	27.14
500-999	37.31	36.64	10.19	24.14	18.03	3.94	1.24	-.74	-.49
> 1000	45.71	45.84	25.10	-11.47	-6.72	-2.16	-10.49	-14.09	-20.65
Total	-8.29	25.76	100	34.04	25.67	100	17.92	11.63	100
A	22.02	30.98		12.55	9.68		4.72	-2.21	
B				80.58	33.35		73.10	10.74	
C		35.29		.03	1.78				

A = Rate of growth of plants with more than 50 employees
B = Growth of plants and employees with less than 10 employees as % of total growth
C = Growth of plants and employees with more than 500 employees as % of total growth
%E= Percentage change in number of employees by firm size/total percentage change in number of employees x 100
Source: ISTAT, Census of manufacturing 1971, 1981

that while they were the 'dominant' classes in the rest of Italy, they were far from being so in the South. Here, the number of firms with less than 20 employees actually declined. Moreover, they account for less than 20% of the new employees registered by the ISTAT in these regions, as against 62% in Italy and 64% in the NEC regions.

Looking at the other end of the spectrum, at firms belonging to the largest dimensional class, we find that over 35% of all new employment in the South has been concentrated in plants with more than 500 employees. In the NEC regions the increase in this class was only 1% of the total and at the national level there was a decrease of employees in plants of this size.

As regards the medium-sized firms, the trends in the South, in Italy, and in the NEC regions were more or less the same, except for the firms with 200 to 499 employees, which had a much higher rate of growth in the South. This further reinforces the conclusion that during the seventies the 'dominant' features of industrial development in the South were different from those in the rest of the country.

Southern Italy

The Growth Of Small Firms In The South By Industry

In spite of the overall negative trend just described, small Southern firms - including those belonging to the smallest dimensional classes - had some interesting characteristics which emerge when the census data is broken down according to industry (Table 2).

As regards the growth in employment, the most dynamic industrial sectors during the seventies, in the South as well as in the rest of Italy, were the Mechanical, electrical and instrument engineering industry and the Vehicles industry. Their growth was particularly marked in the South. There was a 68% increase in the number of plants and a 80% increase in the number of employees in this region, as against increases of 63% and 28%, respectively, in Italy as a whole, and 65% and 50% in the NEC regions. In the NEC regions, this growth was experienced mainly by the small and medium-sized firms: firms with less than 20 employees accounted for 44% of the increase in employment and 94% of the increase in the number of plants. By contrast, the greatest contribution to the increase in employment in the South was made by firms with more than 500 employees, which accounted for 47% of the increase in employment, as against 11% in both the NEC regions and Italy as a whole. Nonetheless, in the South these two industries, as well as the Metal products industry, also experienced a considerable increase in plants and employees in the smallest dimensional classes.

In all three sectors, there were substantial increases in employment in plants with less than 20, less than 10 and less than five employees. In other words, the most significant development of the smallest dimensional classes in Southern Italy took place precisely in those industries where the expansion of very large firms was most pronounced.

As noted earlier, the expansion of very large firms was a direct consequence of the regional industrial policy carried out between 1970 and 1974, whose main objectives were to take pressure off the Northern Italian industrial areas and to diversify the Southern manufacturing sector, which in the early seventies was overtly dominated by heavy industry as a result of the policy interventions of the sixties. It is probable that in the sectors mentioned above the main impetus for the growth of locally based small firms in the South came from the expansion of the subcontracting

Southern Italy

Table 2. Rate of growth (%) of employment in selected industries by firm size, 1971-1981, in Southern Italy, North-East-Centre and whole Italy.

Size of Estab., by no. of Employees	Steel EM	Engineering EM	Vehicles EM	Footwear EM	Clothing EM
Southern Italy					
≥1000	61.82	88.46	80.06	-16.57	
500-999	-33.33	88.46	86.17	-75.63	146.54
10-19	371.67	127.13	306.74	256.56	80.47
5-9	98.93	94.15	247.18	127.64	84.04
1-5	60.05	48.84	284.21	-41.22	-75.10
Total	19.38	66.85	83.81	3.59	-5.82
Central Italy and N.E. Italy					
≥1000	46.31	-8.57	115.62	-33.35	
500-999	75.01	33.07	18.40	-24.72	-13.71
10-19	1.85	88.80	142.48	129.88	82.38
5-9	-4.70	66.05	107.50	100.36	100.67
1-5	-9.96	48.76	203.58	2.28	33.72
Total	-1.47	48.54	58.09	24.17	39.18
Italy					
≥1000	-16.83	-4.87	10.23	-32.53	
500-999	-.82	22.17	55.06	-43.87	-2.86
10-19	-6.84	82.65	121.50	128.14	74.96
5-9	-10.71	62.55	104.65	94.61	76.01
1-5	-8.16	46.46	148.19	-30.00	-38.16
Total	-18.34	29.49	23.51	6.54	12.24

EM = No. of employees
Source: ISTAT

market, which during this period became broader and more dynamic, even if not as rich as in other regions of Italy 2. As we shall see later the sharp decline in interventions in these sectors since 1974 seems significantly to have affected the development potentialities of small firms.

For the very small firms, the increase in the number of plants and employees was smallest in industries such as Footwear, Leather, Timber, Furniture, and so on. These industries were quite dynamic in the rest of Italy, especially in the NEC regions and their growth was characterized by a substantial development of firms belonging to the smallest dimensional classes. In these regions there was a significant growth in the number of employees working in firms with one to five employees, while, in the South, the number of employees working in firms of this size declined sharply, affecting overall performance. Thus in the Clothing industry, the rate of increase in overall employment was -6% and the rate of increase in the number of plants -79%, entirely reflecting small firm decline (Table 2).

Table 3. Percentage growth of small plants compared with the share of employment taken up by plants with more than 500 employees by industry.

	South			NEC		
	Y_0	X	Y_1	Y_0	X	Y_1
	(<10)		(<20)	(<10)		(<20)
A						
Metals	3.29	76.30	4.53	−0.64	51.18	−0.55
Bricks etc.	9.94	11.64	13.61	8.78	7.20	9.68
Chemicals	5.51	53.71	6.32	9.49	48.86	0.89
Chem. Fibres	1.71	82.35	2.14	1.33	96.77	2.47
B						
Engineering	83.58	75.27	90.19	55.22	15.89	63.70
Vehicles	7.17	79.75	9.02	15.98	47.89	20.31
C						
Food etc.	−13.44	5.72	−12.19	−11.37	7.62	−10.65
Textiles	−12.95	14.16	−9.93	60.01	12.50	66.17
Leather	(97.06)	−	(117.65)	(109.71)	−	(125.17)
Footwear	−18.76	8.24	−8.58	−4.47	12.83	6.08
Clothing	−366.94	2.32	−361.33	6.65	3.45	16.46
Furniture	−3.83	0.80	0.85	33.60	2.26	37.42
Timber	82.11	24.37	91.11	39.83	9.87	45.65
Rubber	60.36	9.14	71.44	52.71	2.99	64.53
Other manufacturing	(369.28)	−	(392.16)	(109.49)	8.68	116.14
A	7.05	40.40	9.32	7.59	25.85	8.50
B	n.a.	n.a.	n.a.	n.a.	n.a.	n.a.
C	−73.80	6.63	−68.33	26.47	7.81	32.48
A+B+C	−24.01	21.27	−19.24	31.55	13.86	37.48

$$Y = \frac{\text{Plants (1971-1981)}}{\text{Employees 1971}} \times 1000 \qquad \begin{array}{l} \text{Plants<10 employees} = Y_0 \\ \text{Plants<20 employees} = Y_1 \end{array}$$

$$X = \frac{\text{Employees in Plants (> 500) 1971}}{\text{Employees 1971}} \times 100$$

Southern Italy

We have tried to see whether or not small
local firms in the South were constrained in their
development by the presence of large firms
operating in the same industry. For this purpose,
we have compared the increase of plants with less
than 20 and less than 10 employees (as a % of total
employment in 1971) and the weight of employment in
plants with more than 500 employees (as a % of
total employment in 1971). The results are reported
in Table 3. If the presence of large firms were an
obstacle to the growth of small firms, we would
expect a negative correlation between these two
ratios. As can be seen from the Table, this was not
the case in Italy in the seventies, particularly in
the South.

The Changing Regional Distribution Of Manufacturing Industry In Southern Italy

Let us see how the growth of manufacturing industry
between 1971 and 1981 was distributed among the
eight regions of Southern Italy. On this problem,
there is a firmly rooted idea, according to which
the traditional industrial areas of Southern Italy
(like Campania) experienced a relative decline
during the seventies, mainly as a consequence of a
lower rate of formation of new small enterprises.
The analysis of the Census data does not however
seem to support this conclusion.
In 1971 Campania, with one fourth of the
population of the South, was the most important
manufacturing region, providing work for 33.4% of
all manufacturing employees. Table 4 divides the
manufacturing industries into three broad groups:
the first comprises the heavy industries, the
second, the engineering and vehicles industries,
and the third, the 'traditional' industries (Food,
Leather, et al). From this division, it may be seen
that in 1971 Campania was important particularly in
the second group of industries - that is, in those
which were to be the most dynamic during the
seventies. At the beginning of the decade, Campania
accounted for slightly less than 43% of total
Southern employment in this group of industries.
Ten years later, Campania's share of total
manufacturing employment had indeed decreased very
slightly, to 32.8%. However, while there was a
sharp drop in Campania's share of employment in the
first group of industries, its share remained
fairly constant with respect to the second group,

Southern Italy

Table 4. Regional shares of manufacturing employment by industry group and firm size within the Mezzogiorno.

			1971		
	A	B	C	Manuf.	<50
Abruzzi	8.61	7.19	9.13	8.57	8.29
Molise	.83	.66	1.46	1.13	1.77
Campania	28.82	42.80	31.43	33.43	26.20
Puglia	23.91	19.89	23.76	22.91	23.26
Basilicata	3.47	1.90	2.46	2.56	2.65
Calabria	5.34	2.83	6.45	5.39	7.62
Sicilia	20.70	20.48	18.33	19.39	22.73
Sardegna	8.32	4.06	6.98	6.62	7.48
Mezzogiorno	100	100	100	100	100

			1981		
	A	B	C	Manuf.	<50
Abruzzi	10.75	9.44	12.52	11.18	10.42
Molise	1.31	2.16	1.52	1.68	1.77
Campania	19.90	42.40	31.39	32.77	29.81
Puglia	31.22	19.56	24.33	24.12	24.38
Basilicata	4.55	2.09	2.43	2.73	2.78
Calabria	6.37	2.98	5.67	4.93	7.05
Sicilia	20.79	16.65	15.79	17.03	20.45
Sardegna	17.01	4.72	6.35	7.85	8.04
Mezzogiorno	100	100	100	100	100

A: Metal manufacture; Chemical and allied industries; Bricks, pottery, glass, cement, etc.
B: Mechanical engineering, instrument engineering, electrical engineering, vehicles
C: Food, drink, tobacco; Textiles, Leather, Clothing, Footwear, Timber, Furniture, etc.; Rubber, other manufacturing industries
<50: Regional share of employees in plants with less than 50 employees as % of total southern employment in plants with less than 50 employees
Source: ISTAT

and increased slightly with respect to the third. The slight decline experienced by Campania, the traditional centre for Southern manufacturing, seems to have been determined - contrary to what is usually affirmed - not so much by the weaker development of small firms, but by the fact that

during the decade the large plants in the heavy
industries lost ground. In fact, from Table 4 it
may be seen that in Campania the share of
manufacturing employment of firms with less than 50
employees increased from 26% in 1971 to nearly 30%
in 1981.

Three other regions are worth commenting on:

1. Sicily experienced a dramatic decrease in its
overall share of manufacturing employment,
largely because it lost considerable ground with
respect to the second and third groups of
industries.

2. Puglia does not show, on the whole, the gains in
its relative share of employment that were
expected. In fact, its share of employment
increased by approximately 8 percentage points
in the first group of industries, but remained
stationary in the second and third group. In
addition, its growth of enterprises with less
than 50 employees was no better than Campania's.

3. The most noteworthy changes in the relative
shares of employment took place in Abruzzi. In
fact, Abruzzi's share of overall manufacturing
employment increased by 3 percentage points, and
there were gains in all three groups,
particularly in the third one. In addition, of
all the Southern regions, Abruzzi had the most
significant gain in the growth of small
enterprises.

Thus, an intraregional redistribution of Southern
manufacturing did occur but only to a certain
extent. A much greater 'restructuring' of the
sector would be seen in an analysis carried out at
the more detailed provincial level. The
restructuring process in fact appears to have been
much more intensive within the regions themselves
than between one region and another.

Continuing with the regional comparison, we
arrive at different conclusions if we limit our
analysis to local firms with more than 49
employees. This may be done by utilizing the
IASM-CESAN data, which are particularly useful in
that they specify whether the firms surveyed are
locally-based or not (for the particular
characteristics of the IASM-CESAN Databank, see the
Appendix). The over-fifty employees dimensional
class seems to us to be particularly interesting
because it includes firms which have relatively
more interesting organizational and technological
standards, as well as the best market performances.

Table 5. The pattern of locally-based enterprises (> 49 employees) in Southern Italy.

A

Industry	1981 Plants	1981 Employees
Food, drink and tobacco	33.4	22.5
Bricks, pottery, glass, cement	46.6	36.6
Mechanical and instrument engineering	41.9	15.6
Vehicles, metal products	22.4	6.0
Electrical engineering	100.0	100.0
Footwear	66.7	44.9
Clothing	61.8	60.7
Timber and furniture		
Chemical and allied industries	22.4	6.4
Paper, printing and publishing	54.7	32.7
Total	45.5	21.8

B

	Total manufacturing		Footwear		Clothing		Mechanical and instrument engineering	
	≤1964	>1964	≤1964	>1964	≤1964	>1964	≤1964	>1964
Abruzzi	11.14	17.03	20.00	10.20	15.71	29.21	12.50	12.90
Molise	.97	.55	0	0	2.86	1.12	0	1.08
Campania	45.04	38.19	60.46	71.43	41.43	24.72	47.92	34.41
Puglia	18.65	22.53	16.28	18.37	27.14	35.96	16.67	24.73
Basilicata	1.69	2.20	0	0	1.43	1.12	1.04	2.15
Calabria	3.15	3.57	2.33	0	1.43	2.25	1.04	4.30
Sicilia	15.01	13.19	0	0	10.00	4.49	17.71	17.20
Sardegna	4.35	2.74			0	1.12	3.13	3.23
Total	100	100	100	100	100	100	100	100
Absolute No.	413	364	43	49	70	89	96	93

Data refer to locally-based firms with more than 49 employees.
A: as percentage of total Southern firms.
B: percentage by region, by year of formation.
Source: Iasm-Cesan Data Bank; ISTAT

Moreover, the IASM-CESAN data is extremely helpful - as will be seen in the second section - for specifying the problems of locally-based firms in less developed areas and testing the hypothesis that locally-based firms expanded their activity in the seventies.

Comparing the IASM-CESAN and the census data for firms with more than 49 employees, we can get an idea of the importance within this dimensional class of locally-owned firms, that is, their weight with respect to the class as a whole. Table 5 shows that 46% of all such firms are locally owned, and that they account for 22% of the total employment in firms of this size. These percentages are much the same for all the Southern regions. An analysis of the data by industry shows that only in three industries Clothing, Timber and furniture and Footwear are these firms completely or predominantly locally owned.

Keeping these specifications in mind, we will now go on to the more qualitative analysis of the second section, which exploits the availability, in the IASM-CESAN data, of information on the starting dates of local firms in the South. Before doing so, a few remarks should be made concerning the regional distribution of the locally-based firms which belong to the 50+ employees dimensional class.

We have divided the firms into two categories, those started before or during 1964, and those started since then. This division shows that the firms in Abruzzi and Puglia have been quite dynamic since 1964, especially in the Clothing industry, and - in the case of Puglia - in the Mechanical and instrument engineering industry as well. A further subdivision by five-year intervals shows that more firms of this size were formed between 1970 and 1974 than in any other period. For the Clothing and Footwear industries in Puglia and Abruzzi, the period of maximum formation of new local firms of this size extends to the years after 1974 as well (see again Table 5).

This would suggest - again - that an active industrial policy has been a key factor in promoting the development of locally-based firms in several strategic sectors.

Introduction To Second Section

In this second section the problems of the formation of local firms and the presence of obstacles to their growth will be considered in greater detail. A simple model based on the Markovian process is used to test the hypothesis that the rate of formation of local firms in Southern Italy was higher in the seventies than in the sixties. The validity of the model rests on several strong assumptions; nevertheless, we feel that the results are representative of the trend of the firms which belong to the dimensional classes considered in the model. In any case, it must be remembered that the analysis in this second section refers exclusively to firms which in 1983 had more than 49 employees. The conclusions reached do not necessarily apply to smaller firms, such as those discussed earlier.

Obstacles To Growth And Vertical Integration

It has been suggested that one of the causes of regional inequalities is that in backward areas the rate of formation of local manufacturing firms is too slow and that the growth rate of local companies becomes negligible after they have reached a given size. It will be argued here that these two aspects derive from the fact that the process of division of labour in less prosperous regions is constrained. In general, with the expansion of industry, the firm is able to increase its degree of specialization. The firm will abandon certain productive processes and new firms will take them over. This is Stigler's (1951) explanation of disintegration as industry grows, based on his life cycle theory.

In backward regions as industry grows the following constraints to the expansion of the firm and to the disintegration process are at work (Del Monte 1983):

a. A large supply of gap-filling skills (gap-filler entrepreneurship) but a somewhat smaller supply of input-completing skills (input-completer entrepreneurship) (Leibenstein 1978).

b. A high level of uncertainty with regard to the external world (Schwartzman 1963).

c. A restricted supply of organizational and managerial skills.

As firms grow, problems of adjustment increase and changes in organizational structure are required to ensure an advantageous position in the socio-economic environment. If a firm is not able to make such organizational changes it will not survive or it will not be able to reach a given size. On the other hand if a firm wants to make a change in its organizational structure it needs to employ the right people to implement the change. If the firm is not able to obtain the appropriate people because skills are not available on the market it will not change its organizational structure and therefore it will not grow.

As a consequence the various functions an individual firm carries out in less developed areas have cost curves that begin to rise much sooner than they do in more industrialized areas. Firms of the same size, i.e. having the same number of employees, will show a lower rate of vertical integration in industrialized areas than in backward areas. Moreover, in backward areas, the market is smaller and therefore there are not enough sales to support a specialized producer. Thus, in less prosperous areas the growth of firms will be lower and there will be a higher rate of vertical integration than in developed regions. The lack of specialization reduces the competitiveness of local firms and therefore the rate of growth of local industries, and the rate of formation of new firms.

Obstacles To Growth And Distribution Of Local Firms By Size

We now want to verify the hypothesis that in Southern Italy there are constraints to the growth of local firms, but that these constraints have been less operative since the seventies.

If we assume that the average size of starting firms is about the same in each period, and if we assume that, as Gibrat's law (1931) suggests, equal proportionate increments have the same probability of occurring in a given time interval whatever size the firm happens to have reached, then the average size of older firms will be higher than the average size of younger firms. Otherwise - if the expected value of the rate of growth decreases with the size of the firm - it could still be true that the average size of older firms is higher than of younger firms, but the difference between the average sizes will be much lower, ceteris paribus, than in the case in which Gibrat's law is operative.

The average size, measured in terms of the number of employees, of the Southern Italian firms started before 1965 is higher than the average size of firms started after 1964 (121.1 employees and 101.3 employees, respectively). The difference between these average sizes is not as great as one would have expected, under the hypothesis that any given 'proportionate' size change is equiprobable at all size levels: thus the ratio between the latter and former size values is only 0.84. For different regions, this ratio varies between a minimum of 0.94 for Calabria and Basilicata and a maximum of 0.67 for Sardinia. This relationship is true for all sectors except Timber and furniture. Within each sector this relationship holds for every region. It would seem then that older firms are larger than younger firms and that this relationship follows a fairly systematic pattern. However, it must be remembered that these differences are not as large as one would find in more developed areas.

A further confirmation of the presence of obstacles to growth is the near absence of very large local manufacturing firms in the South: there are only two firms with more than 1000 employees, one started before 1965 and the other after 1964, and only eleven independent firms with more than five hundred employees, seven started before 1965 and four after 1964.

We may obtain further confirmation of our hypothesis by estimating the distribution of firms by size. Many stochastic processes lead to the Pareto Distribution (Simon and Bonini 1958, Steindl 1965). Therefore we have tried to see if the distribution by size of local manufacturing firms in Southern Italy follows Pareto's law, which we write as follows:

(1) $$N(S) = B S^{-a}$$

N(S)=Number of firms with size S

The value of parameter 'a' is regarded as a measure of concentration : a high value of 'a' corresponds to a steeper decline of N(S) with S increasing, and thus, in some sense, to a greater degree of concentration. The coefficients 'a' and 'B' can be estimated by least squares, taking the logarithm of S and N(S).

(2) $$\log N(S) = B - a \log S$$

Southern Italy

The pattern of size distribution for firms started before 1965 and after 1964 was estimated considering a width of 15 employees for firms employing 50 to 500 persons and a width of 100 employees for firms with more than 500 employees. The distribution pattern for all the firms was also estimated. The results are shown in Table 6. The R square is in all cases quite high but the D.W. test shows that the residuals follow a systematic pattern. For firms started before 1965, the residuals are first positive, then negative, then positive. For medium-sized firms the predicted values are higher than the observed values and for firms in the smallest and largest dimensional classes, they are lower.

If we estimate (2) considering only the firms with between 109 and 424 employees there is no autocorrelation. The value of 'a' is 1.95, much higher than that which has been found for advanced countries (Steindl 1965). We encounter the same pattern when equation (2) is estimated for firms started after 1964. In this case, the residuals have a different pattern than was found for firms started before 1964. Residuals are first negative, then positive, then negative. If we do not consider the smallest and largest firms, the problem of autocorrelation disappears. The value of 'a' is 1.98, not much higher than for firms started before 1964. The expected values in the two cases are not very different: 98.51 for firms started after 1964 and 100.51 for firms started before 1965. These regressions show that there is a structural difference between the distribution according to size of firms started before 1965 and those started after 1964. How should this be interpreted? For firms started before 1965, it may be supposed that many firms were not able to grow into the larger dimensional class and remained in the middle classes. For the smallest firms it may be that the probability of failing or of passing into a class with fewer than 49 employees was very high. In other words Gibrat's law works only for medium-sized firms, but not for the largest and the smallest firms. The smaller the firm is - up to a certain point - the higher the probability of failing. On the other hand for medium-sized firms the probability of proportionate increments decreases with increasing size.

As regards the firms started after 1964, the fact that the number of firms belonging to the smallest dimensional class is higher than expected

Southern Italy

Table 6. An estimation of Pareto's law: The distribution of local firms started before 1965 and after 1964, having more than 49 employees in 1983, according to the number of employees.

	no. of obs.	log B	B	R²	D.W.	E (S)
˃64	1-36	– 1.8624 (–48.256)	13.0240 (59.559)	453.159	.9856	.7370	105.82
˃64	5-26	– 1.9896 (–50.000)	13.6402 (62.000)	839196	.9920	1.4816	98.51
˂64	1-33	– 1.95120 (–38.194)	14.0846 (49.544)	13008772	.9792	.3626	100.51
˂64	5-26	– 1.95871 (–68.721)	14.2222 (90.284)	1501870	.9951	1.2646	100.51
MT	1-36	– 1.9866 (–65.459)	14.7085 (85.535)	2442420	.9921	.5986	98.67
MT	1-33	– 1.92082 (–73.267)	14.3675 (98.716)	1736704	.9925	.8493	102.21
MT	5-26	– 1.9686 (–101.611)	14.6643 (136.948)	2336816	.9980	1.9463	99.59

D.W. is the Durbin Watson statistic
The numbers in parentheses are t-ratios
S is the size of the firm (number of employees)
E (S) is the mean of the distribution
˃64 Firms started after 1964
˂64 Firms started before 1965
MT all local firms
Observations between 5 and 26 include firms having between 109 and 424 employees

may be explained by the presence in this group of many firms whose process of growth is still continuing. An interesting element is the existence of a higher number of firms in the largest dimensional class than was predicted by the regression. This could mean that some of the obstacles to growth met by firms started before 1964 were no longer present, or were weaker for firms started after 1964. This suggests that the development process of local firms started after 1964 was different from that of those started earlier.

Changes In The Rate Of Formation Of New Firms Between 1950 And 1983

As mentioned earlier, the IASM/CESAN databank provides information on the starting year and number of employees of local firms in Southern Italy that were still in operation in 1983 and had more than 49 employees at that time. The databank does not give information on the total number of firms surviving in 1983 or on the total number of new firms started in each period because firms with less than 49 employees are not included. Table 7 shows, for 1983, the distribution of the firms included in the IASM/CESAN data, according to firm size and starting date.

The relationship between the number of firms with more than 49 employees and the total number of local firms started in each period has been estimated using a methodology based on Markov chains. The firms have been divided into three dimensional classes: those with less than 50 employees (class 1), those with 50 or more employees (class 2), and those which failed to survive (class 0). For example, a firm which was started at time t and belonged at that time to class 1, at time t+h could still belong to class 1, or it could have become larger and moved to class 2, or it could have failed to survive until t+h, in which case we say that it has moved to class 0. A firm started at time t, belonging at time t+h to a given dimensional class which we will call r, may at time t+h+1 have moved to another dimensional class which we will call s, where r=1,2 and s=0,1,2.

If

X(t) = the number of firms started at time t

X(t,t+h,2) = the number of firms started at time t that at time t+h where in class 2

then

we will have the following relationship

X(t,t+h,2) = b(t,t+h,2) X(t)

where b(t,t+h,2) is the percentage of firms started at time t that at time t+h were in class 2.

Given the following hypotheses:

a. The probability of moving from one dimensional class to another is constant and is independent of time;

b. The probability of moving from one dimensional class to another depends only on the size of a firm, and not on its age;

Table 7. Employment and number of local firms, by
size and starting year, in Southern Italy.

No. of employees	Absolute values					
	50-94	95-199	200-349	350-499	⟩500	Total
⟨1950	6910	5988	2699	880	4475	20941
1950-1954	1677	1793	740	1126	501	5837
1955-1959	1964	2771	1585	896	0	7216
1960-1964	6572	6089	2619	790	0	16070
1965-1969	4853	4431	1758	0	915	11957
1970-1974	7288	4189	2075	781	1266	15599
⟩1975	4580	2349	688	0	1710	9327
No. of firms						
⟨1950	100	45	10	2	6	163
1950-1954	25	12	3	3	1	44
1955-1959	28	20	6	2	0	56
1960-1964	93	44	11	2	0	150
1965-1969	72	34	7	0	1	114
1970-1974	109	34	8	2	2	155
⟩1975	70	20	3	0	2	95

No. of employees	Percentage values					
	50-94	95-199	200-349	350-499	⟩500	Total
⟨1950	.33	.29	.13	.04	.21	1
1950-1954	.29	.31	.13	.19	.08	1
1955-1959	.28	.38	.22	.12	0	1
1960-1964	.41	.38	.16	.05	0	1
1965-1969	.40	.37	.15	0	.08	1
1970-1974	.47	.27	.13	.05	.08	1
⟩1975	.50	.25	.07	0	.18	1
No. of firms						
⟨1950	.62	.27	.06	.01	.04	1
1950-1954	.57	.27	.07	.07	.02	1
1955-1959	.50	.36	.11	.03	0	1
1960-1964	.62	.29	.08	.01	0	1
1965-1969	.63	.30	.06	0	.01	1
1970-1974	.70	.22	.06	.01	.01	1
⟩1975	.74	.21	.03	0	.02	1

Source: IASM-CESAN Data Bank

c. The initial frequency distribution is the same for any starting data t.

we can delete the time index from the percentage of firms started at time t so that

b (t,t+h,2) = b(h,2)

and therefore

X(t,t+h,2)=b(h,2) X(t).

We are interested in knowing how the coefficients b(h,2) changed over time. It is possible to show that given certain plausible values for the transitional probabilities and the initial frequency distribution, b(h,2) was first an increasing and then a decreasing function of h[4]. Therefore, if the number of firms started in each time period had been the same as the number in the preceding period, we would expect, assuming hypotheses a, b, and c are correct, that the starting of firms with more than 49 employees would have been distributed over time as follows:

$$
\begin{array}{ccccc}
1950\text{-}54 & & 1955\text{-}59 & & 1960\text{-}64 & & 1965\text{-}69 \\
X & \langle & X & \langle & X & \rangle & X \\
1983,\!\rangle 49 & & 1983,\!\rangle 49 & & 1983,\!\rangle 49 & & 1983,\!\rangle 49
\end{array}
$$

$$
\begin{array}{ccc}
& 1970\text{-}74 & & \rangle 1975 \\
\rangle & X & \rangle & X \\
& 1983,\!\rangle 49 & & 1983,\!\rangle 49
\end{array}
$$

where the values for X = the number of firms started in each time period (1950-54, 1955-59, etc) which were still operating in 1983 and at that time had more than 49 employees. The number of firms actually started in each time period is reported in Table 8, together with the ratio between this number and the number of firms started in the period immediately preceding it.

From the table it may be seen that the formation of new firms with more than 49 employees was not distributed over time in the way we expected. In fact, the number of firms started between 1970 and 1974 was higher than the number of firms started in the earlier periods, and it appears it is probable that the rate of formation of new firms after 1974 continued at much the same rate as before 1970. The most interesting fact to emerge is that the rate of formation of new local firms in the South increased at the very time when Northern-based firms were most active in establishing new branch offices and plants in the South, that is, between 1970 and 1974. After 1974

Table 8. The number of firms surviving in 1983 with more than 49 employees, by starting date.

Time Period	Number of firms started	Ratio between the number of firms started in the period and that of the previous one
>1974	99	.623
1970-74	159	1.371
1965-69	116	.748
1960-64	155	2.583
1955-59	60	1.333
1950-54	45	

there was a decrease both in the formation of new local firms and in the setting-up of branches by non-local firms. The increased activity in the South of non-local firms did not affect all manufacturing industries equally: rather, the rate of formation of new firms varied from one industry to another. In Table 9 the number of new firms established in each manufacturing industry in the time periods 1965-69, 1970-74, and 1975-83 has been calculated individually.

Food, beverage, tobacco and coal, petroleum, chemical and allied industries seem to have been least affected by the increased activity of non-local firms in the South, and their ratios show that few new firms were being established in these sectors between 1965 and 1974. Clothing and footwear and leather were the most active sectors overall, and seem to have been largely unaffected by the activity of outside firms in as much as the number of new firms formed in these sectors remained fairly constant. For all other sectors, the rate of formation of new firms was greatest between 1970-74, although in some cases the increase in the number of new firms was modest. The most interesting case is that of the mechanical engineering sector. Here there was a dramatic increase in the rate of formation of new firms during the period 1970-74, and a sharp drop in their formation after that. The decline after 1974 was such that, of the firms still in operation with more than 49 employees in 1983, the ones which had been established between 1965 and 1969 far outnumbered those established after 1974. The values of the ratios also point to the conclusion that fewer new firms were set up in this sector

Table 9. The distribution of local manufacturing firms in the South, by industry and starting date.

	1965–69		1970–74		1975–83	
	N	R	N	R	N	R
Food, beverage, tobacco	13		9	0.69	5	0.56
Bricks, pottery	14		15	1.07	12	0.80
Mechanical engineering, vehicles, metal goods	28		48	1.71	17	0.35
Electrical engineering	4		10	2.50	6	0.60
Clothing	27		30	1.11	31	1.03
Footwear, leather	13		17	1.31	16	0.94
Paper, printing	3		6	2.00	0	0
Timber, furniture	5		12	2.40	4	0.33
Coal, petroleum, chemical, allied	7		5	0.71	3	0.60

N = Number of firms
R = ratio between number of firms in one period and in the previous period.

after 1974 than had been set up either between 1970-74 or between 1965-69. It should be noted that the considerable difference is very unlikely to be explained by the shorter period for new firm growth to above the 49 employee threshold of this study, which has been available to post-1974 new firms, since the post-1974 period is in fact nearly twice as long (9 years) as the earlier ones (5 years each).

The temporal pattern identified in the formation of new local engineering could have been determined by the activity of Northern-based firms which was mentioned earlier. From about the end of the sixties until the mid-seventies there was a substantial increase in the number of large engineering plants set up by Northern-based firms in the South. For new, local - and smaller - engineering firms this meant an increase in the number of subcontracting orders; and likewise, an increase in the number of medium-sized engineering firms. Similarly, with the decline in the establishment of large plants by firms based outside the South, there was also a decline in the subcontracting market after 1974, and a concomitant decline in the formation of new locally-based firms. Other sectors (e.g., Clothing, Leather and footwear, Bricks) were not as affected by the activity of non local firms in the area because their markets - in particular the markets for the firms of the size we are considering here - are located outside the South.

Conclusions

In Southern Italy the formation of firms in the smallest and largest dimensional classes over the last twenty years has been quite different from the rest of Italy. Nevertheless, there is a strong correlation between the growth rates of plants belonging to these two dimensional classes, particularly in the strategic group of mechanical, electrical, and instrument engineering and vehicle industries.

When we consider the growth of the larger local firms (with more than 50 or 100 employees), we find that the obstacles to growth for firms in this dimensional class appear to have been less strong during the seventies than they had been previously. In addition, the analysis strongly supports the view that the positive effects of active regional industrial policy have significantly affected the rate of formation of firms of this size in the strategic industries.

Notes

1. For this problem see Fondazione Brodolini (1985), AA.VV. (1985)
2. See A. Del Monte (1979), R. Varaldo (1979), G. Bianchi-R. Bosco-R. Cibin-A. Giannnola (1985)
3. The value of 'a' is lower than 2 and the size distribution does not have a finite variance, however in reality any observed size distribution has a finite variance. The questions remain whether the same distribution was accompanied by a distribution with a finite variance or not.
4. Our example is founded on the following transition matrix estimated from a survey we conducted in the province of Caserta (a province of Southern Italy) for a four-year period.

Southern Italy

$$A = \begin{array}{c c} & \begin{array}{c c c} 0 & 1 & 2 \end{array} \\ \begin{array}{c} 0 \\ 1 \\ 2 \end{array} & \left[\begin{array}{c c c} 1.00 & 0 & 0 \\ .23 & .73 & .04 \\ .10 & .10 & .80 \end{array} \right] \end{array}$$

Appendix

A note on the IASM-CESAN Databank

The population: The Iasm-Cesan Databank covers all manufacturing establishments operating in the South that are managed by firms with a total of 10 or more employees. While this source is completely reliable for larger firms, it is much less so for smaller firms. For the larger firms, the Iasm-Cesan data is reasonably comparable to the Census Data excluding firms formed after December 1981. As for the regions, we have considered the standard Southern regions: Abruzzi, Molise, Campania, Basilicata, Puglia, Calabria, Sicilia and Sardegna. The data is symbolically referred to 31 December 1983.
Sources: Information on ownership comes primarily from the direct interviews routinely conducted by the CESAN, which are especially crucial in assessing the ownership of smaller plants.
We have considered as 'local' or locally-based firms those firms having Southern ownership. They include all establishments owned by Southern-based firms or Southern entrepreneurs, regardless of the size and articulation of the firms. Firms that are legally based in the South, but the majority of whose shares are owned by non-Southern corporations or entrepreneurs, are not considered to be local firms.

References

AA,VV (1985) Crisi Industriale e Sistemi Locali nel Mezzogiorno, F. Angeli, Milano
Bianchi G., R. Bosco, R. Cibin and A. Giannola (1985) Grande impresa e artigianato: ipotesi di integrazione verticale e verifica empirica, Franco Angeli, Milano
Cramer, J.S. (1969) Empirical econometrics, North Holland
Del Monte A. (1979) 'Piccola impresa e sviluppo economico', Contrattazione, mar. giu

Southern Italy

Del Monte A. (1983) 'Il Processo di Divisione del Lavoro e la Crescita Dimensionale delle Imprese nell 'Economia Meridionale', Rassegna Economica, nov. dic.

Fondazione Brodolini (1985) Potenziali di Sviluppo Industriale Endogeno nel Mezzogiorno d'Italia, Marsilio, Milano

Gibrat, R. (1931) Les inégalités economiques, Paris

Kemeney, J.G. and J.L. Snell (1960) Finite Markov chains, D. Van Nostrand Company

Leibenstein, H. (1978) General X efficiency theory & Economic Development, Oxford University Press

March, J.C. and H.A. Simon (1958) Organizations, Wiley

Schwartzman, D. (1963) 'Uncertainty and the Size of the Firm', Economica, v. 30, pp. 287-296

Simon, H.A. and C.P. Bonini (1958) 'The Size distribution of Business firms' A.E.R., v. 48, pp. 607-617

Steindl, J. (1965) Random process and the growth of firms, Griffin

Stigler, G.J. (1951) 'The Division of Labour is Limited by the extent of the Market', Journal of Political Economy, June

Turker, I.B. and B.P. Wilder (1977) 'Trend in Vertical Integration in the manufacturing sector', The Journal of Industrial Economics, September

Varaldo, R. (1979) Ristrutturazioni industriali e rapporti tra imprese, Franco Angeli, Milano

Chapter fourteen

SMALL MANUFACTURING FIRMS AND REGIONAL DEVELOPMENT
IN GREECE: PATTERNS AND CHANGES

Evangelia Dokopoulou

The Importance Of Small Firms

Most attention today in Greece is concentrated on
the poor financial performance of the country's
relatively few large manufacturing companies and
the large plants which they operate; small-scale
firms and plants have not attracted much interest
or concern. There is thus a need to initiate
research into the small-firm dimension of regional
and industrial change in Greece as a guide for
policy-making in this field. New small firms have
been even less an object of investigation. Unlike
other EEC countries, no studies of new firm
formation or entrepreneurial characteristics are
available in Greece for the last 20 years. So this
study has perforce to be based on aggregate figures
obtained from the national censuses of
manufacturing establishments. The most recent of
these is for 1978, and provides data for
establishments, not enterprises. Virtually all
small establishments (less than 10 employees) in
Greece are however independent single-plant firms.
Census small-establishment data therefore affords a
valid picture of small-firm distribution and
characteristics.
    Trends in the 1970s must be understood in the
context of the favourable impacts from Greece's
association with the EEC since 1962, with tariffs
on imports of Greek manufactures to EEC countries
having been abolished in 1968. Trends in the 1980s
may be different following Greece's full membership
of the Community because tariff barriers with other
member countries had to be phased out by 1984 for
most industrial products. However, sectors such as
textiles, food products and engineering still enjoy
substantial protection through non-tariff barriers.

Table 1. Employment change in small establishments 1969-1978.

	Total	Mining	Manufac- turing	Industries Gas water electr.	Restaur. Hotels Commerce	Transp. Stor. Commun.	Real estate insur. banking
	(1)	(2)	(3)	(4)	(5)	(6)	(7)
Small plants: Employment 1978 000s:	782.8	3.6	264.1	2.4	429.4	20.3	26.3
Change 000s:	78.0	-0.9	+16.6	+0.1	+55.7	+4.0	+8.9
Annual growth rate:	+1.17	-2.49	+0.72	+0.49	+1.56	+2.49	+4.70
All plants: Annual growth rate:	+2.91	-0.49	+3.30	+4.14	+2.13	+4.82	+5.69
Small plants: Distribution:	100.0	0.5	33.7	0.3	54.8	2.6	3.4
% in sector:	51.7	17.0	39.3	9.2	82.2	13.3	36.8

Sources: National Statistical Service of Greece (NSSG), 1981, Résultats du Recensement des Industries Manufacturières-Artisanats, du Commerce et autres Services, effectué le Septembre 1978, Athens; and NSSG (1971), Recensement des Etablissements Industriels et Commerciaux, effectué le Septembre 1969, Athens.

In 1978, small establishments[1] (defined throughout this chapter as plants or firms employing 1-9 persons) accounted for 96.2 per cent of establishments in all industries excluding agriculture. Their employment share was 51.7 per cent compared with 17.0 per cent in medium sized (10-49) and 31.3 per cent in large scale establishments (over 50)[2]. As Table 1 indicates, small establishments were important in four sectors which accounted in 1960 for 56 per cent of the national gross domestic product: commerce and tourism; miscellaneous services; manufacturing; and real estate, insurance and banking. The annual increase in employment in small-scale establishments between 1960 and 1978 was however two and a half times lower than the increase of employment in all establishments. Small establishments recorded relatively lower growth rates in all industries. Within the small-firm sector, the three fastest-growing industries in employment terms were all services. Tourism contributed most to the employment gains in small

establishments recorded in Table 1, with
manufacturing second.

Family entrepreneurial initiative and support
is vital in small manufacturing plants since self-
employed and unpaid family members constituted in
1978 60.8 per cent of their personnel, and 84.9 per
cent of this was males. Female participation is
under-represented too in the waged and salaried
workforce of small-scale manufacturing, only 22.4
per cent being women.

There are significant structural and
organizational differences between small, medium
and large manufacturing plants in Greece. First, as
shown in Table 2, family entrepreneurial initiative
decreases substantially as plant and firm size
grows.

Second, the low productivity of small-scale
manufacturing in Greece is reflected in its low
value-added contribution, which in 1974 (the most
recent estimate from the National Statistical
Service of Greece) was only 19 per cent of all
manufacturing, less than half its share in jobs.
Mechanisation, measured as installed HP (horse
power) per employee, was in 1978 only 46 per cent
of the level of plants of over 10 employees (NSSG
1981). Around 15 per cent of employment in small
manufacturing plants is actually engaged in non-
manufacturing activities, though classified as the
former. These activities include marble cutting and
repairs of shoes, engines, cars, motorbikes, office
machines, watches, cameras and boats: their

Table 2. Status of persons[+] employed in
manufacturing in 1978[+] by size of
establishment.

Size of plant (employees)	Self-employed and non-remunerated persons per plant	Salaried and waged persons per plant	Percentage of plants owned by personal firms*
	(1)	(2)	(3)
1- 9	1.36	0.88	97.6
10-49	1.46	18.71	68.4
over 50	0.29	180.13	15.1

* Firms not having the status of Societe Anonyme, Limited
  Company, and which are not cooperatives or State-owned.
+ Refers to employment on the day of Census.
Source: NSSG (1981) op. cit.

inclusion in manufacturing reflects the absence of an ad hoc code number (NSSG 1981, Vl, p.X).

Traditional and labour-intensive assembly operations are the main areas of specialisation of small manufacturing firms. Together, the food, garments, wood, furniture, printing, leather, metal products, assembly of non electrical machinery and buses and miscellaneous industries accounted in 1978 for 82.3 per cent of all employment in such firms. The first three of these recorded between 1973-1978 the largest decline in employment share within the small firm sector, a total of 2.9 percentage points. The largest increase in share was in transport equipment assembly, of 1.9 percentage points, but most of this is due to the growth of employment in repair shops.

In 1978, the sectoral distributions of both small-scale and total manufacturing employment at 2-digit level (20 sectors) had a strong positive association, r=+0.868, which suggests that the problems of small plants are closely interlinked with those of the industrial structure of Greece as a whole. Thus sectoral policies for restructuring and diversification of manufacturing are likely directly to influence the country's small plants and firms. Intra-sectoral linkages may also be implied by the above strong association.

A number of workers have argued that small plants have only limited potential to generate jobs, relative to large firms, which suggests that small firms are not likely to be a major force in industrial development in Greece. Research by Gould and Keeble (1984, 199) has supported this view in the case of the United Kingdom. As Table 3 shows, the annual rate of employment growth of small plants in Greece during 1973-1978 was less than half that of medium, and less than one-fifth that of large plants. The share of small plants in the growth of manufacturing employment represented only 13.5 per cent of the total increase (see column 4), compared with their 39 per cent share of employment. Average small firm size declined due to a larger percentage increase in establishments than in jobs. This may partly reflect a lack of job growth or upward mobility to the next highest size class, although this is contrary to evidence found elsewhere as in Ireland (O'Farrell 1985, p. 41). Larger plants have been considerably more important in employment change. Possibly, small establishments substituted capital for labour, since per worker installed HP rose between 1973 and

Greece

Table 3. Changes in manufacturing 1973-1978.

	Average Size (emps.)		Esta-blishm.		Employment	
	1978	% aver. annual	% aver. annual	net change	% aver. annual	rate: per an. /1000 in man.
	(1)	(2)	(3)	(4)	(5)	(6)
1- 9	2.19	-0.54	+1.18	+9124	+0.71	+3.02
10-49	19.49	+0.24	+1.49	+11500	+1.74	+3.87
over 50	175.51	-0.19	+4.11	+46832	+3.91	+15.50
Total	5.21	+0.91	+1.23	+67456	+2.13	+22.39

Sources: NSSG, 1975, Resultats du Recensement des Industries Manufacturières-Artisanats et des Industries Extractives, effectué le Septembre 1973, Athens: NSSG (1981) op. cit.

1978 by 4.18 per cent per annum, compared with only a 0.21 per cent increase in plants with more than 10 workers (NSSG 1975 and 1981).

Patterns

Fig. 1 shows that in 1978 the regional distribution of manufacturing employment in Greece was polarised: industry is concentrated in the two most prosperous regions of Greater Athens and Macedonia which contain between them 64.2 per cent of all manufacturing jobs and 63.2 per cent of that in small firms (Table 4). Very little manufacturing is located in the islands and the rural regions of Ipiros and Thraki, these accounting for only 8.7 per cent of all manufacturing jobs and 14.7 per cent of those in small-scale industry.

The coefficient of correlation between the distribution of jobs in small establishments and in total manufacturing in the 10 regions is r=+0.988. This shows a strong positive locational association and could suggest linkages between small units and larger manufacturing plants. It also implies that the centralised pattern of Greek manufacturing in the prosperous, more urbanised and most accessible areas has conditioned the location of small establishments.

As Table 4 shows, urban-industrial centres, excluding Greater Athens[3], account for 17.6 per cent of small-scale industry, which is less than their share of total manufacturing employment (19.7 per cent). Adding Greater Athens' share to that of

Greece

Fig. 1.   Distribution of manufacturing employment
by size of establishment and by regions
in Greece, 1978.

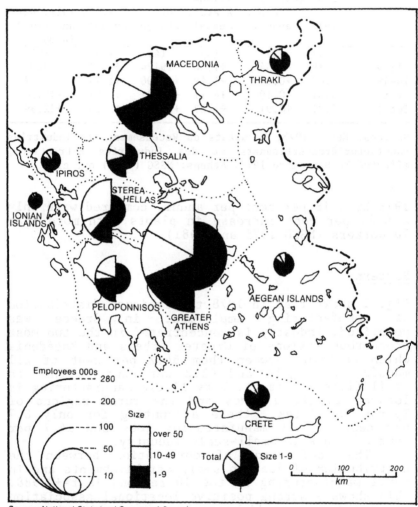

Source: National Statistical Service of Greece

urban-industrial areas, the proportion of jobs in
small plants in the urban-industrial centres is
57.9 per cent. A considerable percentage of small-
scale manufacturing is therefore located in the
hinterland: 42.1 per cent. It is not clear,
however, how much of this is satellite to the main
urban areas in terms of proximity.

As Fig. 2 indicates, the largest urban areas
of the country, Thessaloniki, Patras, Heraklion,

Fig. 2. Distribution of manufacturing employment by size of establishment and urban-industrial centres* in Greece, 1978.

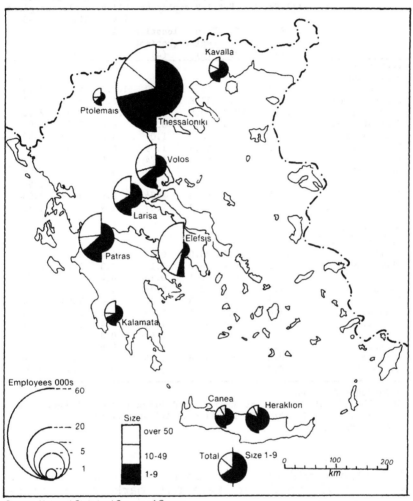

Source. National Statistical Service of Greece

Larissa and Volos, contain the largest shares of employment in small scale plants. Not surprisingly, the distribution of jobs in small establishments within the set of urban areas is strongly and positively associated with that of total manufacturing (r= +0.998).

Fig. 1 shows that the most rural regions of the mainland, Ipiros and Thraki, and all the islands, specialise in small-scale industry (this

Table 4.   Small manufacturing establishments in
            Greece in 1978.

	All Est.	Employment Est.1-9 employees			Esta-blish. 1-9	Average Size employees/plant	
	%	%	% in region	location quotient	%	All	1-9
	(1)	(2)	(3)	(4)	(5)	(6)	(7)
Regions (in empl. rank)							
Greece	100.0	100.0	39.3	1.00	100.0	5.21	2.19
Greater Athens	42.0	40.3	37.8	0.96	36.1	5.95	2.46
Macedonia	22.2	22.9	40.6	1.03	22.8	5.03	2.20
Rest of Sterea	13.8	8.0	23.0	0.58	8.8	7.99	2.02
Peloponnisos	7.7	8.0	40.9	1.04	8.8	4.60	1.99
Thessalia	5.6	6.1	42.8	1.09	6.4	4.60	2.08
Creta	2.7	4.7	68.7	1.74	5.5	2.65	1.87
Aegan Islands	2.0	3.5	66.5	1.69	4.3	2.62	1.78
Thraki	1.7	2.5	55.3	1.40	2.8	3.38	1.95
Ipiros	1.5	2.4	61.5	1.56	2.6	3.19	2.03
Ionian Islands	0.8	1.6	81.2	2.07	1.9	2.25	1.85
Urban-Industrial* Centres (in empl. rank):	19.7	17.6	35.0	0.89	16.4	6.19	2.36
Thessaloniki	8.3	9.2	43.2	1.11	8.3	5.16	2.44
Elefsis	2.9	0.5	7.1	0.18	0.4	28.47	2.81
Patras	2.3	1.7	29.1	0.74	1.6	7.44	2.39
Volos	1.8	1.3	28.3	0.72	1.4	7.00	2.12
Larissa	1.4	1.3	35.1	0.89	1.1	6.54	2.54
Heraklion	0.9	1.4	64.5	1.64	1.4	3.16	2.12
Canea	0.6	0.8	52.8	1.40	0.8	3.93	2.15
Kalamata	0.6	0.6	38.2	0.97	0.6	5.92	2.34
Kavalla	0.6	0.6	38.6	0.98	0.6	5.12	2.16
Ptolemais	0.3	0.2	28.0	0.71	0.2	6.93	2.01

* Excludes G. Athens
N.B. The classifications of Regions and Urban-Industrial Centres are
     those used by the NSSG in all official statistics.
Source: NSSG (1981).

is also evident in Table 4). The lack of
substantial local or regional markets is almost
certainly one reason for the lack of large plants
in these peripheral areas. But other constraints on
growth no doubt also play a part, including poor
accessibility, lower rural incomes which diminish
capital availability for entrepreneurs wishing to
enlarge their manufacturing plants, and unbalanced
labour market structures and shortages of younger
and skilled workers caused by the outmigration of
population.
        The fact that these peripheral areas are
predominantly rural and specialise in agriculture

also constrains manufacturing growth in various
ways. Manufacturing has to compete with agriculture
for the few younger people who work on family
property in crops and orchards. Rural areas have an
above-average percentage of aged population with
little education or motive for entrepreneurial
activity which is so essential to start a small
firm. Indeed, the employed work force in
agriculture in rural areas in 1983 represented 70.2
per cent of the total compared with 37.3 per cent
in semi-urban and 3.4 per cent in urban areas. Of
all those engaged in agriculture, 30 per cent of
Greece's workforce, only 5,7 per cent had finished
any class beyond primary school; only 16.0 per cent
were under 30 years of age; and 96 per cent were
working on their own property (NSSG 1984). It is
likely that the indebtedness which characterises
families engaged in agriculture has been another
factor preventing farmers from starting another
type of business. Parents may be unable to release
land for sale to help provide capital for younger
family members wishing to set up a new enterprise.

Specialisation on small-scale plants in
regional manufacturing employment seems to increase
inversely with the region's share of Greece's
employment (Fig. 1). Regions with the smallest
share of Greece's manufacturing jobs, such as
Ipiros, Thraki and the islands, have over half of
their employment in small plants: their small firm
location quotients range between 1.40 and 2.07
(Table 4). However, statistically the association
between the share of small scale industry in
regional employment and the share of each region in
Greece's manufacturing is relatively weak, r=
-0.60. So regional specialisation in small plants
is perhaps to be explained more by other factors
than by the region's share of national
manufacturing activity.

The share of small establishments in the
urban-industrial centres excluding Athens is 35.0
per cent, not much smaller than that for Greece as
a whole, 39.3 per cent. Only Thessaloniki and two
island cities, Canea and Heraklion, exhibit a
relative specialisation on small-scale industry
(Table 4, column 4). Elefsis, the closest centre to
Athens, was one of the pre-war assisted areas
designated for decentralisation of industry from
the national capital. Though in proximity to it, it
specialises in large-scale manufacturing (Fig. 2)
which indicates that it is not a satellite location
for small firms subcontracting to Athens plants.

The two most developed regions, Greater Athens and Macedonia, and the industrial centres as a whole, had in 1978 the largest plant size within the small establishment sector. By contrast, lower average sizes of small manufacturing establishments are found in the islands and the less developed periphery, which is characterised by mountainous districts, dispersed towns, poor accessibility and peripheral communications to the major North-South highway and the capital of Athens; these areas are Ipiros, Thraki, Peloponnisos and the central parts of Sterea and Thessalia. The smaller industrial centres, those located on islands like Canea and Heraklion and those off the main highway like Ptolemais, Kavalla and Volos, also have below-average sizes of small firms.

Nine out of the eleven urban-industrial centres, including Greater Athens, are ports which indicates the significance of sea transport rather than roads. In fact, more than 94 per cent of commodity imports and 89 per cent of exports by volume are transported by sea. Proximity to the main highway may be less important to small firms which are likely to be relatively more flexible locationally, in the sense of being able to operate successfully in a variety of different areas of Greece, for a number of reasons. First, labour can be obtained locally since most of their personnel comprises family members and the waged labour they use is generally limited; despite this the supply in rural areas may be less than sufficient. Roads could become important to small peripherally-located plants if they grow in size and thus need access to more labour which has to be drawn from dispersed locations. Finance institutions, notably banks and authorities giving subsidies for regional development, tend to be centralised and located in Athens. Access to capital and subsidies may thus require extra personnel to be sent and stay in Athens. The cost involved for small plants located in the periphery would be relatively high and the same whether they are located close to main roads or not. There is certainly a need to decentralise financing for small firms to local authorities and to provide local sources of capital for them. Communes and municipalities have as yet no authority to promote industry in their areas, not have they any funds to do so. In addition, the building of plants in peripheral assisted areas reduces or removes altogether taxes otherwise payable to local authorities, themselves prospective investors, and thus in fact diminishes local funds for development.

It can be argued that small firms are capable of operating successfully in ports or in relatively remote locations with poor infrastructure provided there is a decentralisation in the administration of subsidies away from the central government in Athens. However, the coastal development of small plants could create environmental problems given the weak protection from water and air pollution, which have become major problems in all the ports of Greece. This may affect tourism and recreation, the most important source of employment growth amongst small firms in recent years as noted earlier (see Table 1).

Finally, small plants outside the main urban-industrial centres are basically responding to local market opportunities and not to export-processing. The great majority sell their products in their isolated locality rather than serve the national or international market. Likely contacts are exchanged with other nearby firms, and their products are distributed more widely, if at all, through kinship ties in particular towns or through travelling salesmen. This pattern of distribution is found amongst firms in olive oil, building materials, repairs, publishing and furniture. In the urban-industrial centres, export processing and subcontracting to larger firms may take place because the industrial agglomeration of diversified industries facilitates frequent contacts of small firms with their customers for orders, and urban external economies exist which are unattainable in peripheral towns and mountainous districts.

The dividing mountains of Greece do disintegrate the national landscape both physically and economically. But it may be argued that the centralisation of the administration of subsidies to manufacturing has been even more important in discriminating in favour of larger, more centrally-located plants, and against smaller firms in isolated and peripheral locations. The type of subsidies which are given are moreover suitable only for large capital-intensive processes rather than for the labour-intensive ones in which small establishments specialise, due to the limited finances of family firms. Partly for this reason, small plants tend to engage in subcontracting, a low-level entrepreneurial activity, with small value added because it has minimum capital requirements; no purchase of materials and no organisation for marketing and distribution is involved.

Changes

Changes in the geographical distribution of small manufacturing firms in Greece between 1973 and 1978, and more recently, perhaps reflect three main influences. First, there was a strengthening of incentives during 1971-1978 for the industrial development of the peripheral regions and the decentralisation of manufacturing from Greater Athens[4]. Thus the boundaries of the assisted areas altered four times in that period. Investment in Greater Athens received no assistance; its commuting hinterland and Thessaloniki were favoured as area B; and the rest of Greece, area C, enjoyed the largest government subsidies. However, firms located in Athens could receive subsidies to the extent that they relocated or invested outside it in a branch plant. Since 1973 the most favoured areas have been less developed peripheral regions and a 20 kilometre-wide border zone. Subsidies have however been biassed in favour of capital intensive plants, with deductions of a percentage of investment costs from profits. Mergers have been encouraged to increase firm size, while since 1971 financial support has been available to cover R&D costs. Initially, regional subsidies were given subject to a requirement that investments would be realised between 1973 en 1982. However in 1978 the time limit was extended to 1985, before being abolished altogether in 1981.

The second influence has been the development of industrial estates. Until 1977 there were only three such estates in operation in Greece and these were all in cities: Thessaloniki, Heraklion and Volos. Together, these received 81 new plants between 1975 and 1977 (HIDB). Since 1975 investment in industrial estates has increased considerably and there were ten more in operation in 1982.

The third factor influencing small firm trends has been the impact of international events, notably the post-1974 recession, and the phasing-out of tariffs on imports into Greece from other EEC countries which was to be effected for most products by 1984[5]. Little or no survey research has been carried out on the effect of these trends on industrial restructuring and firm organisation in Greece. However it does appear that while major plants have modernised in the face of intensifying competition, investment in manufacturing as a whole has declined. This suggests that small firms have been affected more severely than large businesses, partly perhaps through reduced linkage or subcontracting opportunities.

Between 1973 and 1978, manufacturing industry experienced a decentralisation from Greater Athens and Thessaloniki, these two dominant centres recording, as Table 5 shows, a decline of 5.0 percentage points in their share of Greek manufacturing employment. This was the largest loss experienced by any region and urban industrial centre, with the exception of the Aegean islands.

All the islands and the peripheral region of Ipiros also recorded declining shares of national manufacturing activity. Employment was redistributed amongst the intermediate regions. Intermediate-sized urban-industrial centres as a group also gained marginally in shares. The decentralisation of manufacturing is marked by the very rapid growth rates of employment outside Greater Athens and Thessaloniki.

The share of small firms in total manufacturing employment declined everywhere in Greece except Greater Athens and Thessaloniki. It declined less rapidly in the urban-industrial centres than in their hinterlands but the most peripheral cities of Kavalla, Canea and Kalamata lost relatively heavily in this respect.

Small firms became relatively and absolutely more important in the two major cities of Athens and Thessaloniki during 1973-1978, as these were losing shares of larger-scale industry. Fig. 3 shows that employment in small plants grew fastest in the urbanised regions of Greater Athens and Macedonia, together with one peripheral region, Thraki. Other urban areas which recorded above-average small firm growth rates included Elefsis, Patras and Larissa, all of which are accessible and centrally-located towns. The rapid growth rates in Greater Athens and northern Greece suggest that greater accessibility to other EEC countries may have been important, a point also noted by Wagstaff (1983, 27).

Small scale manufacturing in the Ionian and Aegean islands declined faster than anywhere else in Greece, the Aegean region losing no less than 150 small plants during the period. This trend almost certainly reflects their relative isolation from the major national ports and urban-industrial

Table 5. Urban and regional changes in small manufacturing establishments 1973-1978.

	Employment			Aver. Size (empl./plant)		Establishments
	Total	1-9				1-9
	Growth rate per annum	Growth rate per annum	Change of share in region*	Growth rate per annum All plants 1-9		Growth rate per annum
	(1)	(2)	(3)	(4)	(5)	(6)
Regions						
Greece	+2.13	+0.71	-2.9	+0.91	-0.54	+1.18
Greater Athens	+0.14	+1.15	+1.8	-1.81	-1.10	+2.26
Macedonia	+4.29	+2.10	-4.5	+1.67	-0.27	+2.43
Rest of Sterea	+5.75	+0.33	-6.9	+5.24	+0.40	-0.10
Peloponnisos	+2.97	-0.36	-7.3	+2.29	-0.10	-0.24
Thessalia	+3.10	-0.78	-9.1	+3.46	-0.29	-0.49
Crete	+0.58	-0.54	-3.9	+0.27	-0.42	-0.10
Aegean Islands	-3.45	-3.93	-1.7	+0.61	-1.19	-2.71
Thraki	+8.62	+2.51	-18.6+	+5.55	-0.10	+2.61
Ipiros	+1.65	-0.41	-6.7	+1.64	-0.29	-0.12
Ionian Islands	-1.07	-1.20	-0.5	-0.26	-0.43	-0.81
Urban-Industrial Centres	+2.45	+1.29	-2.1	+0.26	-0.91	+2.21
Thessaloniki	+0.57	+1.51	+1.9	-1.69	-0.96	+2.48
Elefsis	+6.10	+5.49	-0.2	+1.24	+2.54	+2.91
Patras	+3.79	+3.40	-0.6	-1.09	-1.59	+5.11
Volos	+5.18	-0.37	-8.9	+4.56	-1.00	+0.67
Larissa	+3.64	+2.52	-1.9	+0.09	-0.92	+3.43
Heraklion	+1.32	+1.21	-0.4	-0.86	-1.00	+2.25
Canea	+1.50	-0.63	-5.9	+1.10	-0.82	+0.17
Kalamata	+3.01	-2.43	-11.0	+5.08	-0.42	-2.05
Kavalla	+2.78	-1.35	-8.8	+1.55	-2.17	+0.88
Ptolemais	-0.91	-1.15	-0.4	-0.71	-0.78	-0.36

* The share of employment of small plants in the regions manufacturing employment in 1978 minus the corresponding share in 1973.

+ Employment in small manufacturing establishments in the region of Thraki rose from 5795 in 1973 to 6561 in 1978, an annual growth rate of 2.51 per cent; but this was only one-third as fast as the growth of total manufacturing in the region (8.62 per cent per annum). As a result, the share of small establishments in the regions manufacturing employment fell from 73.9 to 55.3 per cent, giving a change in share of -18.6

Sources: NSSG (1975 and 1981), op. cit.

concentrations, and the impact of competition from larger firms in these concentrations with their economies of scale.

The above discussion thus indicates that the 1970s witnessed a redistribution of small manufacturing firms towards Greater Athens and Thessaloniki (see Fig. 4), together with a decentralisation of large-scale industry from the

former. This redistribution may indicate that the
increasing costs of labour and materials in Greece
have led small establishments to seek external
economies in urban areas. In addition, it may well
reflect high urban new firm formation rates,
because of rapid market and population growth, and
selective immigration of younger, more educated
potential entrepreneurs.

Small firm losses in the Greek periphery (see
Fig. 4), with the exception of Thraki, also suggest
that the small manufacturing workshop cannot be
viewed as a source of employment growth in these
isolated rural regions. Although it is suited to
the periphery's physical and human resources, and
is a more flexible operating unit, the small
workshop cannot be relied on to absorb unemployed
or underemployed workers from agriculture. Thus
where policies for reorganisation and
intensification of agriculture are implemented,
there will be a need to consider other sectors
suitable for employment creation to absorb the
surplus labour which will be created. Tourism and
services have been largely neglected fields in this
respect, though they arguably possess much higher
employment creation potential than manufacturing.

There are indications of an increasing
concentration of manufacturing activity in Greece
into larger units, a trend which is occurring most
rapidly outside the urban-industrial centres. Thus
the average size of manufacturing plants increased
faster between 1973 and 1978 in Greece as a whole
than in the cities (Table 4). The size of small
plants declined in all regions and urban centres
except in Sterea, a region which is the hinterland
of Athens, and Elefsis, the closest city to Athens,
clearly indicating a decentralisation process. The
rate of decline in size of small plants was most
marked in the urban industrial centres, -0.91,
appreciably faster than the rate of decline of
small plants in Greece as a whole (Table 4).
Indeed, the size of small-scale establishments in
the industrial centres declined whereas the size of
all urban plants increased. Concentration into
larger units, though faster outside the urban-
industrial centres, is thus a general trend
affecting cities as well as smaller towns and rural
areas.

Finally, Table 4 reveals that between 1973 and
1978, the number of small manufacturing firms in
Greece increased by 6742. At the regional level,
this was entirely due to substantial increases in

Fig. 3.   Employment growth of small manufacturing
           establishments by regions in Greece,
           1973-1978.

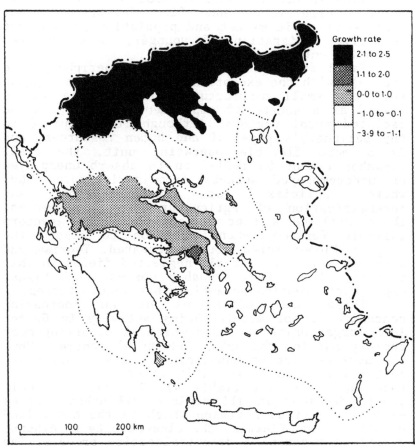

Growth rate
2·1 to 2·5
1·1 to 2·0
0·0 to 1·0
-1·0 to -0·1
-3·9 to -1·1

0   100   200 km

Source: National Statistical Service of Greece

Greater Athens, Macedonia and to a lesser extent
Thraki. All other regions recorded losses of small
plants, with a particularly heavy decline in the
Aegean region. On the other hand, only two Greek
cities experienced a decline in numbers of small
manufacturing firms, the remaining eight recording
gains. As noted earlier, this strongly suggests
that the cities have acted as small firm
incubators, perhaps due to the external economies
they afford, opportunities for linkages and
subcontracting, the growth of markets and
immigration of potential entrepreneurs, and their
generally relatively diversified structures.

Fig. 4.   Employment change in small manufacturing
establishments   by   regions   in   Greece,
1973-1978.

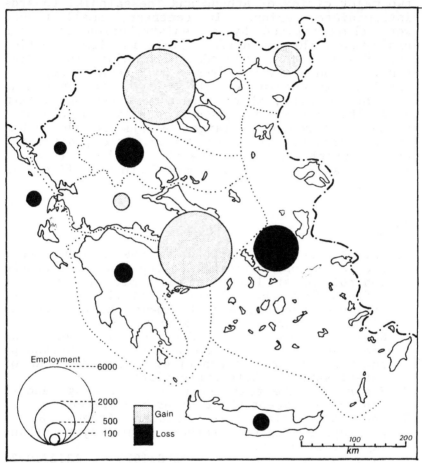

Source: National Statistical Service of Greece

Conclusions

Although   small   firms   and   establishments   are   an
important   component   of   Greek   manufacturing,   they
are   not   likely   to   be   a   major   force   in   employment
creation,   and   in   regional   and   industrial
development.   The   problems   of   small   plants   are
associated   with   the   sectoral   distribution   and
spatial   concentration   of   Greek   manufacturing
industry.   Entrepreneurial   initiative   and   the
development   of   small   enterprises   in   rural   regions
are   constrained   by   the   structural   problems   of   these

Greece

areas.

During the 1970s, a redistribution of total
manufacturing employment took place away from the
two major cities of Athens and Thessaloniki towards
intermediate regions. In contrast, small plants
were characterised by a redistribution of their
employment, through differentials in firm formation
and death rates, towards the major industrial
centres and away from peripheral regions.
Particularly evident was the polarisation on Athens
and Thessaloniki, which gained most new small-firm
jobs. This perhaps suggests a satellite development
of small firms near larger plants in the urban
areas. Certainly it is the major cities, not rural
areas, which appear currently to be the chief
incubators of new small manufacturing firms in
Greece.

Notes

1. Establishment is defined as one economic unit
   located in one building and engaged under single
   control in at least one economic activity. It
   differs from the enterprise, which may consist
   of more than one establishment. Establishments
   with less than 10 persons are classified by the
   National Statistical Service of Greece as
   small-scale units. Offices, premises, workshops
   and plants are alternatively used instead of
   establishments where appropriate.
2. Figures in the text refer to the average annual
   employment except where otherwise stated.
3. The NSSG classifies Greater Athens as a
   geographic region, rather than major urban-
   industrial centre.
4. Legislative Decrees 1078/1971, 1312/1972,
   1377/1973, 289/1976 and 849/1978.
5. By the 1961 association agreement between Greece
   and the original EEC members, tariffs on all
   products were to have been phased out by 1984.
   However, in 1979 Greece signed an agreement for
   full membership from 1.1.1981. This extended the
   phasing-out of tariffs for all products for
   which tariffs still existed by that date to
   1.1.1986, the end of the entry transition
   period.

Greece

References

Gould, A. and D. Keeble (1984) 'New Firms and Rural Industrialization in East Anglia' Regional Studies, 18,3, 189-201

Hellenic Industrial Development Bank (HIDB), undated, The contemporary idea of industrial development (in Greek)

National Statistical Service of Greece (NSSG) (1975) Resultats du Recensement des Industries Manufacturieres-Artisanats et des Industries Extractives, effectue le Septembre 1973, Athens

NSSG (1981) Resultat du Recensement des Industries Manufacturieres-Artisanats, du Commerce et autres Services, effectue le Septembre 1969, Athens

NSSG (1984) Survey of the Labour Force (Employment) of the Year 1983, Athens, (in Greek)

O'Farrell, P.N. (1985) 'Manufacturing Employment Change and Establishment Size', Area, 17,1, 35-43

Wagstaff, J.M. (1983) 'The Geographical Setting', in Clogg, R., (ed), Greece in the 1980s, Macmillan Press Ltd, London and Basingstoke

INDEX

Index

Index

Index

Index